Dr John G. Taylor is a sociologist who was educated at the University of Sussex and the City University. He has held a variety of teaching appointments since 1974, most recently as Principal Lecturer in Social Sciences at the South Bank Polytechnic, London, where he is also Director of the Centre for Chinese Studies. For many years, John Taylor has been associated with the Open University as a tutor and academic adviser in Development Studies. South East Asia and China have been his principal areas of research concern. He is the author of *From Modernisation to Modes of Production: A Critique of the Sociologies of Development and Underdevelopment* (Macmillan, London, 1979) and co-editor (with Andrew Turton) of *The Sociology of Developing Societies* (Macmillan, London, 1988). In the late 1970s he was active in the British Campaign for an Independent East Timor. He currently edits *Timor Link* for the Catholic Institute for International Relations on whose Education Committee he also serves as an adviser.

At a time when Washington has been leading a massive 'international' military effort to reverse Saddam Hussein's brutal annexation of Kuwait, it is salutary to be reminded of Washington's complicity in Suharto's even more brutal annexation of the former Portuguese colony of East Timor. John Taylor's thoroughly researched book, covering developments up till 1990, is an impressive analysis of East Timor's ordeal, under Portuguese fascism, Japanese invasion in World War II, and Indonesian occupation since 1976. Drawing on a wide range of documentary sources he explains cogently why the United States, Australia, and the Western democracies have abetted the Indonesian regime's aggression, and in harrowing detail, describes the campaign of counter-insurgency warfare, torture, disappearances, forced resettlement, and planned famine that over fifteen years have cost at least 200,000 East Timorese lives. Particularly enlightening are his account of the reasons for the astonishing stamina of the East Timorese resistance, and his balanced judgment of the various East Timorese leadership groups' successes and failures.

Professor Ben Anderson
Director
Modern Indonesia Project
Cornell University

A path-breaking work that manages, as no previous study of East Timor has done, to perceive events through the eyes of those who actually lived through the brutalities of the Indonesian invasion and military occupation . . . fills an important gap on Third World regional conflicts.

Peter Carey
Trinity College, Oxford

Indonesia's Forgotten War

The Hidden History of East Timor

John G. Taylor

Zed Books Ltd
London and New Jersey

Pluto Press Australia

Indonesia's Forgotten War was first published by Zed Books Ltd,
57 Caledonian Road, London N1 9BU, UK and 165 First Avenue,
Atlantic Highlands, New Jersey 07716, USA, and in Australia
and New Zealand by Pluto Press Australia, PO Box 199,
Leichhardt, NSW 2040, Australia.

Copyright © John G. Taylor, 1991.

Cover designed by Andrew Corbett.
Cover photograph © TAPOL, 1983.
Typeset by EMS Photosetters, Thorpe Bay, Essex.
Printed and bound in the United Kingdom
by Biddles Ltd., Guildford and King's Lynn.

A catalogue record for this book is
available from the British Library

A catalogue record of this book is
available from the Library of Congress

ISBN 1 85649 014 9
ISBN 1 85649 015 7 pbk

In Australia
ISBN 0 949138 66 5 (pbk)

Contents

Acknowledgements

In acknowledging those who have helped me in the preparation of this book, my greatest debt is to the East Timorese refugees who have provided such a substantial amount of detailed information. Without them the following account would have been impossible. I would also like to express my gratitude to those, directly involved in the events dealt with in this book, who have allowed me to interview them, particularly officers in the Portuguese Armed Forces Movement and politicians, lawyers and economists working in Indonesia. Many others have helped me in a whole number of ways, by supplying information and providing me with ideas. In this, I am indebted particularly to Abilio Araujo, Carmel Budiardjo, Peter Carey, Guilhermina dos Santos, Jill Jolliffe, Arnold Kohen, José Ramos-Horta and Kevin Sherlock. For their general support and help throughout the project, I would also like to thank Robert Archer, Elaine Capizzi, Shepard Forman, Anthony Goldstone, Helen Hill, Korinna Horta, Sidney Jones, Klemens Ludwig, David Macey, Robert Molteno and Torben Retbøll. Needless to say, none of these people bear any responsibility for the positions taken or the conclusions reached.

John G. Taylor
London
June 1990

Introduction

Some wars make the world's headlines, others do not. This book is about a war on an island east of Java and 400 miles north of Australia that has been fought for 15 years, since Indonesia first invaded East Timor in December 1975. This invasion and subsequent annexation has resulted in the most appalling brutalities and loss of life, inflicted by Indonesian troops. At least a quarter of East Timor's 690,000 population has been killed since 1975. The effects on the country's social and economic life have been horrendous. The agricultural system has been undermined, the population resettled in strategic camps and villages, and all areas of society controlled in the interests of a thoroughgoing Indonesianization.

Little of this has been told. The Indonesian military imposed a blockade of the country after the invasion, and until very recently only selected foreign journalists and observers have been allowed entry. Most coverage has had to rely on reports from these observers, and on official military statements. There has, in addition, been a general unwillingness by many of the governments in the international community to undertake any detailed investigation of what has been happening in East Timor, not, as one might imagine, because it is small and insignificant but, on the contrary, because of its importance to them in a number of areas — economic, political and strategic. Whether regarded from an American, Australian or Japanese perspective, there are crucial reasons why East Timor should remain within the Indonesian orbit and why, therefore, one should not rock the boat by criticizing the Indonesian Government too strongly.

The analysis that follows deals both with this and with the East Timor reality that has been hidden. Using visitors' reports, documents, letters and radio broadcasts from the independence movement, Fretilin, and other opposition groups, intelligence service reports from governments allied with Indonesia and, above all, descriptions given by East Timorese refugees in Portugal and Australia, I have tried to reconstruct what has happened since the Indonesian invasion. In this, I have discovered a history which cries out to be told. It is nothing less than an act of genocide committed by the Indonesian military. A country which could have developed as a viable and successful nation-state is being moulded brutally in the Indonesian image, at a terrible cost to its population.

Despite attempts to downplay the war in East Timor, the issue will not go away. Resistance continues, both from Fretilin and from regular outbursts of protest against Indonesian incorporation, particularly by the most recent generation who have been raised during Indonesian rule. Internationally, pressure remains on the Indonesian Government to solve the problem of a war which it seems unable to win, and which is tarnishing its image at a time when it is heavily reliant on the industrialized states for the development of its manufacturing base. After accommodating the Indonesians in the years after the invasion, the former colonial power, Portugal, is now campaigning successfully in the European Community (EC) states for a negotiated settlement and a referendum on self-determination. Within the United States Government there is growing support for free access, a monitoring of human rights and a negotiated settlement of the war. Recently almost half of the members of the Senate signed a document to the secretary of state voicing their approval of these measures. A similar lobby has developed in recent years in the Japanese Diet. The Vatican, too, has a strong interest in East Timor; most of the island's population remains Catholic, and its priests are highly critical of the Indonesian occupation. Consequently, the Vatican is committed to finding a solution to the conflict in the near future.

Currently, the barriers to reaching a settlement are, of course, the Indonesian Government itself, but also governments such as those of Australia which remain fully committed to the Indonesian position. In this case the determining factor is the Indonesian Government's willingness to negotiate agreements with the Australians which provide oil companies entry into the oil-rich deposits of the Timor Sea, inside East Timor's maritime boundaries. Similarly committed, for ideological reasons, are many of Indonesia's fellow Islamic states.

When the Indonesian military first invaded East Timor, the view of its leading generals was that resistance would be dealt with swiftly, and that the territory would be incorporated into the Indonesian Republic with relative ease. Some 15 years later, despite massive troop deployments and vast expenditures, the movement for independence continues, maintaining itself under the most difficult conditions. This resistance by the East Timorese people to the Indonesian occupation for such a long period of time is, ultimately, the most important factor in keeping the issue alive internationally into the 1990s. This, however, has been achieved at incredible cost, and the impact of the Indonesian occupation on the East Timorese themselves has been devastating. I would like to illustrate this by citing a particular case from the many experiences of the refugees whose accounts have contributed so much to this book. It is an extraordinary, yet in the light of events in East Timor, a very ordinary case of two people caught up in the events after the invasion. It first appeared in the Australian paper, the Melbourne *Age*, on 22 June 1985. Slightly abridged, it runs as follows:

Tali and Bi Halik have not been able to tell their story before. Even now, they cannot reveal where they live because they fear for the safety of their remaining family and friends in their homeland — East Timor. Tali and Bi lived relatively normal lives until December 1975, when the world as they knew it came to a halt and they started a life filled with starvation, torture, raw fear and death. Indonesian forces had invaded East Timor. Ten years and more than US$20,000 in bribes later, the couple managed to migrate to Australia four weeks ago. Through a Portuguese interpreter the couple recounted their life.

In 1974, Tali was teaching in a junior high school in Dili — the lush, coastal capital of East Timor. At 23, he was thinking about furthering his career by joining the airforce and continuing his study through its academy. His girlfriend Bi was studying at the Dili High School. Tali was a member of the Frente Revolucionara Timorense de Libertacao e Independencia (Fretilin). He was involved in communications work and Bi joined a women's group. At 4 am on 7 December, the Indonesians made their move. Tali related the sequence of events: 'The first parachutists landed in Dili about 4 am. There was a lot of bombardments going on in the outer suburbs, as the Indonesians were trying to stop Fretilin — who had their headquarters here — from getting into the centre of Dili. At 7 am, the Indonesians took every one of the army units and they asked for everyone to surrender. They were told to form a line and then they were all shot, killed there and then. Two people survived the massacre and one is living in Perth.'

Fretilin moved into the mountains behind Dili. Groups of Fretilin supporters made their way to various mountain villages. Tali and Bi and about 500 others went to Dare. Indonesian troops caught the group by surprise and they fled again, without supplies. At this point, Tali and Bi were separated from Tali's parents. The young couple managed to get to Aileu — about 80km from Dili. The central Fretilin committee was set up in Aileu and the people organized themselves into groups with specific responsibilities. The Indonesian troops soon took over Aileu and Fretilin moved higher into the mountains. Tali and Bi were responsible for more than 500 people, many of them young children. Fleeing from village to village, Fretilin had few supplies. Bi said many children had to be carried. Their food was whatever they could find and they sheltered in caves or under covers made from coconut and palm leaves. 'In some villages, we were able to use the fresh vegetables from the garden', Tali said. In Same, Tali and Bi decided to get married. The village people found Bi a traditional Timorese blouse and cloth skirt. Same was their home for two months, but again the Indonesian troops took over the village. They left the area and moved to another village at the top of the Timorese mountains — Samora. Bi was heavily pregnant at this time with their first child. 'We were very short of food by this time — the people were starving', Bi said. 'I needed food for myself and the baby, so Tali would travel 80km through mountainous country for two days and nights to get some food from another village for me and the others.' The birth was difficult and Bi was very weak, as her only food for weeks had been a sort of porridge of dried corn and coconut. Her son died one hour after birth.

Indonesian troops were close at hand and so the population was forced to move yet again, this time to Mt Calcaissa — an area untouched by fighting. 'This was a good place for us. We were there nine months and were able to grow gardens and get back some health', Tali said. During this time, Bi gave birth to her second son, Luan Halik. The peace was shattered one day when they heard that the Indonesian troops were getting too close and the community would have to leave that night. So 50,000 people had to be shifted through dense, hilly jungle area. They moved at night to avoid being spotted. During the day they hid in long grass, sitting in mud and slush for hours. Bi had to carry her son and three other babies in a cloth apron with four large pockets. They headed for a swampy mosquito area called Lagoa ne Lagas, on the north of the island. Hundreds died during the trip — either drowned crossing rivers or caught by the Indonesians. Tali was carrying a very sick, elderly woman and bundles of food. Bi was trying to breastfeed the four children on little food. They finally reached Lagoa ne Lagas, but the swampy area provided little food, and thousands died of starvation and malaria. Tali became very ill with malaria and so did their young son. The couple set out for Teras, a small mountain village, in the hope of finding some Fretilin commanders. Their trip back through swamp and river areas was a nightmare: 'All I can remember are dead bodies and bones. Bones everywhere, rotting bodies, bodies with maggots crawling all over them', Bi said. In one clearing, Bi spotted what she thought was a beautiful pool of water. She wanted a drink so she gave the baby to Tali. Gulping water down, Bi didn't look round her for a few minutes. When she did, she saw a dead body only inches from where she was drinking. The couple continued on to Teras, but their child grew more ill. Bi's milk dried up in her breast and all she could feed the child was a little tapioca: 'When we were crossing a river, I knew the baby was dying, but I didn't want Bi to panic, so I told her he wanted to go to sleep', Tali said. 'I held him very close to help him sleep and that's where he died', Bi said. The couple baptized their dead child and Bi carried him for three days until they found a place to bury him. They eventually met up with 100 other Fretilin, including four commanders. Starving and ill, the group searched the jungle for food. On one of these searches, two of the group surrendered to the Indonesians and told them about the Fretilin community in the hope of saving their own lives. Indonesian troops surrounded the group and the Fretilin commanders were killed. The others were arrested and taken to Turiscai, where Bi and Tali were treated by Australian Red Cross workers. 'We were told that our poor health probably saved our lives, as we were of no use to the Indonesians', said Tali. When the couple were well enough, they were taken to Dili. There, Tali was interrogated for days because of his senior Fretilin position. Bi never recovered from the last month in the jungle, she conceived another baby, but this died soon after. Tali was given a job where he worked for three years without wages. They were forced to learn Indonesian, and Tali was made an Indonesian citizen.

Finally, Tali was allowed to go to Jakarta to study. He arranged for Bi to follow a year later on the grounds that she needed medical treatment. From that time in early 1981, the Haliks started bribing various officials to get papers to come to Australia. Their fourth son, Luan Noruk, was born in 1982 and was forced to learn Indonesian from birth. Bi's family, which had headed for Australia before the fighting began, sent thousands of dollars, year after year, to try and get the couple out to Australia. Four weeks and six days ago, Bi and Tali were told they could go if they handed over another US$2000. 'Now we must fight and try to save the others so that they too can tell their stories', Tali said.

I hope that what I have written in this book will also in some way contribute to this objective. The experiences of Bi and Tali are typical of thousands of East Timorese since the Indonesian invasion. Typical not only in terms of their suffering but typical also in their determination to resist. The history of East Timor needs to be recounted because of its concealment, but just as importantly because it is one of the most impressive and striking attempts ever by the people of a small nation to resist incorporation by the government of a large, powerful, aggressive military state, with all the necessary resources at its disposal. In many ways — through their policies for independence, their organization of resistance and their creation of a nationalist movement, culturally, socially and politically — the experiences of the people of East Timor are an inspiration and a guide for the peoples of other nations, in Southeast Asia, the Pacific region and elsewhere, who are striving to achieve self-determination and independence.

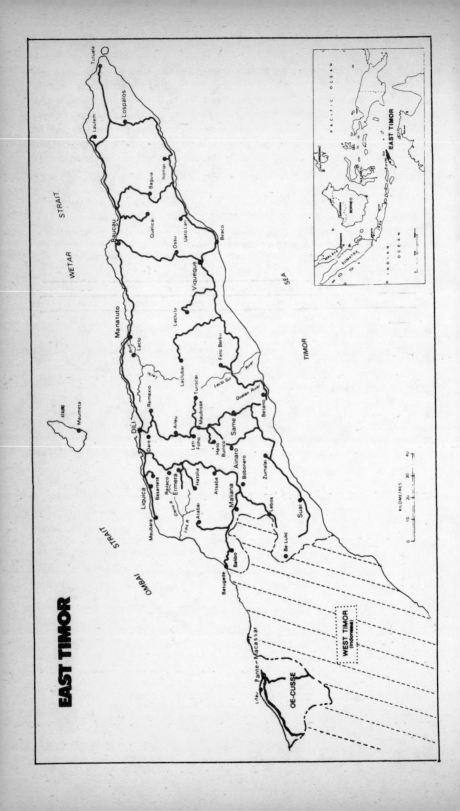

Indonesia's
Forgotten War

1. Colonial Failure

The history of Timor is written largely from a European perspective. It documents the events through which Dutch and Portuguese colonialism extended their control over the island, and it charts the level of resistance to this extension. From the Portuguese capture of Malacca in 1571 to the final attempt at pacification of Timor in the beginning of the twentieth century, this history documents faithfully the shaping of its people into the colonial mould. The Timorese exist only in their encounter with colonialism. Less well known is that, contrary to colonial assumptions, Timorese ethnography and anthropology present a rich tradition of oral history, recounting both the precolonial period and the varied development of Timor's kingdoms and regions during the 400 years in which Portuguese colonial influence was largely formal. Drawing on this tradition often provides us with a more adequate means for understanding twentieth-century developments than does a primary reference to the texts of colonial history. Certainly, it helps us answer the crucial question of why Timorese society was able to resist colonial incorporation for over four and a half centuries; of why its basic social and economic systems were able to survive, despite all attempts by Portuguese colonialism to undermine their reproduction. Only by answering this will we understand why the people of East Timor were able subsequently to build a successful independence movement, and resist Indonesian incorporation during the post-colonial period.

Settlement and exchange

Long before the Portuguese and Dutch entered the region, the island of Timor formed a part of the trading networks centred politically on East Java and then on the Celebes (Sulawesi). These networks were tied into commercial links with China and India. The commercial value of Timor is highlighted in documents published during the Ming dynasty in 1436. The island is described as one in which 'the mountains are covered with sandal trees, and the country produces nothing else'.[1] Duarte Barbosa, one of the first Portuguese to visit Timor, wrote in 1518: 'There is an abundance of white sandalwood, which the moors in India and Persia value greatly, where much of it is used'.[2] The Dutch administrator and anthropologist, Schulte-Nordholt, illustrates the value of Timor's sandalwood trade for the Portuguese. He points out that in the world maps drawn by Gerelamo de Verrazano in 1529, currently located in the Vatican Museum, the map of Southeast Asia mentions only Sumatra and the 'Spice Islands' including Timor, whilst it omits Java. Consequently, although other commodities, honey, wax and slaves, were exported from Timor, its trade was focused primarily on its rich sandalwood reserves.

At first glance, it seems that Timor's role in the sandalwood trade influenced markedly the structure and development of its political systems. Schulte-Nordholt cites early sixteenth-century reports which seem to indicate that the predominance of coastal kingdoms in the north and south coasts were a direct result of this trade. Each area appeared to be under the control of a chief who supervised all commercial dealings. In a similar vein, van Groeneveldt cites a Chinese report of 1618 which claims that trading could not begin until a figure he calls 'the King' appeared, to whom taxes were paid daily: 'When they (the Timorese) see their King, they sit down on the ground with folded hands'.[3] This example illustrates the forms in which Timorese political organization appeared initially to Asian traders, as societies with political hierarchies relying heavily on commerce. Colonial history took this form and adopted it as the basis for its subsequent analyses. Yet behind it there seems to have been a much more complex political organization. This needs to be uncovered if we are to understand the basic structures of Timorese society.

A Timorese myth recounted to the ethnographer Middelkoop, begins: 'A long, long time ago there was one ruler of this island in Baliko-Babali' (the southern coastal plain). The ritual ruler of this realm appears to have had three subordinate rulers (*liurai*) immediately under him, each of whom exercised executive power in his own territory.[4] The first *liurai* was located in South Belu (the coastal plain), the second in Sonbai (in the west of the island). This triad of in Suai-Kamanasa (in the south-centre of the island). This triad of heads under one ruler had its origins in a substantial migration dating from the early fourteenth century. Myths describe how the original Melanesian inhabitants were displaced in this period by invaders coming from Malacca via Makassar in the Celebes and Larantuka in eastern Flores. These newcomers, of Malay origin, settled in the southern coastal plain, and moved northwest and northeast displacing the original inhabitants, and forming the three kingdoms heads under dominated by 'Baliko-Babali'.

These kingdoms were neither unified nor centrifugal in any sense which would be familiar to European contact. They combined loosely-knit localized territorial groups in a general hierarchy of clans, each related through exchange. Clans were ruled by chiefs who received tribute and organized marital alliances with neighbouring clans. Each clan paid tribute to the kingdom in which it existed. At all levels, then, an exchange of goods, people and sacred objects pervaded this system. Consequently, when these localized groups began to trade with the Dutch and Portuguese in the sixteenth century, their encounter with a relatively more developed economic system which itself operated through exchange enabled this latter system to transform the clans' ties with their kingdoms by directing their exchange systems externally. Chiefs who could organize labour to produce and trade in commodities such as sandalwood received in return from the Portuguese trade items such as cloth, guns and iron tools. This supply from the Portuguese enabled coastal groups to assert their identity over their erstwhile kingdom rulers. The resultant shifts in political control introduced major changes in the distribution of power in the sixteenth and seventeenth centuries. These changes formed the backdrop to the turbulent events of this period, which centred on resistance to European invasion. Before examining the effects of these intrusions on the reproduction of Timorese society, we need to recount briefly the course of events.

Colonial interplay

At the beginning of the sixteenth century, Malacca, on the western coast of the Malay peninsula, was in the words of historian D. G. E. Hall: 'a political power of the first rank . . . the most important commercial centre in Southeast Asia as well as the main diffusion-centre of Islam'.[5] The port controlled trade along the route from the Spice Islands of eastern Indonesia to India and China. European and western Asian commodities found their way to the Far East through Malacca's seasonal trading fairs. Malacca was thus a primary strategic target of the Portuguese in their struggle for God and Mammon against the religious and economic pursuits of the Ottoman Empire in Asia. It was seized in 1511. The Portuguese fleet then began to move eastwards, with the aim of setting up factories in the lucrative Spice Islands, focusing on islands such as Ambon and the Moluccas.

The first Portuguese settlement in the proximity of Timor was on the island of Solor. In 1566 Dominican friars built a fortress which they garrisoned with their recent converts from Solor and Flores. At this stage the Portuguese made annual trips to Timor to collect sandalwood and trade in finished goods. When their trading rivals, the Dutch, managed to capture Solor in 1613, the population of the fortress moved to the neighbouring island of Larantuka. Whilst Solor interchanged between Dutch and Portuguese rule in the seventeenth century, Larantuka remained firmly under Portuguese control.

This relatively settled period of Portuguese rule witnessed the consolidation of a group which was to dominate Timor's development in the seventeenth and eighteenth centuries. The Dutch termed them the 'Topasses' or 'Black Portuguese', a designation whose origins historians have seen either in their role as interpreters (from the Gujerati word *tupasse*, interpreter) or their mode of dress (from the Indian *topee walas*, hat-men). The Topasses first appear in colonial history as a 'mixed race . . . the off-spring of Portuguese soldiers, sailors and traders from Malacca and Macao, who intermarried with the local women of Solor',[6] and who moved with the Portuguese to Larantuka. After the move, the Topasses, initially with the help of groups of Dominican friars, began to control the trading networks between Solor, Larantuka and Timor, in particular the lucrative sandalwood trade. In this process, they started to settle in Timor itself, although their presence was not really felt until after 1642.

This mid-seventeenth century date marked a watershed in Timorese history since it was during that year that the Portuguese invaded Timor in strength, attempting to extend their influence beyond the coast to control the island's internal trade. Justifying their attack by the need to defend recently christened coastal rulers, the Portuguese moved directly against the western kingdom of Sonbai and its parent kingdom Babali, or Wehale as they called it. Their main objective was the latter, since the Portuguese rightly viewed Wehale as the religious and political centre of Timor. Victory was swift and brutal. An observer described the campaign of the commander, Captain Major Francisco Fernandes of Solor in the following words:

> Laying waste the regions through which he marched with his troops, the Captain Major held out in the face of pursuit by the enemy up to the place where Wehale had his residence; after reducing everything to ashes there he withdrew to Batimao.[7]

Topasse migration to Timor increased markedly after this. The Topasse community was centred at Lifau (now Oecusse) on the northern coast. From here the Topasses prepared to quell any internal threat to their position, from either local people or the Dutch, encroaching on Timor from the west.

In 1653, the Dutch defeated the Portuguese garrison at Kupang in the west of the island, followed by the landing of a substantial military force in 1656. Unlike the earlier Portuguese invasion, the Dutch met with stiff resistance: western kingdoms controlled by Topasse families were provided with the appropriate military equipment to contain the Dutch advance. With a detailed knowledge of the rocky terrain, they were able to rout the Dutch in a short and brutal battle which forced them to move to the neighbouring island of Roti, thus giving effective control of Timor to the Topasses.

Political opposition to Topasse rule could now come from only three groups: Portuguese merchants, Dominican friars, and the Timorese themselves. The merchants tried to wrest control of the sandalwood trade from the Topasses, with the blessing of the Portuguese crown; the Dominicans attempted to build an independent power base; and the Timorese kingdoms rose in periodic revolt against both the 'white' and 'black' (Topasse) Portuguese. Throughout the late seventeenth and early eighteenth centuries, this triangular conflict was interspersed with periods in which its participants united in opposition to the spread of Dutch influence.

After the fall of Kupang, the Portuguese embarked on a campaign of enticing chiefs away from the Topasse sphere. This culminated in attempts to introduce a governor on to the island in Lifau in 1695 and again in 1702. On both occasions he was forced out by the combined efforts of the Timorese and Topasses. In a subsequent attempt, in 1720, the Dominicans were largely responsible for removing the governor. In 1729 another governor and his forces were besieged and defeated in Manatuto, after which the Portuguese withdrew until 1748.

Meanwhile, the Dutch had once again begun to reassert themselves in the western half of the island. Their spread of influence amongst local tribes using Dutch support against the Topasses in the 1730s culminated in their rebuilding Fort Kupang by 1746. Unlike earlier conflicts, the campaigns against the Dutch in 1735 and 1745 had only a limited impact. Hence the Topasses turned to the Portuguese for assistance, mounting a joint invasion of the Dutch areas in 1749. The outcome of this was a ferocious engagement which came to be known in Timor as the battle of Penfui. An outright victory for the Dutch, it led to a tremendous strengthening of the Dutch presence in the western part of the island. Indeed, with Dutch assistance, the kingdom of Serviao was able to evict its Topasse masters. Penfui finally laid down the territorial division of Timor: the Dutch in the west and the Portuguese in the east. The fact that the Topasses had been forced to request Portuguese assistance ensured the latter a definite presence on the island, and led to a reduction in Topasse power. The healthy respect engendered by the one for the other meant that neither attempted to extend their influence beyond the kingdom level, leaving Timorese society relatively free from incursion and disruption. The result of these events was that the Timorese had effectively guaranteed their future by playing off one foreign group against another, though this is hardly recognized in the annals of colonial history.

The structure of Timorese society

The Timorese had successfully maintained a society with specific characteristics, distinct from neighbouring societies in the Southeast Asian region. At all levels, economic, political and ideological, its reproduction was maintained by a number of complex mechanisms, unified through an elaborate system of exchange. The basic structure of this system can best be illustrated by focusing initially on its economy.

The organization of production was influenced profoundly by the distinctive nature of the Timorese terrain. The main topographical feature of the island is its rugged mountainous backbone, interspersed with fertile valleys and permanent springs. To the north, mountains protrude into the sea, whilst in the south they give way to a broad coastal plain. Lowland areas are also found in the west and northwest. In this terrain the flow of water is seasonably based. In the dry season (May to October) rivers are no more than stony corridors, whilst in the monsoon season (November to April) they become torrents of often impassable water. The vegetation produced by the climate and terrain varies from savanna and grassland in the plain areas, to bushland on the hill slopes, and to evergreen and tropical forests in the mountainous areas. Under these conditions, only a limited amount of land-use was possible. Irrigated cultivation could be undertaken only where water supplies were available from flood plains, in the vicinity of springs, or on swamp land. Most agricultural production was of the slash and burn type, with land-use being rotated to preserve the soil. Several crops were grown: rice, maize, cassava, yams, sweet potatoes and a variety of fruits. Livestock, such as pigs, goats, sheep and buffalo, were grazed on the hill slopes. Production was mainly for local subsistence, but goods were regularly exchanged at local markets. The only goods exchanged externally were sandalwood and beeswax.

The units in which production occurred were the household garden, the field and the irrigated *padi*. Economic organization was based primarily on the extended family, responsible for the maintenance of each type of unit. This base was constantly extended, however, throughout the agricultural cycle, since the low technical level necessitated extensive co-operation in the use of labour. For example, in wet-rice cultivation the tasks of irrigating, sowing, harvesting, threshing and winnowing could only succeed with the co-operation of many workers in a fairly sophisticated division of labour. Production thus occurred in both extended kin and village contexts, each being characterized by distinct sexual divisions, and governed by ritual. In the cycle of rice cultivation, for example, planting was undertaken by women and harvesting by men. Outside agriculture, weaving was a female task, whilst the males produced iron implements, and so on.

Economic relations were not influenced merely by divisions in the production process, however. They were also influenced by a system of exchange, involving both goods and individuals. Goods were exacted from Timorese communities as tribute due to the chiefs of the various princedoms and kingdoms. In the Wehale kingdom, for example, through his officials the *nai boot* (lord of the land) granted land to families for their use, in return for which they paid a token rent, a *rai teen* (excrement of the land). Goods were also exchanged for women and men in marriage. This exchange ensured an appropriate balance between the land and its cultivators in an economic unit, so that the size and capability of the labour force provided by these exchanges would be adequate to meet the subsistence needs of the local population. The exchange was only possible if the goods required could be produced in return for the provision of women and men in the village unit. Villagers had to work beyond the time required to produce their own subsistence crops, in order to produce the goods to be exchanged. The products of surplus labour-time were thus exchanged for means of reproduction (women and men), and the elders, through their role in exchange, were responsible for distributing these products. In addition, therefore, to the economic relations generated by production were those generated by exchange and the consumption of goods exchanged.

These relations were expressed in systems of kinship and status distinction between various groups in each of Timor's kingdoms. Although these systems varied somewhat, their basic essentials were the same, having a common structure of production and exchange. For example, by the end of the seventeenth century, there appears to have been a geographical transition from a patrilineal kinship system with patrilocal residence in the north and east to a matrilineal system in the south. In the south, there was also matrilineal kinship with uxorilocal residence, in which the young man left his family and went to live with that of his wife. This kinship pattern reflected the decline of the kingdom of Wehale; in areas where its influence remained, matrilineal kinship and the religious and ritual power of women seemed much stronger. Indeed, from most available accounts, Wehale was a matriarchal society in which feminine attributes governed the exercise of both political and economic power. There was a strong focus on these attributes in many different areas, but particularly in the religious sphere.[8] Whatever the form taken by kinship, the exchange of women and men between groups was channelled through the tribal elders, who arranged an exchange of women for goods which were either designed for luxury use or as means of production, from buffaloes and horses to swords and gold ornaments. Consequently, just as the chiefs of the princedoms were able to gain status from their collection of surplus labour through tribute, so also were elders through their role in the system of kinship exchange. Although status accrued to individuals in other ways, such as size and fertility of land cultivated, knowledge of tradition, possession of sacred objects, accumulated wealth and age, the most important hierarchy remained that generated by production and exchange. This meant that, in Timor's political system, the predominant positions were occupied by the most elevated individuals in the tribute and exchange systems.

This political structure had three main administrative levels: the village, the princedom and the kingdom, each with its own head. Other sources of political power resided in clan leadership, and a royal and aristocratic status accorded to some kingdom leaders. The village comprised several hamlets, spread over a wide area. Each hamlet contained the members of a particular clan, the latter generally tracing itself to six generations. Ruled by a headman in association with a council of elders, the village was part of a princedom (*suco*) headed by a family which was itself subject to the ruler (*liurai*) of the kingdom in which it existed. In kingdoms and princedoms where the *liurai* and princes possessed a royal or aristocratic status, the extended royal and aristocratic families distinguished themselves from the mass of the population, divided into commoners (*dato*) and slaves (*ata*), mostly captured in wars between clans, princedoms and kingdoms. In this system, those with the greatest political power were those in receipt of the most tribute and/or those in the most strategic positions in the kinship exchange system. For example, in the kingdom of Wehale, the lord received tribute as the ultimate owner of the land, and was the ultimate arbiter of marital exchanges in the system embracing the royal families. Royalty conferred certain powers upon him, but his role in production and exchange gave him power in addition to his royal status. Similarly, councils assisting in village administration seem to have had a preponderance of elders with senior positions in the kinship system.

Each Timorese kingdom, princedom and clan possessed value systems whose ideologies highlighted the importance of exchange, and justified the hierarchy influenced by this exchange. In the kingdoms of Belu and Serviao, for example, tribute paid to the rulers controlling trade focused particularly on gifts at the end of the harvesting period. These gifts were called *poni pah* (rice baskets of the land). Similarly, gifts of homage (*tuthais*) were given to rulers whose political prominence had been established by their success in arranging marital exchanges. This exchange of gifts in return for access to means of production (land) and reproduction (the creation of new family units) was also expressed in the rites accompanying birth, marriage and death, all of which were combined in a value system relating these acts to the place of the tribe in the cosmos. In death rites, for example, the dead person's descent group acted as an intermediary between wife-givers and takers, co-ordinating exchanges between them, making 'death payments' to the deceased person's matrilineal kin. Just as marriage was characterized by an exchange of gifts for means of reproduction, so too were death rites part of a value system whose ethos centred on the notion of exchange. In marriage, food was exchanged for means of reproduction; in death, it was offered to spirits who, in exchange, ensured the fertility of the earth. The products of this fertility were then offered to different spirits who ensured the best climatic conditions for growth, and so on. Life was viewed as a system of inter-linked exchanges whose enactment was essential for the maintenance of economic and social stability.

Reproduction and resistance

The entry of the European powers had a marked effect on the reproduction of Timorese society. Examining the events we have recounted earlier from the history of the sixteenth and seventeenth centuries, in the light of our knowledge of Timorese economic and social structure, a number of trends emerge.

Whilst trade in the pre-sixteenth century period had led to a gradual increase in the amount of surplus labour-time devoted to the cultivation of goods for export, the political and social effects had been minimal, largely confined to a limited increase in the political influence of the heads of coastal princedoms. Inserting themselves into existing trade patterns, the Portuguese intensified this process, with the long-term aim of undermining the Timorese kingdoms to produce smaller less powerful units, more amenable to European control. Throughout the sixteenth century, these Portuguese efforts at divide and rule had only very limited success, and it was not until the mid-seventeenth century, with the defeat of the Wehale kingdom, that the control by the kingdoms over their princedoms was lessened.

This decline in the kingdoms' powers enabled the invading group of Topasse families to take over the senior positions occupied previously by kingdom and princedom heads in the exchange of tribute, services and women and men between clans and villages. In this way, during the course of the eighteenth century, the Topasses were able to exercise political influence within the Timorese princedoms.

The emphasis on the value of exchange in pre-Portuguese Timor was thus reinforced by the Portuguese spreading the net of exchange economically downwards from the kingdom level, and by the Topasses reinforcing the system of kinship exchange for the purposes of their own political control. The entry of a European economic system operating through the medium of exchange thus resulted in the strengthening of the dominant values of a society itself based on the notion of exchange in the cultural, social, political and economic spheres. Consequently, although the Timorese economy was increasingly diverted to external needs, and although control of its political system shifted to an external grouping, the concrete effects of these changes were limited. What, in other societies, might have produced fundamental structural changes resulted paradoxically in the strengthening of the basic aspects of Timorese society. This conclusion is of fundamental importance in understanding contemporary Timorese society, since it indicates how its indigenous economic, social and cultural systems were able to reproduce themselves intact, despite being subject to foreign control. Once established, the co-existence of external control with indigenous structural reproduction continued throughout the eighteenth and nineteenth centuries. The history of this period is thus marked by the success of Timorese communities in restricting Topasse and European influence and control to the political sphere of princely kinship alliances.

This resistance took many forms. Throughout the eighteenth century, opposition focused largely on the Portuguese, with attacks on Portuguese troops launched from sheltered mountain areas. One of the most renowned battles took place in the mountains of Cailaco, in 1726, when four thousand troops under Portuguese command were encircled by a handful of Timorese.[9] As a result of such encounters, by the middle of the eighteenth century the Portuguese had given up their attempts to administer the territory as a whole. In 1769 they were routed in Lifau and moved their administrative centre, with its 1200 inhabitants, eastwards to Dili. With the Portuguese threat reduced, the Timorese then found themselves defending their territory against the Topasses, who tried constantly to extend their political control through kinship agreements. Topasse families tried to entice Timorese kingdom rulers by awarding them Portuguese titles such as *coronel* or *brigadeiro*, and providing them with military support in tribute-exaction. Their success, however, was limited. Resistance continued into the nineteenth century as evidenced in eye-witness reports.

In 1825, a Dutch lieutenant visited Dili. His account illustrates both the depth of Timorese resentment of the Portuguese and Topasses, and some of the reasons for this resentment:

> Slaves were frequently offered to me on sale, the Commandant (of Dili), among others, wishing me to purchase two children of seven or eight years of age, who were loaded with heavy irons. These unfortunate people are kidnapped in the interior, and brought to Dili for sale, the Governor readily providing the vendor with certificates for sale. Many of the inhabitants of Dili expressed to me their strong desire to be freed from the hateful yoke of the Portuguese.[10]

The English traveller Wallace spent several months in Timor during his travels in the Malay Archipelago, at the end of the 1850s. Witnessing one of the regular Timorese attacks on Dili, he concluded: 'Timor will for many years to come remain in its present state of chronic insurrection and mis-government'.[11] When the naturalist, H. O. Forbes, travelled in Timor in 1882, he reported that the country 'is apportioned out under certain chiefs called Rajahs or Leoreis (*liurais*), each of whom is independent in his own kingdom'.[12] Their independence was attested by Forbes being conducted through the country without the presence of any Topasse or Portuguese, except in Dili. He noted that the Timorese had learnt many of the customs of the Portuguese, in order to be able to outwit them more effectively. Forbes' observations on the independence of the Timorese kingdoms, and on their ability to control Topasse or Portuguese encroachment, illustrate the constant complaints of Portuguese officials in the nineteenth century that they were unable successfully to maintain military and administrative posts in the interior.

Pacification: the two political systems

At the end of the nineteenth century, this situation appeared to change dramatically. After centuries of purely formal rule, the Portuguese tried to establish effective control over their colony. Colonial history documents this as a reaction to the assassination of a newly appointed governor in 1887, but its causes were more fundamental. In 1898, a Portuguese Royal Commission completed its report on the country's colonial possessions. It concluded:

> The state . . . should have no scruples in *obliging* and if necessary *forcing* these rude Negroes in Africa, these ignorant Pariahs in Asia, these half savages in Oceania to work, that is, to better themselves by work, to acquire through work the happiest means of existence, to civilise themselves through work.[13]

Such emphatic policies towards its colonies stemmed both from an inability to control them, and an increasing awareness that greater control was needed to assist the economy of the mother country. Whilst a large part of Western Europe had developed industrially by the end of the nineteenth century, Portugal remained an agrarian-based feudal backwater, its landowning class restricting successfully the development of manufacturing industry in order to maintain its political power. Faced with the rapid economic development of other European powers, Portugal tried to bolster its position by a systematic exploitation of its colonies, including Timor, which had thus far been little more than a trading post. This exploitation required the extraction of raw materials and the cultivation of cash crops for export, together with the development of an internal market, both for home-produced and imported goods. Consequently, in both its African and Asian colonies, Portugal introduced measures aimed at transforming subsistence economies into cash crop systems, which could become more integrated into the world economy. In Timor, these policies aimed to focus initially on the production of a surplus from a subsistence economy, through the use of forced labour to develop the infrastructure, cultivate crops for export and extend the trading system.

The success of these policies required a more widespread Portuguese political control than had existed hitherto. Yet the extension of Portuguese authority encountered a fundamental barrier. This was described by the governor of Timor in 1882 in the following terms:

> Marital exchange is our Governor's major enemy because it produces . . . an infinity of kin relations which comprise leagues of reaction against the orders of the Governors and the dominion of our laws. There has not yet been a single rebellion against the Portuguese flag which is not based in the alliances which result from marital exchange.[14]

The centrality of exchange in Timorese society, which had been reinforced during earlier periods of Portuguese influence, was now clearly seen by the colonial power as a barrier to control of its colony.

Portuguese policies at the end of the century thus had two objectives: to undermine the indigenous system of kinship exchange and to create a basis for a systematic economic exploitation of its colony.

Between 1884 and 1890, a programme of road construction was organized with the use of forced labour. In 1899 a company was set up, named *Sociedade Agricola Patria e Trabalho* (SAPT) — Society, Agricultural Fatherland and Labour. It introduced coffee plantations into Ermera, in the northwest. From 1908 a head tax was levied on all Timorese males between the ages of 18 and 60. The only way in which this could be met, of course, was by peasant families producing and selling goods for the market, over and above their subsistence needs. Between 1911 and 1917, an additional cash crop, copra, was introduced.

The introduction of these measures, particularly the use of forced labour, produced widespread resentment amongst the Timorese. Kingdoms united under the leadership of a *liurai* from the southern district of Manufuhi (Same) named Dom Boaventura. The rebellion simmered for sixteen years, culminating in an uprising which engulfed the colony for two years, from 1910–12. The Portuguese were forced to bring in troops from Mozambique and a cannonship from Macau. Boaventura's forces were defeated in August 1912. An Australian paper, the Melbourne *Argus*, reported that 3000 Timorese were killed and 4000 captured.

With resistance quelled, the Portuguese introduced their policies to undermine the system of political alliances produced by kinship exchange. The position of the *liurais* was undercut by the abolition of their kingdoms. The colony was re-divided into administrative units, broadly based on the *suco* (princedom). A measure of administrative power was thus given to the unit below the kingdom level in the indigenous hierarchy. This enhanced the position of the leaders of the *sucos*, although their election as administrators was subject to Portuguese approval. The Portuguese created two new administrative levels: the *posto*, comprising groups of *sucos*, and the *concelho*, controlling *postos* via a Portuguese administrator. By these means, the Portuguese tried to replace the Timorese political system with one whose structure and hierarchy could be independent of kinship alliances. The essence of Portuguese 'pacification' was its attempted destruction of a crucial aspect of Timor's social system, whose reproduction limited the influence of Portuguese control.

During the same period in which pacification campaigns occurred in Portuguese Timor, they also took place on the Dutch side of the island, east of Kupang. The Dutch similarly introduced a new political system and restructured the entire economy down to the smallest family unit, introducing cattle-ranching and the cultivation of cash crops in all areas. The entire population was dispersed, and relocated in smaller settlements which inhibited the development of any general opposition.

With pacification, the Dutch and Portuguese administrations completed their border discussions with the *Sentenca Arbitral*, agreed in 1913 and signed in 1915. The treaty divided the island almost equally, with the Dutch in the west and Portuguese in the east. The Portuguese retained the enclave of Oecusse Ambeno on the northwest coast (the site of the eighteenth-century Portuguese capital, Lifau) and the islands of Atauro and Jaco.

Politically, the Portuguese thus appeared finally to have implanted an effective framework of colonial rule throughout East Timor. The appearance, however, was deceptive. The impact on the subsistence sector of the economic policies required for cash-crop cultivation was relatively minor, as were the social effects of these policies, with the exception of the regular demands for forced labour. Furthermore, although the kingdoms were formally abolished, the ideologies legitimizing the traditional political hierarchy and the rituals of exchange were perpetuated. *Suco* heads, for example, always had to ensure that they were supported by the *liurai* and his retinue. Consequently, two political systems, the colonial and indigenous co-existed. Whilst the former was sanctioned through coercion and the use of force, the latter was sanctioned by a powerful cultural tradition. Where the two systems met, in the office of *suco* head or of village chief, for example, the Timorese tradition gave some legitimacy to the colonial hierarchy, but, in general, both co-existed in a rather uneasy truce.

Japanese invasion and occupation

Although the emergence of a fascist government in Portugal had little effect on the indigenous political system, it produced some important changes in the colonial sector[15] through its incorporation of small groups of Timorese into the administrative and clerical élites.

Established after a military coup in 1926, the *Estado Novo* of Antonio Salazar began to formalize Portugal's 'civilizing mission' in its colonies by creating new institutional relations between them and the fatherland. The Colonial Act of 1930 centralized political control over the colonies, bringing them under direct rule from Lisbon. Legislative councils were set up representing local colonial élite interests: the administration, the church, Portuguese plantation owners and the army. Their powers of influence, however, were limited, being confined to twice-yearly consultations with the governor. More important for Timor's political future was the creation by the act of two categories of people in the colony: *indigenes* ('unassimilated' natives) and *nao indigenes* including *mesticos* (whites) and *assimilados* ('assimilated' natives). To gain *assimilado* status, and its accompanying Portuguese citizenship, a Timorese had to speak Portuguese, earn sufficient income to maintain his family, and prove he possessed a good character. For those in administration and business, these criteria were waived. Unlike the overwhelming majority of the population, *assimilados* could vote in elections for the Portuguese National Assembly and the local legislative council. This *indigines/nao indigenes* distinction, together with a limited recruitment of Timorese into the colonial political system was to have an important effect on the emergence of indigenous political élites during the post-Pacific War period, and on the struggle for independence itself.

Of similar importance was the incorporation of the Catholic Church into Salazar's corporatist colonial system. After 1941, education in the colonies was entrusted to the church under the tutelage of the state. As an earlier Vatican–Portuguese accord of 1940 had put it: 'Portuguese Catholic missions are considered to be of imperial usefulness; they have an eminently civilizing influence'.[16] Timorese children subsequently learnt colonial values through a socializing encounter in Catholic missions. Again, this was to be of some importance in the later emergence of Timorese political élites in the 1950s and 60s. Aside from these measures, there were few other changes in Timor. As the Portuguese economy stagnated under the impact of depression and war, its exploitation of East Timor gave way to neglect. The colonial state's only contribution was a limited programme of road construction, largely to ease the transport problems of the colonial community.

This system was shattered by the Pacific War. The Japanese invasion of the island, prompted by the Allies' use of Timor as a forward base for the defence of Australia, profoundly affected both the colonial system and Timorese society. After the Japanese invasion of Pearl Harbor, 400 Dutch and Australian commandos landed in Dili, against the wishes of the Portuguese governor. Their aim was to pre-empt a Japanese takeover which the Allied Government considered imminent. As a result of this action, the Japanese became convinced that the Allies planned to use Timor as a forward military base, and sent 20,000 troops to take the island.

According to most accounts, the outcome was a gallant two-year guerrilla war carried out by 400 Allied troops, who inflicted 1500 casualties on the Japanese, against overwhelming odds, until they were forced to retreat to Australia in January 1943. History has duly recorded their feats. What it failed to record was the fact that this success would have been impossible without the support of a Timorese population who paid the price for their loyalty to the Allies' cause when the Australians departed. Personal accounts of the Allied campaign document the crucial support given by the indigenous population. Typical is the following from one of the Australian commandos:

> We relied on the natives to act more or less as a buffer between us and the Japanese; they more or less protected us by letting us know when the Japanese were moving about and where the Japanese were going . . . part of my job was to collect food to send away to our headquarters that lived in an area where there was no population. I would go around with the local chief and we'd collect the food. On occasions when the food was scarce the *chefe* would order the householders to give us food which they had ready to eat that night — they would have to go without because the *chefe* said we had to be strong to fight their enemy, the Japanese.[17]

During this campaign, many towns, villages and hamlets were destroyed by both Allied and Japanese bombing. But worse was to come. When the Australian troops were evacuated in February 1943, the Timorese carried on fighting, and their eventual defeat by the end of the year resulted in the Japanese exacting a brutal toll for their Allied support. In areas where the Australians had been active, villages were burnt and families executed. The population was resettled and subjected to forced food deliveries to the Japanese. By the time the Japanese surrendered some 60,000 Timorese, or 13 per cent of the population, had died as a result of the war.[18] Most of the main towns and villages had been destroyed, the livestock population was at a third of its 1939 level and most people were starving. An Australian Services Reconnaissance Department Report of August 1945 concluded that in most parts of Timor the hamlets has disappeared altogether.[19]

As the Japanese left, the Portuguese returned, in the hope that they could resume their traditional pattern of colonial rule. Control was reasserted ruthlessly. The economy's infrastructure was rebuilt with compulsory labour, extending the chiefs' powers to recruit forced labour from their *sucos*. The use of workers from each *suco* for at least one month per year in the construction of roads, buildings and port facilities led to a decline in agricultural output, since at least some of the male population was always absent from the village. Faced with economic decline at home, coupled with international isolation for its support for Franco's policies, the Portuguese were forced to rely on such compulsory labour to rebuild their distant colony. A typical description given by visitors during this period was provided by a member of the Australian War Graves Commission, which went to East Timor in 1947: 'Forced labour under the whip goes on from dawn to dusk, and the Portuguese colonists . . . live with the same mixture of civility and brutality as they had 350 years ago'.[20]

With these basic economic and political tasks complete, Portuguese rule returned to its pre-war objectives. Production of agricultural commodities increased, a few more Timorese were allowed to participate in the political system and educational provision was extended through the Catholic schools. Secure in the belief that the independence movements overturning colonial rule throughout post-war Southeast Asia would never spread to their orderly society, administrators counselled Timorese against bowing or saluting whenever they encountered a Portuguese; such 'feudal' practices would be rather embarrassing for foreign guests . . .

The Portuguese need not have been so concerned. The energies of the Timorese had been spent in reconstructing their rural economy, shattered in many areas by war and occupation. Resistance to the Japanese had been organized through the same indigenous political system that had resisted colonial influence. It continued to reproduce itself intact during the post-war period. Social reorganization was at times necessary as a result of Portuguese economic demands, but the fundamental structure of traditional society remained solid. Despite attempts at colonial transformation, the salient features of East Timorese society remained in the mid-twentieth century much as they had been at the time of the Portuguese arrival. All the basic elements ensuring the reproduction of indigenous society were still firmly in place — kinship systems, ideologies legitimizing traditional rule, a self-regulating political system, a self-sustaining subsistence economy and a culture based on notions of reciprocity and exchange. Just as the East Timorese had created a framework in which resistance to colonial occupation could be organized, so too would they use this in the coming struggle for independence.

Notes

1. Groeneveldt, p. 116.
2. Ibid. p. 117.
3. Middelkoop, 1952, p. 202.
4. Groeneveldt, 1960.
5. Hall, 1968, p. 211.
6. Boxer, 1960, p. 351.
7. Cited in Schulte-Nordholt, 1971.
8. See Francillon, 1967.
9. Boxer, 1960, p. 355.
10. D. H. Kolff, *Voyages through the Southern and Little Known Parts of the Moluccan Archipelago, and along the Previously Unknown Coast of New Guinea, 1825–6*, ed. G. W. Earl, Madden & Co., London 1840, p. 35.
11. Wallace, 1964, p. 153.
12. Forbes, 1883, p. 404.
13. Anderson, 1962, p. 95.
14. Forman, 1976, 1978.
15. The Pacific War was the term used for World War II in Southeast Asia.
16. Cited in Hill, 1978, p. 22.
17. Interview with C. Morris, former commando, on ABC Radio, Melbourne, 6 April 1977, printed in *Retrieval*, No. 36, April–May, p. 14; see also Callinan, 1953.
18. J. S. Dunn indicates that the census of 1947 showed that the population of East Timor had fallen from 472,221 in 1930 to 433,412 in 1947. Allowing for a normal population growth, he estimates that the population fell by 60,000 between these two dates. See Dunn, 1983, p. 26.
19. Intelligence Reports, Operation SUNLAG, Service Reconnaisance Department, 21 August 1945, cited in Dunn, 1983, p. 4.
20. Glen, Francis, 'Slavery in Timor', *Observer* (Australia), 29 October 1960.

2. East Timor and Indonesia: Political Developments from the Pacific War to the Portuguese Revolution

During the period following the Pacific War, political power in East Timor was held largely by a grouping of élites whose authority derived from their positions both in the colonial structure and in the indigenous kinship system.

In the indigenous system, political power was exercised by *liurai* and *suco* chiefs. Despite their political displacement in the early years of the twentieth century, the *liurai* (and most notably those with royal status) maintained a powerful control over their former subjects. They dominated the 'replacement' *suco* leaders promoted to positions of local power by the colonial administration. *Liurai* and *suco* bases thus formed the loci of power; status accruing to groups on grounds of religion, landholding or age continued to be of lesser importance.

In the colonial system, power rested on administrative, military or economic foundations, the latter in trade or plantation holdings. In addition to these power centres, there was also one founded on a commercial base, located in the Chinese community. Chinese formed about 2 per cent of East Timor's population during the post-war period.[1] Their contacts with Timor dated from their fifteenth-century involvement in the sandalwood trade; settlement came later, with Portuguese and Dutch 'pacification' at the beginning of the twentieth century.[2] Many Chinese subsequently married into Timorese families. Although not all Chinese were involved in trading, they nevertheless dominated East Timor's commercial sector, notably in retailing. By the end of the 1960s, 397 of the 400 retail outlets were run by Chinese families, who also played an important role in the buying and selling of grain. Most Chinese were educated in Taiwanese schools, and remained Taiwanese citizens, as in many other areas of Southeast Asia. Being to a degree institutionally separate, and often located at the end of a commercial chain, directly linked with consumers and producers, Chinese were often stereotyped by Timorese as wealthy profiteers who ultimately owed their allegiance to a foreign state. Although this stereotype undoubtedly corresponded to members of the commercial élite in the Chinese community, it often bore little relation to the reality of life for many poorer, non-trading Chinese in the villages. Membership of the élites in the colonial sector was extended as a result of post-war changes introduced reluctantly by an increasingly impoverished colonial power. These changes occurred mostly in the areas of education and administration.

Catholicism pervaded education; the first schools in Timor had been established in the eighteenth century by missionaries and, by the mid-1960s, the church still controlled 60 per cent of primary-school education. The colonial administration organized schools for Portuguese *assimilados* and *mesticos*, whilst the Chinese and Moslem communities ran their own institutions. The Portuguese army groomed Timorese through their network of training schools in the rural areas. Aiming to consolidate its rule, the colonial power began to train Timorese for administrative positions by raising educational levels. Typically, they left it too late and did too little. Although the numbers attending primary schools increased from 8000 to 57,000 between 1954 and 1974, this expansion seemed to have little effect; 93 per cent of the population remained illiterate by 1973.[3] The reasons for this are not hard to find. As one observer noted in 1975: 'Education is a tremendous economic burden and confers only dubious benefits on a rural family. Students' parents must pay for books and uniforms, and many large rural families can afford to send only a couple of children'.[4]

Furthermore, the sort of education children received was often both irrelevant and alien to their home life. Surveying primary education in the early 1970s, another observer wrote:

> The first year in *posto* and *suco* schools run by the missions was a preparatory year aimed at giving children a grasp of the Portuguese language. Those who did not succeed in this year were severely handicapped in the rest of their education. As rural Timorese generally spoke no Portuguese at home this would have been a high percentage. The curriculum of the next four years consisted of reading, writing, arithmetic and the history of Portugal. Even in the remotest villages children were required to commit to memory the rivers, railways and cities of Portugal. Timorese culture and traditions were not mentioned in the classroom and neighbouring Asian countries rarely mentioned. There was a very high drop-out rate even at the primary school level.[5]

With this sort of content and organization, the results were two-fold: an increasing alienation from colonial culture and a marginal improvement in the level of basic literacy skills. Both these developments were influential in the emergence of the differing ideas about independence which developed in the countryside in the early 1970s.

Equally influential were the changes that took place in the secondary and tertiary sectors of education. Although the actual increase was relatively small at the secondary level, the result was the creation of small, educated urban élites, based in towns such as Maubisse, Lospalos and Baucau but mainly in the colonial capital, Dili. Very few Timorese went on to tertiary education, which after 1970 involved entering either one high school, one army-team training centre, one technical school or attending university in Lisbon. Before 1970, only two students per year attended university, but by 1974 there were 39 students in attendance.

Most of these tertiary-level students eventually took up posts in government administration, the health service, education or the army. In all these areas there was a limited 'Timorization' from the mid-1960s onwards, as élite membership was extended minimally to the indigenous population. In this process educated Timorese soon came up against the all-too-familiar realities of their childhood: rigid political control, colonial hierarchies, propaganda masquerading as education in sparsely resourced schools[6] and a rural sector where basic diseases such as tuberculosis, malaria and leprosy were endemic, resulting in a 50 per cent death rate for children under the age of five.[7]

At the same time, it was all too apparent that Portugal would not relinquish its colonial control unless forced to do so. 'Portugal would no more give up Timor than America would give up Hawaii', declared a government official to a visiting journalist in 1964.[8] Since the early 1950s, the United Nations had put increasing pressure on Portugal to expedite a policy of decolonization,[9] but to little effect. Indeed, one of the main reasons for the limited developments occurring in Timor in the 1960s was the increasing success of the independence movements in the African colonies and the ensuing heavy burden of defence expenditure on the Portuguese government. Hence a restructuring of the imperial system took place to provide for greater autonomy for the colonies, the ultimate aim being to delay the achievement of independence by creating a federal framework in which the 'overseas territories' could co-exist under a benevolent Portuguese tutelage.

The prospect before Timor's newly-educated élite groups of a lengthy Portuguese presence co-existed with an increasing awareness on their part of the country's potential for development. Post-war expansion in the cultivation of export crops and the improvement in the infrastructure, together with increases in investment from abroad, held out possibilities for national development, if the capital accumulated from trade and commerce in the controlling Portuguese companies of SAPT and SOTA (*Sociedade Orientale do Transportes e Armagens*), could be diffused into the domestic agricultural sector. This conclusion was reinforced by the discovery of potentially rich off-shore oil and gas deposits in the late 1960s, followed by the awarding of concessions to international corporations by the Portuguese government.[10] From the mid-1960s onwards, three themes dominated discussions amongst the newly recruited members of East Timor's élite: the potential for economic development; the lack of any social or political initiative by the colonial power; and the seeming eternity of Portuguese rule.

Although the members of these élites occupied positions in areas like education or administration, whose institutions enshrined colonial values, they nevertheless formulated their ideas in terms which frequently owed as much to their socialization in Timorese culture as to the values generated by their recent education and training in the colonial system.[11] This was reinforced for many by their being related directly to families holding economic and political power in the local élite. Consequently, it seemed possible that the separation which colonialism had attempted to create and perpetuate between rural indigenous and urban-based colonial-oriented élites could begin to be undermined by developing ties between these groups. In this process, it seemed likely that the dominant values of the indigenous system would be influential, particularly given this system's ability to express novel political and cultural values in traditional ideological forms. In the mid-1960s, it thus seemed possible that new social and political groups could emerge, with an ability to express their increasing knowledge of the values of national development in the framework provided by the values of indigenous society. This, however, depended on two factors: the ability of the Portuguese administration to plan a phased process of decolonization, and the ability of the élites in Timor to develop viable rural-based political parties. If these could be achieved, then political independence was possible; and, with the support of a powerful, cohesive indigenous sector, East Timor could become a successful developing state in Southeast Asia. The success of this scenario depended not only upon internal developments, however, but also upon the international and, more particularly, the regional context — the Southeast Asian framework so blithely ignored by Portuguese colonialism since the defeat of the Dutch in the seventeenth century and, most importantly, within this framework, East Timor's vast and populous neighbour, Indonesia.

Indonesia

In the aftermath of the Pacific War, with the demise of Dutch colonial control, Indonesia rapidly became the lynch-pin of Southeast Asian security. Containing the world's fifth largest population, with an abundance of raw materials and fertile soils, and strategically placed between the Indian and Pacific oceans, the newly independent Indonesian state commanded attention. So much so that the major influence supporting its independence in negotiations with the Dutch was none other than the United States government itself.

Despite its potential, the new state nevertheless faced major problems. Colonialism had undermined the economic basis for its national development and left it without any viable administrative structure. Both these had to be created rapidly by the populist leaders of the independence movement. At the same time they had to weld together a tremendous variety of indigenous cultures into a viable national entity. Dutch colonial rule had been based overwhelmingly on the populous central island of Java, and much of the remainder of the country had developed very unevenly under the exploitative tutelage of a centralized administration. From the strictly Moslem areas of North Sumatra to the tribes of Borneo and the Christian islands of the east, a variety of social and economic systems faced very different problems for their development. The catchphrase of the new regime, 'Unity in Diversity', expressed more of a hope than a reality.

Indeed, the first independence government after 1945, under the charismatic leadership of Sukarno, immediately faced a number of regional rebellions, from Islamic movements in Java and Sumatra, and from Christian groups in the South Moluccas. Dealing with these, and attempting to build up a sense of national unity for political and economic reconstruction, consumed the energies of the groups of nationalist, communist and military politicians who held state power by the middle of the 1950s. They dealt superficially with the problems generated by regional inequality rather than focusing on the underlying structure of regionalism itself; and as inequalities worsened, politics at the centre became factionalized with élite politicians, and most notably the military, voicing regional demands as a means for outflanking their opposition within the élite. The ensuing atmosphere of ideological confrontation was heightened by Sukarno's use of anti-colonial rhetoric as a substitute for coherent economic or political planning. Stress was laid on the external enemy, be it the Dutch, the neo-colonial state of Malaysia or the machinations of American imperialism. Indeed, internal opposition came to be defined primarily in external terms. When in 1958, areas such as North Sulawesi and Central Sumatra rebelled against a central government which they saw as restricting their cultural, economic and political development, the suppression of their revolt was legitimized by its supposedly pro-imperialist stance. Similarly, the lack of any referendum offered to the people of West Irian (West New Guinea) in the discussions leading up to the UN-sponsored New York agreement of 1962 was justified by a simple emphasis on the need to wrest the territory from the colonial yoke and restore it to Indonesia. In the early 1960s, foreign policy was again dominated by a sloganized posturing which portrayed the formation of Malaysia (from the states of Sarawak, Sabah and Malaya) as a Western plot to destabilize Indonesia. As the economy declined from lack of serious national planning, and as factional divisions intensified in the Indonesian political élite, the emphasis was increasingly placed on externally induced threats and on which group could deal with them most effectively.

In this political climate, one might have assumed that East Timor would have been given some importance in foreign-policy calculations. After all, what could have been more suitable than a relic of colonialism, bordering Indonesian territory and controlled by a fascist government? According to most analysts, however, this was not the case.[12] East Timor was either ignored, or its status confirmed. As Foreign Minister Subandrio stated: 'We have no claims on Portuguese Timor, nor on North Borneo or any other territory outside of the former Dutch East Indies'.[13] In a similar vein, but more specifically, a UN document on East Timor, published in 1962, stated that: 'For its part the government of Indonesia has declared that it maintains friendly relations with Portugal and has no claim to Portuguese Timor, which has never been part of the Dutch East Indies and therefore is not of the same status as West Irian'.[14] Basing themselves upon such statements most commentators concluded that, although exceptional to the trends of the period, it appeared as if Indonesia had little interest in East Timor.

Yet, contrary statements are relatively easy to find, and a very different account can be presented, one which indicates a continuing interest in East Timor by sections of the Indonesian hierarchy throughout the period. As early as 1950, Mohammed Yamin, Minister of Justice and Education in the 1950s, argued that Indonesia should incorporate the Dutch East Indies, North Borneo and the whole of Portuguese Timor.[15] At a later date, in 1961, Ruslan Abulgani, Vice-Chairman of Sukarno's Supreme Advisory Council, stated that Indonesia's 'eyes and heart are directed towards Portuguese Timor . . . fill your hearts with hatred not only for Portuguese colonialism, but for all colonialism still existing on Asian and African soil'.[16] In 1963 Mokoginta, a high-ranking general, was rather more specific: 'If the people of East Timor today or tomorrow started a revolution . . . we would support them . . . After independence, if they wanted to stay independent, fine — if they want to join Indonesia, we will talk it over'.[17]

Rebellion

Beyond such statements, there is also evidence of more supportive action. The 1962 UN report on East Timor cited the existence of a 'Bureau of Liberation of the Timor Republic', in Jakarta. In spring 1963, the Bureau claimed to have established a government, with twelve minsters in Batugade inside East Timor. It appealed for recognition from other governments. These events coincided with reports of a military build up in East Timor, with a thousand new troops reportedly being sent in by Portugal.

The emergence of this Indonesian-sponsored movement in the early 1960s seems to have been related to events a few years earlier in East Timor in 1959. In that year, fourteen Indonesian military officers landed on the East Timor coast, and requested political asylum; they were from southeast Sulawesi, and had been involved in a rebellion in 1958 against the government. The Portuguese allowed them to settle, ten in Bacau and four in the southern area of Viqueque. In these areas, and particularly in the regions of Uatolari and Uatocarabu near Viqueque, the Indonesians began to ally themselves with groups opposed to Portuguese rule, whose objective seems to have been unification of Indonesia with Portuguese Timor. As one of the group's leaders subsequently stated: 'We never regarded ourselves as part of Portugal. We are not interested in the government of Indonesia, but in the integration of East and West Timor. We have ancient links — we never had a border before Portugal colonized Timor'.[18] An uprising was launched on 7 June 1959, with attacks on Portuguese *postos* in Uatolari and Uatocarabu. In order to isolate these *postos* telephone links with Baucau were cut. A revolt was also planned in Dili, but details of it were leaked to the Portuguese administration by an informer; a truckload of arms was stopped by the Portuguese just prior to its arrival in Dili's central barracks. Fighting in the Viqueque area was intense; the Portuguese flew in a company of one hundred Goan troops from India to suppress the rebellion, which ended on 14 June. Estimates of deaths varied between 160 and 1000, but all reports agreed on the brutality with which the Portuguese put down the revolt — villages were burnt, families killed and most of the leadership were executed. Fifty-eight Timorese were exiled to Angola and Mozambique after having been told that they were being sent for trial in Lisbon.

Reports of the degree of Indonesian involvement in the rebellion varied considerably, some even arguing that the fourteen officers were direct agents of the Indonesian Government, sent to organize the overthrow of the colonial administration.[19] What seems most likely is that they were genuine dissident regional leaders who tried to mobilize local discontent as a means for rebuilding their base in East Timor. What is indisputable is that they were assisted both by the Indonesian consul in Dili and by supporters in Kupang in Indonesian Timor, who had agreed to supply arms. These facts indicate, at the very least, that there already existed an integrationist lobby which had the support at some level of the Indonesian Government. News of the ease with which fourteen soldiers could organize an internal rebellion in such a short period of time must have spurred on any members of the Indonesian political élite who hoped to extend national boundaries. Certainly, it would have encouraged them to support a 'liberation bureau' trying to set up an alternative Timorese government. Hence the prominence of the bureau in the early 1960s, and its proof of its success to its supporters with the formation of a 'government' inside East Timor in 1963.

Despite such successes this project seems to have suffered a temporary demise during the next few years, resurfacing in the late 1960s. This is obviously related to the tumultuous turn of events in Indonesia during the middle of that decade.

On 30 September 1965, a group of junior army officers launched a coup to pre-empt what they claimed was an impending takeover of the Sukarno Government by a pro-Western 'Council of Generals'. On the same day, the armed forces, under the leadership of a group of major generals, notably the commander of the army's Strategic Reserve (KOSTRAD), General Suharto, staged a counter-coup, quickly defeating the earlier attempt. Implicating prominent nationalist and communist politicians in this attempt, and fuelling the widespread resentment of the communist party amongst Indonesia's Islamic groups, the military gradually took over the government, completing this with the effective resignation of Sukarno on 11 March 1966. In this process, the military oversaw the creation of an authoritarian corporatist state, purging and then strictly controlling political parties and trade unions. In the months following the military takeover, at least 600,000 people were killed in sectarian violence. The formation of Indonesia's *Orde Baru* (New Order) state was characterized by an increasing militarization of all spheres of economic and social life, and by a highly centralized system of political rule based on a Javanese military élite. In the run-up to the coup, foreign-policy issues such as East Timor had disappeared from the political scene as the infighting between nationalist, communist, military and Islamic élites intensified. After the coup, the military's energies were totally consumed in political reconstruction and consolidation of state power. Foreign-policy issues were again effectively shelved until the end of the 1960s. Furthermore, the ideological affinities between the Caetano regime in Portugal and the Suharto Government were such that problems potentially bringing them into conflict, such as border clashes and smuggling between Indonesian and Portuguese Timor, were usually resolved quite quickly.

However, within the military, and in its higher echelons, the 'problem' of Portuguese Timor soon resurfaced as an issue. The integrationist perspective gained influence. By late 1969, it had been taken up by BAKIN, the army's central co-ordinating intelligence agency and think tank and, more particularly, by OPSUS, Suharto's special operations unit headed by his closest political adviser, Brigadier General Murtopo. OPSUS studies concluded that since an independent Portuguese Timor could pose a security threat to eastern Indonesia, the military would prefer to incorporate the island into the republic if Portuguese rule became unstable or unviable.[20] As OPSUS saw it, the problem lay less with the decision to incorporate than with the decision on how incorporation could be achieved.

Despite such unofficial conclusions, however, the official position of the Indonesian Government remained as before. Even as late as April 1974, on the eve of the coup that was to overthrow the Caetano regime, Indonesian policy remained officially one of 'non-interference' in Portuguese Timor. Indonesia's Foreign Minister, Adam Malik, even went as far as to welcome the progressive character of the post-Caetano Government, since he claimed it had 'an intention to give independence'. The only hint of any dissent at official government level had come in April 1972, when the state-controlled press had carried reports of an insurrection in East Timor a few days before an official Indonesian delegation was to visit Dili to discuss the setting up of a border commission. Although the report was later denied, the objective was achieved, namely the blocking of a formal government contact which would directly recognize the border on the ground in Timor. It was a significant gesture, recognized by most senior members of the military as emanating from OPSUS.[21]

In a sense, this incident typified post-war policy towards Portuguese Timor. Behind the official statements of the recognition of Portugal's position, and of the acceptance of the right of non-interference, there was intermittent pressure for annexation. This had grown to significant proportions in the intelligence service by the early 1970s. Furthermore contrary to the opinions of many observers, it had also become a very determined lobby, as was shown by subsequent events.

Notes

1. This figure includes both Chinese and Mestico ('mixed blood' Chinese).
2. Most Chinese in East Timor are Hakka, originally from Fukien province. See Hill, 1978.
3. Ranck, 1977, pp. 17–29.
4. Ibid., p. 20.
5. Hill, 1978, pp. 44–5.
6. According to Dunn, the number of students in secondary schools by 1974 was still only 1200. See Dunn, 1983, p. 31.

7. For general data on the health situation in East Timor, see *The World Health Statistics Annual, 1973–6*, Vol. III, UN Publications, New York, 1976.

8. Nilsson, K., 'Sleepy Island Due to Wake Up', *Straits Times*, 19 June 1964.

9. Most notably in 1955, from which date Portugal was required to report regularly on the progress of its decolonization (it refused), in 1961 when Portugal was openly condemned for its colonial policies, and after 1963, when Portugal was expelled from all UN bodies.

10. In the late 1960s two companies were drilling offshore: Timor Oil and International Oil, both Australian based. They were joined by other American companies in the early 1970s.

11. See, for example, the early debates amongst members of these groups in journals such as *Seara*, a Catholic newspaper, *Voz de Timor*, mostly circulating in Dili.

12. Writing in 1966, a pro-Indonesian American academic stated: 'In conclusion, we can say that in a sense Portuguese Timor is a trust territory, the Portuguese holding it in trust for Indonesia'. Weatherbee, pp. 683–95.

13. See *Antara*, Indonesian Government news agency, 2 October 1962.

14. United Nations Document A/AC 108/L.13, 3 December 1962, paragraph 35.

15. *Antara*, Indonesian Government News Agency, 1 February 1950. Feith comments that Yamin's 'stature as a nationalist ideologue was second only to that of the President himself' (see Feith, 1962, p. 342).

16. Ruslan Abdulgani, speech to the Afro-Asian Solidarity meeting, Jakarta, 1961.

17. General Mokoginta, interviewed in the *Washington Post*, 10 May 1963.

18. José Manuel Duarte, a Timorese leader of the Viqueque uprising, interviewed in Lisbon, by Jill Jolliffe, 11 November 1978 (from a transcript in the author's possession).

19. José Martins, a leader of the pro-Indonesian KOTA party, argues that the 'refugees' were sponsored by the Indonesian Government, who, through the Indonesian Consul in Dili, won the support of Timorese through bribes. See Martins, J., Affidavit submitted to the UN Secretary-General, 23 March 1976.

20. See Dunn, 1983, p. 106.

21. For details of this event, see Reece, B. 'Portuguese Timor, 1974', in *Australia's Neighbours*, Canberra, April–June 1974.

3. Changing Strategies: The Emergence of Political Parties and the Indonesian Response

On 25 April 1974, the Portuguese Armed Forces Movement (AFM) overthrew the Caetano regime. Weary of defending an archaic feudal power clinging to the last vestiges of its colonial empire, army officers replaced a fascist government with one committed to capitalist modernization and decolonization. Whilst the new head of the 'Junta of National Salvation', Antonio de Spinola, favoured progressive autonomy for the colonies within a Portuguese framework, most army officers, fresh from their experience of fighting Africa's liberation movements, preferred some form of independence.

News of the April coup filtered to East Timor through radio broadcasts and military messages, but no official pronouncement was forthcoming. The governor, understandably, was reluctant to make any statement. A strong supporter of the Caetano regime, he had publicly denounced the AFM two days before the coup. Portuguese radio promised the disbanding of the secret service, the reform of the administration, and the freedom to organize political parties. Governor Aldeia held firm, however, convinced that the coup was ephemeral. Soon he was forced to react. The Portuguese company, SAPT, had sacked some of its workers who were requesting an increase in their US$10 monthly salary. The company appealed to Aldeia, who would have reacted with the normal coercive Caetanoist policies had it not been for the arrival of two AFM delegates from Lisbon. The delegates assessed the case, awarded the workers a 100 per cent wage rise and rebuked the governor.[1] This event, symbolizing the momentous changes occurring in Lisbon, galvanized Timorese politics. Associations and groupings that had led a shadowy, partial existence amongst the indigenous members of the colonial élites rapidly emerged to put forward their ideas for independence and development. The coup had taken them by surprise, and the rather vague and general notions they had been discussing since the middle of the 1960s now had to be concretized in specific ideas for popular discussion.

The coup had also come as something of a surprise to other interested parties, all of whom were to play a crucial role in the events of the next two years: Indonesia, where the intelligence services were pressing the government to annex East Timor; neighbouring powers, such as Malaysia and Australia, staking out their place in the region's rapid development; and the industrialized nations of Western Europe, Japan and the United States, concerned about strategic and economic interests in Southeast Asia.

All these actors, however distant, were to influence markedly East Timor's decolonization. The struggle for the emerging state's independence soon became a dynamic interplay of these powerful forces whose interests shaped, restrained and determined the outcome.

The most immediate issue for the East Timorese in the early dry season of 1974 was, however, independence — what it was and how it could be gained.

Party formation

Whilst the changes in Lisbon had little immediate impact on rural society with its well-tried means of protecting itself from colonial interference, they nevertheless had a profound impact on Timor's élites, and particularly on sections of the administrative élite centred on the towns, and notably in Dili. Opposition to aspects of Portuguese rule amongst the urban élite had centred largely on a small group of students and administrators meeting clandestinely in the capital.[2] The main outlets for their ideas had been Catholic newspapers with a tiny circulation, such as *A Provincia de Timor* and *Seara*. Their conclusions had been piecemeal, general and rather vague. Topics such as traditional marriages and the education system were discussed. There was little in the way of overall critique, and little offered as an alternative. Their political inexperience was perhaps best illustrated by their approaches made to the Indonesian Government in 1973 to assist in the struggle against colonialism. This student–administrator group together with more senior bureaucrats who had been incorporated into colonial politics by standing for the Legislative Assembly[3] in the 1960s, as well as leading Timorese landowners, formed the bases for the two main political parties organized in Dili after the April coup.

What was initially the most popular party titled itself the Timorese Democratic Union (UDT). Its programme called for democratization, income redistribution, human rights, but above all, for 'Self determination for the Timorese people oriented towards a federation with Portugal with an intermediate stage for the attainment of independence', and a 'Rejection of the integration of Timor into any potential foreign country'.[4] The union's organizing members illustrated its leadership. Its president, Mario Carrascalao, was a forestry engineer and coffee-plantation owner. Two other senior members, Lopez da Cruz and Domingos d'Oliveira were customs officials. Both da Cruz and Carrascalao were formerly representatives of the only political party allowed in East Timor, the Caetanoist *Accao National Popular*. UDT was the first party to be formed, on 11 May, and it soon became the most popular. Basing itself firmly on two groups — Dili's senior administrative élite and leading plantation owners — it also drew support from a range of *suco liurais*, most notably in the areas of Ermera, Maubara and Maubisse. Using their positions of power in the kinship system, these *liurais* built up support for the UDT in their areas. The Portuguese flag, revered as a sacred object (*lulik*), was used skilfully to attract members from the countryside. UDT thus welded together traditional and administrative élite centres of power in a coalition which promised development within a familiar framework — 'Proceeding in the shadow of the Portuguese flag', as their programme put it.[5]

In the months that followed, UDT's leadership often appeared divided between those whose positions in the civil service led them to stress the benefits of a continuing Portuguese role and those who focused more on the need for independence, an idea born from their growing awareness of the benefits to their commercial concerns of economic diversification beyond the Portuguese orbit. In May, however, they presented a united, self-confident front.

Just as the UDT combined the interests of urbanized with rural-based élites, so too did a second party, the Timorese Social Democratic Association (ASDT), but it did so in a rather different way. Comprised mostly of the newly recruited members of the urban élites, most of ASDT's founders lived in Dili, although they retained ties with their rural areas of origin, and several of them were from *liurai* families. The oldest member of ASDT's organizing committee was its 37 years old future president, Xavier do Amaral. The average age of the committee was twenty-seven. Most of its members were employed in the government service, as administrators or teachers. Many were Catholics trained in the Jesuit seminary of Dare, near Dili. The programme of the ASDT, published at its inception on 12 May, was 'based on the universal doctrines of socialism and democracy', and committed the party to 'the rejection of colonialism'. One of its founding members stated subsequently that the essence of the programme: 'called for gradual independence, preceded by administrative, economic, social and political reforms. A period of three to eight years was what was thought to be necessary in preparing the country for independence'.[6] In the words of another of its founding members: 'ASDT was social democratic, with the emphasis on democratic. It was formed to defend the idea of the right to independence'.[7]

Although ASDT's programme was rather general, its members agreed on a whole range of specific issues as attainable conditions assisting the achievement of independence: the need for literacy programmes, a priority for agricultural development, the fullest participation of Timorese in the political structure, the reassertion of Timorese culture and a widespread health programme. During the months that followed, ASDT members worked intensively, trying to see how these conditions could be developed. In this, they travelled outside the capital to provincial areas, where their ideas began to attract support. At the same time, in June and July, ASDT began to make tentative diplomatic contacts in the neighbouring countries of Indonesia and Australia. Its reception at ministerial level enhanced its status in East Timor as a more systematic alternative to UDT. It began to draw support from all levels of the rural social structure and, most importantly, from a number of prominent *liurai*.

Meanwhile, a third political party had been formed. Its title directly expressed its aims: 'the Association for the Integration of Timor into Indonesia'. For popular consumption, following its founding meeting on 25 May, it changed its name to the Timorese Popular Democratic Association, or

Apodeti. Its manifesto called for: 'An autonomous integration into the Republic of Indonesia in accordance with international law', and 'the teaching of the Indonesian language as a compulsory subject'. It promised human rights, freedom, a just income distribution, free education, free medical treatment and the right to strike.[8] Apodeti's most important leaders were Guilherme Gonçalves, a *liurai* from the border area, Arnaldo dos Reis Araujo, a southern-based cattle-rancher, and Osario Soares, a schoolteacher and administrative official. Support for Apodeti came mostly from Gonçalves' *sucos* but also from Dili's small Moslem community. The prominence of these particular individuals in Apodeti was of some significance. As noted earlier, the Indonesian intelligence service BAKIN, had been committed to the integration of East Timor for some time. During the 1960s it had built up an information network in East Timor, which worked through traders, customs officials and agents in Dili's Indonesian consulate. Gonçalves, Soares and, to a lesser extent, Araujo dealt with these agents in return for favours, sanctuary in the event of conflict and cash payments.[9] These three, together with a number of other pro-Indonesians, received financial support immediately after Apodeti was founded. Furthermore, before the Lisbon coup, BAKIN had already trained a number of pro-Apodeti East Timorese in radio broadcasting and interpreting. Apodeti was thus very much an Indonesian creation from its inception. It attracted minimal support. Whilst UDT and ASDT membership grew rapidly into the thousands, Apodeti never had more than 300 members throughout the whole of 1974.

Three further parties were created hurriedly, but they had little impact: 'the *Klibur Oan Timur Aswain* (KOTA) ('Sons of the Mountain Warriors') traced its roots to the Topasses, and wished to restore the position of *liurais* who could trace their ancestry to the Topasse period; the *Partido Trabalhista* (Labour Party), which like the KOTA party had no programme, had eight members, all of whom comprised one family; and the *Associacao Democratica Integracao Timor–Leste Australia* (ADLITA) collected money in return for promises of integration with Australia, but declined rapidly when the Australian Government rejected the idea at the end of 1974. None of these parties ever had more than a handful of members and played no part during decolonization.

Effectively there were two genuine political parties vying for popular support, and one created by Indonesia for its own purposes. Politics, which in Timorese society previously had meant representations to lineage elders and a complex set of discussions based on reciprocal obligations, now had a new referent — a choice between two general perspectives for the future, represented in conventional Western party forms. Initially, these different forms of politics existed in an uneasy truce, with those holding power in the indigenous sector being wary of the rather vague and general notions of the new parties, and those in the latter viewing rural politics as a tradition-bound system requiring modernization.

The perspectives of those in both systems soon began to change as external and internal events began to limit the scope of the possibilities envisaged by their leaders.

Diplomacy

On 12 June Deputy President of the Indonesian Parliament, John Naro, a member from Eastern Indonesia, argued in parliament that Indonesia should: 'Work out a special policy on Portuguese Timor so that finally that area will once again return to Indonesian control'.[10] Coming shortly after the formation of Apodeti, and with the growing awareness amongst Dili's élite of its ties with Indonesia, Naro's statement caused near panic. Most ASDT leaders still viewed Indonesia primarily in its role as founder member of the Non-Aligned Movement (NAM), and most of its members had been confident of a 'Bandung spirit' type support for independence from Portugal. Similarly, the UDT felt they had no reason to be concerned about their neighbour, many members hoped for trading and investment links with Indonesia.

In haste, a newly appointed diplomatic nominee from Fretilin's founding committee was sent by the ASDT to Jakarta to investigate. José Ramos-Horta was well received, or so it seemed. Naro appeared conciliatory, stressing his respect for the East Timorese people to choose their future. Foreign Minister Adam Malik was more direct and succinct. He recorded in writing three principles to which his government would adhere:

> That the independence of every country is the right of every nation, with no exception for the people in Timor; that the government had no intention of expanding or occupying other territories; that whoever governed in Timor after independence could be assured of Indonesian friendship and co-operation.[11]

Nothing could be clearer. Horta returned from Jakarta jubilant; armed with reassurances, he left for Australia.

As far as both ASDT and UDT were concerned, the situation in Australia seemed even more favourable. A party from Australia's Foreign Affairs Department had visited East Timor in June. One of its members, James Dunn, the Australian Consul to Dili from 1962–4, had reported back to Canberra that there was a strong case for independence. Indeed, it was 'inconceivable that the Timorese would freely choose any form of integration with Indonesia'.[12] It was thus a considerable surprise to him when Horta found himself snubbed by the Foreign Affairs Ministry. Throughout July, he was refused meetings with both the Minister and the head of the Southeast Asia Department. Despite many requests from parliamentarians, the church and academics, the government refused to make other than confused, disclaiming and disinterested statements; it had no knowledge of the situation, and it was beyond its concern. Horta was advised to focus on Indonesia and Portugal.

Meanwhile, Lisbon was showing little interest in this diplomatic manoeuvring. Alves Aldeia had been replaced by Nivio Herdade, a lieutenant-colonel who had implemented Spinola's ideas in Guinea-Bissau, but he was not given any brief for decolonization when he took up his post in July. Beset by the urgent and pressing problems of war and decolonization in its African colonies,

Portugal seemed to be drifting with the tide in its 'land of good coffee'.[13] Indeed, although the Portuguese Government in June had made public the idea that 'three choices' would soon be presented to the East Timorese, these were not forthcoming, and on 4 August 1974, in a joint communiqué with the UN on decolonization, it referred only to its African colonies.

Consequently, in Dili and the other centres of administrative and *liurai* power in the middle of the dry season, it was assumed that the Portuguese were committed but preoccupied, the Australians uninformed and unconcerned, and the Indonesians supportive and secure. Confident in the strength of their perspectives, the country's increasingly popular parties, ASDT and UDT, planned their campaigns for the coming months.

BAKIN and its allies

Berita Yudha is an Indonesian newspaper, reflecting the army's view of events. At the end of August, it analysed the situation in East Timor, concluding that the right to self-determination 'cannot be separated from general world strategies'. More specifically, it accused ASDT of 'seeking communist support'. Although *Berita*'s ideas were not taken up by any other newspaper, they were as significant as Naro's retracted parliamentary statement after the April coup. Both indicated that behind Indonesia's official pronouncements, a very different future was being mapped out for East Timor.

The driving force behind this was BAKIN. Since its commitment to integration in the 1960s, the Indonesian intelligence service had built up a widespread network of which the Apodeti leaders were a part. BAKIN represented the views of a highly influential grouping within the military, whose hallmarks were its concern for national security (and hence territorial expansion to ensure this security), a strong state and a corporate society. In the 1970s it spanned the major ministries and was the leading light in Suharto's inner cabinet. Its spokesmen were: Major-General Ali Murtopo, also head of OPSUS, the special operations unit which had masterminded Suharto's most successful operations (to overthrow former president Sukarno, to manipulate political parties and incorporate West Papua New Guinea in 1969); Lieutenant-General Yoga Sugama, close associate of Suharto and a leading figure in both OPSUS and KOPKAMTIB (the Operational Command for the Restoration of Security and Order, and the army's security command and interrogation unit); Admiral Sudomo, head of KOPKAMTIB; and, above all, Major-General Leonardus Benjamin Murdani, head of both military intelligence operations and KOPKAMTIB's special-tasks intelligence unit. He was the military man with the closest CIA contacts in Indonesia.[14]

In essence, these men and the network of military officials surrounding them were the godfathers of Indonesia's New Order regime. They had a tremendous influence in areas such as foreign affairs, diplomacy, defence and internal security. They were even able to set the terms of the country's academic debates through think tanks such as the Jakarta based Centre for Strategic and

International Studies (CSIS). They were intimately involved in the state's economic planning, and, like all military officers, had carved out niches in the extensive structure of economic pay-offs based on Indonesia's mineral wealth, oil deposits and investment potential. Not that they represented any particular sections of trade, agriculture or industry. In Indonesia the military itself constitutes the dominant fraction in each of these areas, to which other economic groups — financiers, indigenous entrepreneurs, landholders — are all subordinate.

Although in the late 1960s the views of the BAKIN group were not held by any other military groupings, with the exception of some members of the eastern Indonesian parliamentary lobby, such as Naro, they began to spread rapidly from the time of the April coup onwards. Events spurred this movement in 1974, events which themselves often owed much to the work of BAKIN and its operatives.

As early as the middle of 1974, BAKIN had finalized the general details of its plan to integrate East Timor. The scheme was entitled *Operasi Komodo* (Operation Giant Lizard), and, according to its founding documents, non-military means of annexation were preferred. *Komodo* employed several leading operatives, each with specific aims. Elias Tomodok was the Indonesian consul in Dili and part of the eastern Indonesian lobby. He came from the island of Roti, off the west coast of Indonesian Timor. Since 1968 he had transmitted diplomatic messages from Dili to Jakarta, exaggerating support for integration and emphasizing the worst aspects of Portuguese colonialism. Similarly, the governor of Indonesian Timor, El Tari, was an early 1970s recruit to BAKIN's plans. Together with a BAKIN agent from West Timor named Louis Taolin, he played a key role in early contacts with Apodeti members and East Timorese in the border areas. Outside Indonesia, the task of drumming up diplomatic support for integration in the United States and Western Europe was handed to a Sumatran, Liem Bian Kie (also known as Jusuf Wanandi). The director of CSIS, Harry Tjan Silalahi, took care of Australia and Portugal. A number of army officers was chosen specifically to organize a military campaign from the border if necessary. The most prominent of these were colonels Sugianto, Hernoto, Sinaga, Dading and Kasenda, assisted by a major named Andreas. Finally, an Indonesian Timorese, Lieutenant-Colonel Alexander Dinuth, was dispatched to Kupang to take charge of propaganda directed to East Timor. The Indonesian news agency, *Antara*, was organized to disseminate propaganda on East Timor to an international audience.[15]

The *Berita* article and the Naro statement were the opening salvoes of the *integrasi* campaign. *Komodo* was initiated in late August, when its actors began to play out their roles in earnest. Early in September, El Tari invited the leaders of Apodeti to Kupang, after which he released a press statement stating that the provincial government intended 'to assist the struggle of Apodeti'.[16] In mid-September, one of Indonesia's leading generals, Amir Machmud, claimed that although Indonesia was not territorially ambitious, it had no objections to integration. Clearly, the BAKIN bandwagon had started to roll, and in the next few weeks more leading figures began to support integration. One of the most surprising converts in this was none other than the Foreign Minister, Adam Malik, who three months earlier had supported independence and who had always been staunchly opposed to Murtopo's opportunistic manoeuvring. On 18 September, he publicly supported Apodeti. Why this sudden change? To explain this we have to turn to Timor's 'uninformed and unconcerned' neighbour Australia, fresh from its urging Ramos-Horta to 'look westward'.

To a *kabupaten* capital 60 km from the Indonesian city of Jogjakarta, in September, President Suharto travelled to develop his growing friendship with Australia's Prime Minister, Gough Whitlam. Before arriving in Wonosobo, Whitlam had met with a coterie of generals, spending most of his time chatting to BAKIN officers, and notably Yoga Sugama. During their discussions in Wonosobo, Suharto tentatively raised the subject of East Timor and was staggered by Whitlam's resolute answer. The Australian prime minister was fully briefed, personally involved and disarmingly forthright: 'An independent East Timor would be an unviable state, and a potential threat to the area',[17] he said. He offered Australia's services in making a joint approach with Indonesia to Portugal, urging integration. At the end of the meeting, the Foreign Affairs Department published a briefing paper, which stated:

> Australia appreciates Indonesia's concern about the future of the territory and shares its belief that the voluntary union of Portuguese Timor with Indonesia, on the basis of an internationally acceptable act of self-determination, would seem to serve the objective of decolonization, and at the same time the interests of stability in the region.[18]

As one commentator noted: 'Mr. Whitlam went much further, one suspects, than his Indonesian hosts required'.[19] Murtopo and his coterie must have been overjoyed, as Suharto returned to Jakarta mulling over BAKIN's advice that Indonesia would not necessarily be isolated internationally if it was to integrate East Timor. Clearly, the Australian Government was neither 'uninformed' nor 'unconcerned'. Adam Malik drew his own conclusions, and drifted tactically in the appropriate direction by supporting Apodeti. Some two months later in Jakarta's Foreign Press Club, he was to argue that integration was the only serious option for East Timor.[20]

Fretilin's programmes

The significance of increased Indonesian diplomatic activity and of the Wonosobo meeting had little immediate impact on Dili's political activity. After the diplomatic successes of June and August, the parties had turned inwards, consolidating their programmes and strengthening their support. The most fundamental changes were taking place in ASDT.

During July and August, ASDT had done well in most areas of East Timor. Although still not the largest party, it had increased its support among some of the more strategically placed *liurai*. This was symbolized in its leaders' meeting with the widow of Dom Boaventura, the *liurai* who had led the 1912 rebellion. In its campaigning, ASDT repeatedly encountered the demand for a more immediate transition to independence than suggested in its programme. This, together with a changed atmosphere in Lisbon, where Spinola seemed to be being outflanked by more radical army officers such as Otelo and Gonçalves, and an increasing knowledge of the successful models of independence movements in Angola and Mozambique, led ASDT members to change their organization's structure and objectives at a conference held in Dili on 12 September 1974.

The nature of the change from ASDT to a new political organization named Fretilin (Frente Revolucionara do Timor Leste Independente) is most aptly described by one of its founding members: 'ASDT was formed to defend the idea of the right to independence; Fretilin was formed to fight for independence'. This formation required a very different type of politics, one based on mobilizing mass support for independence. Fretilin's structure and programme were directed primarily to this end. The programme called for ultimate *de jure* independence from Portugal, with *de facto* independence being sought for first, through a rapid process of decolonization. It pinpointed the main areas for decolonization: the administration and control of the state, institutional racism, cultural transformation, education and economic organization. Fretilin's structure, although still centred on the Dili political élite, had now devolved a certain amount of decision-making to regional sub-committees responsible to a central committee in the capital. There regional sub-committees dealt with particular areas such as education, health and economic development, and were also seen as springboards for the mobilization of support in the rural areas.

With this programme finalized, Fretilin leaders began to develop their ideas on the means for decolonization, by working with their supporters through the avenues provided by regional sub-committees. During these months, Fretilin's popularity increased rapidly. By the end of the year, it was undoubtedly the largest party, easily surpassing the more conservative UDT. Its success lay in its commitment to independence, its presentation of concrete policies for change and the implementation of these policies and their operation in the countryside. Looking at some of these policies in the rural areas gives us some insight into why Fretilin increased its popularity in such a short space of time.

Whilst Fretilin leaders recognized that the development of East Timor's economy depended on building up a solid agricultural base, the September programme had made little reference to the role of agriculture in economic development. In later revisions of the programme, however, systematic policies were offered for the transformation of the agricultural sector, concentrating on land reform, technology, mechanization, agricultural co-operatives and trade. These were largely the result of the accumulated experiences of Fretilin members, who had given up their jobs in Dili in September and moved to the rural areas to work with regional sub-committees, assessing the possibilities of different strategies for agricultural development. One such individual was a founding member of ASDT, Nicolau Lobato, who left his post in the Finance

Department and moved to his home region of Bazar-tete, some 30kms outside Dili, to try and set up an agricultural co-operative. In October, an Australian journalist visited Bazar-tete and described Lobato's work:

> The co-operative is small, comprising about fifty people who share instruments and collectively work their private plots. 'The people are still suspicious of the idea', says Lobato. 'They have been drawn into similar collective projects before by either the Portuguese or the Japanese only to find themselves dispossessed. We have started off with a small number so that we can work out the problems that arise easily, and when it has shown itself to be successful then others will follow quickly. It demands a great deal of trust amongst the members that all decisions taken by the co-operative be taken democratically'. He was involved in what they call a 'production co-operative', and when things get off the ground they hope also to create 'consumer co-operatives' to market their goods and to break the present commercial stranglehold of the Chinese.[21]

Similar methods could be seen working in other co-operatives, in Bucoli, west of Baucau, and in Aileu. In the former, Vincente S'ahe, a Fretilin member and former engineering student in Lisbon, returned to the region where his father was the local *liurai*, and began to set up a distribution co-operative. A journalist visiting Bucoli in October reported:

> Bucoli people were planning a co-operative for next year's harvest. Villagers will pool their surplus crops (after deducting family needs) for sale in Dili for higher prices than they would get through Chinese middlemen. The receipts will be used as the villagers decide, to buy a truck perhaps, or build a co-operative store, to buy wholesale basic necessities or to buy a small tractor.[22]

These accounts illustrate the Fretilin approach. Beginning with rather vague and general notions, ideas for future development were concretized through the accumulated experience of their members. The results were proposals that were directly relevant, realizable and popular, emerging from specific forms of co-operation with the rural population. Consequently, in Fretilin's subsequent agricultural policies, areas were targeted to be worked co-operatively at the *suco* level, using shared implements. Half the crop was to be delivered to the consumer co-operative and half to the families involved in production. The consumer co-operative would then purchase what was agreed on by the producers themselves from other co-operatives via the Dili administration. The main areas for co-operation would be fertile lowland areas (such as Maliana in the west) and, as production increased, poorer subsistence areas could be brought into the system.

A similar process was at work in the educational system. At the time of the April coup, the illiteracy rate in East Timor was about 93 per cent.[23] Fretilin's commitment to the attainment of literacy in the process of decolonization was embodied in both ASDT and Fretilin programmes, but it was not until mid-1974 that they began to prepare the ground for this, by collecting material for a literacy handbook in Tetum, the most well-known of Timor's many languages, which served as its *lingua franca*. Organized by one of Fretilin's most intelligent and articulate members, the former Lisbon student, Antonio Cavarinho (who subsequently adopted the name Mau Lear), areas were selected from which teachers could be recruited to train in Paulo Freire's well-known techniques for language acquisition. A handbook entitled *Rai Timur Rai Ita Niang* (Timor is our country) was eventually produced for use by such teachers. It contained 50 words in common use, which were illustrated, written in Tetum, broken into syllables and then placed in context with associated words. An exponent of Freire's ideas who observed the literacy handbook in use, concluded that although the use of Freire's method was somewhat propagandist: 'Nevertheless there were some fairly dramatic successes not only with people learning to read in three months, but also in encouraging people to write short stories, and generally write of their experiences'.[24]

The way in which this literacy campaign was built up similarly characterizes Fretilin's approach in the post-September months — general themes were enshrined into popular policies through continuous work in the countryside. By such means Fretilin was able to formulate a systematic programme for East Timor's decolonization and post-independence development. As distinct from the rather general notions of the earlier ASDT policies, a programme published by Fretilin at the end of November 1974 was detailed and comprehensive, with concise proposals for areas such as health, education, justice and economic reconstruction.[25]

The growing awareness in Timor's regions that such policies could be achieved, produced a substantial swing to Fretilin in the later months of the year. Whilst the UDT retained its generalized programme and confined its campaigning to Dili and the *liurai* of areas such as Ermera, Maliana and Maubara, Fretilin expanded into new regions, drawing on all sections of the rural population. By the end of the year, Fretilin's claim that it was based on 'the support of all Timorese patriots'[26] across the social and regional spectrum seemed a reasonable description of what was rapidly becoming a truly nationalist party.

Paradoxically, appearances tended at times to conceal this trend. For example, when Almeida Santos, Minister for Interterritorial Co-ordination, made the first serious visit by the Lisbon Government to Timor in the middle of October, he noted a strong support for UDT in the colony, and what he called 'the deep love the Timorese have for Portugal'.[27] Santos based this conclusion on the constant waving and presentation of Portuguese flags to him during his visit. He saw it as a sign of support for a federation with Portugal, which was also the main item of UDT's programme at this stage. What he had encountered, of course, was the traditional presentation of *lulik* objects to a foreign visitor, of which ancient Portuguese flags and bibles were often the most important; but this didn't lessen Santos' apparent conviction, nor UDT's enthusiasm for it.

Realism — Portuguese style

On his journey back to Portugal, Almeida Santos made two stops, in Jakarta and then in Canberra. There he met the relevant officials and presented a rather different face to the one he had shown in East Timor. Indeed, in Canberra he stated explicitly that whatever happened in East Timor had to be acceptable to the Indonesian Government. He was to say much the same when he reiterated Portugal's 'three choices' policy before the UN General Assembly in early December. Yet the same minister could still state in March that Indonesia had no territorial ambitions on Portuguese Timor.[28] Thus, on the one hand, for Timorese consumption, Lisbon's representative condoned a federal solution entailing eventual independence, and on the other he insisted to his government's allies that this solution must be acceptable to a state which had already made clear in several arenas its hostility to independence and its desire for integration. Clearly, there was something more to Santos' expressions of affection than was immediately apparent.

Earlier, on 5 October, the *Komodo* group had scored a major victory. Suharto had authorized Murtopo to handle all negotiations with Lisbon on East Timor. Within a few days, a meeting had been arranged with Portuguese leaders and Murtopo arrived in Lisbon on 14 October. He and his entourage booked into the Lisbon Sheraton Hotel, where they were welcomed by the State Secretary for Foreign Affairs, Dr Jorge Campignos, an old university friend of the Indonesian ambassador to Brussels, himself a friend of Murtopo. Murtopo was worried that the resignation of Spinola and his replacement by more radical officers might make the Portuguese Government less sympathetic to the Indonesian position. He need have had no cause for concern. The new president, Costa Gomez, described independence for East Timor as 'unrealistic' and Prime Minister Vasco Gonçalves reportedly exclaimed that the independence notion was 'nonsense'. Gomez concluded that there were only two options for East Timor: integration with Indonesia or self-government under the aegis of Portugal, whilst Gonçalves simply seemed to prefer integration.

By the end of Murtopo's trip to Lisbon, Almeida Santos had already left for East Timor. In fact he may well have been about to make his 'affection' speech when he received the following telegram from the prime minister:

> In contact with the President and the Prime Minister, the Indonesian delegation led by General Murtopo stated its conviction that the only formulae acceptable for Timor's future will be links with Portugal or Indonesia, which prejudice the independence option. In keeping with this, the Prime Minister considers it convenient for you to abstain in public from declarations giving emphasis to or even referring to the independence solution on a plane with other solutions.[29]

Santos' support for the UDT, with its ideas of continuing co-operation in a federated system, and his constant reference to the traditional links with

Portugal, are thus perhaps explained more adequately by the aims of his mission than by any 'affection' for the Timorese. His trips to Jakarta and Indonesia were similarly an integral part of this mission. Independence was rejected from his very first contact with the Indonesians. Indeed, Santos too probably thought it was 'nonsense'.

Delighted by the outcome of the Lisbon meeting, Murtopo returned to Jakarta. As ministers such as Malik fell into line with his integration proposals, Murtopo began the first serious stage of the *Komodo* campaign. The objectives were clear:

- to build up support for Apodeti and to discredit the other parties in preparation for either a potential Portuguese referendum or a transitional administration involving the three main parties; and
- to prepare the ground for military intervention across the border from Indonesian Timor in the event of Apodeti proving unpopular and parties unfavourable to integration coming to power in East Timor.

The propaganda barrage now began in earnest. In November, *Berita Yudha* exposed supposed 'Chinese involvement' in East Timor, notably in Fretilin. Radio broadcasts from Jakarta and Kupang announced that Apodeti favoured integration, had the support of 70 per cent of the population, and was supported by Indonesia. UDT was described as 'neo-fascist', and it was reported that 'violence' was spreading through the territory.

Meanwhile, the Portuguese Government again presented its public face: 'Let Timor choose', said Costa Gomez in an interview with the Romanian press on 12 December.[29] In keeping with its public persona, the government appointed a new governor of East Timor, Colonel Lemos Pires, to oversee a process of decolonization. Significantly, he was given no systematic brief by the president, who nevertheless insisted to him that no compromise had been made with the Indonesian Government.[30] On his arrival at the end of November, Lemos Pires had with him a team of officers, some of whom were to play crucial roles over the coming months, most notably two younger officers who had previously served in Timor, majors Jonatas and Mota. One of Lemos Pires' first tasks was a letter of introduction to the governor of East Timor. Thanking him, El Tari replied: 'Together we can build the integration of East Timor with Indonesia'.[31] Clearly El Tari must have thought that Costa Gomez had conveyed the 'unofficial' view to Lemos Pires.

Along with El Tari, others were also trying to build alliances. In December, a party of American officials travelled to Lisbon on behalf of the Oceanic Company of Denver, Colorado, to sign an agreement with the Portuguese Government. An earlier agreement had been signed with another American company, Adobe Oil and Gas. Both agreements were for off-shore oil concessions south of East Timor, in the Timor Sea. Neither concession seemed large, nor immediately profitable. They attracted little attention, except amongst Australian oil interests and their political lobbyists, who subsequently devoted considerable resources to reversing these agreements.[32] Some twelve months earlier, Indonesia and Australia had tentatively agreed a maritime boundary, following the Timor Trough, a sea-bed boundary some 40 miles off Timor's south coast, which marks the end of Australia's continental shelf. The boundary could not be finalized, however, because part of it came under East Timor's jurisdiction. Since drillings had begun to indicate that the sea-bed between Timor and Australia could contain substantial oil and gas deposits,[33] the Australian companies were anxious to finalize the boundary. Hence their dismay at Portugal granting concessions to American companies. Their vested interests strongly favoured Indonesian annexation, to keep the American companies out. They thus began an intense campaign of backroom lobbying for integration, powerfully orchestrated in Canberra throughout the coming year. Little of this was known at the time, but it began to exercise an increasingly important influence on the Australian Government's support for Indonesia's position.

Coalition

Whilst the new leaders of the AFM seemed prepared to acquiesce in the integration of East Timor into the Indonesian Republic, the team sent to oversee the process of decolonization seemed to have rather different views. As a supporter of Spinola's ideas, Lemos Pires was committed to the achievement of East Timorese independence, but within a Portuguese cultural (or Lusitanian) federation. Despite the absence of a brief for his governorship, Pires thus aimed to maintain peace, create the conditions for democratization and organize an act of self-determination within this framework. His main political advisors, Mota and Jonatas, had served in East Timor.[34] Both were committed to self-determination and independence in a fuller sense than Pires. Their problem was to transform this general commitment into strategies which could create the conditions in which the Timorese population could realistically participate in a process of self-determination, and to do this against their minister's preference for integration.

After a brief assessment, the AFM team formulated a general strategy by the beginning of 1975. Summarized, it was as follows: to create the conditions for a successful transition to independence over a period of years by promoting literacy, democratic processes, nationalist values and a basic development of the economic infrastructure.

Pires placed great stress on the training of a political–administrative élite to oversee the long-term creation of a new state. Both he and Jonatas were particularly concerned at conflicts between political parties restricting the emergence of such an élite. Although they soon came to regard Apodeti as a lost cause, they were particularly worried about potential conflicts between UDT and Fretilin. Pires concluded that a coalition between them would be 'the best buffer to Indonesia'.[35] Similarly, Jonatas felt that 'the coalition was the best way to proceed'.[36] Consequently, one of the first actions of the governor was to set up a Decolonization Committee on which the three main political parties were invited to sit.[37] After Apodeti's immediate refusal, UDT and Fretilin began discussing Portuguese proposals for a coalition. Not that this was a new step, of course. Fretilin had suggested such a move previously, but it had been rejected by the UDT leadership. This time the situation was rather different. The colonial administration was pressing for an agreement, Indonesian attacks on both parties had intensified and, above all, Fretilin was in a much stronger position. Indeed, a little later, in February, an observer noted: '(UDT) is thought to have about 10 per cent of the people . . . Apodeti supporters are said to be few, perhaps only 5 per cent . . . Fretilin could possibly command about 60 per cent of the vote'.[38]

Whilst this probably exaggerated Fretilin's strength, it had undoubtedly become the leading party by the beginning of 1975. Its work in the countryside and the appeal of its programme had led to a very rapid increase in its popularity.

Consequently, the coalition was agreed in mid-January, and by mid-March had published proposals for a transitional government. The coalition partners agreed on 'total independence, rejection of integration, repudiation of colonialism, and recognition of decolonization'.[39] Fretilin rescinded its claim to be the 'sole legitimate representative' of East Timor but, as can be seen from the programme's points, the UDT moved to Fretilin's policies in most areas. Indeed Jonatas, who supervised the coalition negotiations, later went so far as to claim that the transitional government proposals were written by Fretilin members.[40] When published, these proposals called for a government with equal representation from UDT, Fretilin and the Portuguese Government, to be transitional for three years after which general elections would be held for Constitutional Assembly.

The coalition was established at some internal cost to both parties. Both the left of Fretilin and the right of UDT were initially highly suspicious. The former argued that it was detrimental for Fretilin's development to ally with a declining party which had never firmly supported genuine independence, and the latter feared that UDT would gradually drift leftwards.[41] The opposition of these two factions was to have a critical influence on developments over the next few months. In the short-term however, the overwhelming majority of the two parties' supporters seemed delighted with the coalition.[42]

Soon after its formation, the coalition sent a message to the Indonesian Government, requesting an improved basis for relations. It stated:

The major political forces in Timor have formed a coalition for national independence. Being a country of Southeast Asia and a close neighbour of Indonesia, we are aware of our great responsibility for the maintenance of peace and political stability in this area. Thus we are anxious to establish a basis for mutual understanding of our common problems. We can assure you that now and in the future, after independence, we shall endeavour to promote friendship, good neighbourhood [sic] and co-operation for the progress of the people of Indonesia and of East Timor for world peace.[43]

A reply was soon forthcoming. Shortly after the message was sent, two Australian daily papers, the Melbourne *Age* and the *Sydney Morning Herald*, reported that Indonesia was planning a takeover of East Timor, with amphibious landings in Dili harbour, and an aerial assault on Baucau.[44] The origin of these reports seems to have been a military exercise held in South Lampung, Sumatra, where a simulation of an air- and sea-landing on East Timor was enacted on 18 February 1975. The Australian Defence Department reported this as an immediate precursor to an invasion, and journalists covered it as such. In actual fact, it was part of an escalation of *Operasi Komodo*, designed to convince the Portuguese and Timorese of the seriousness of the invasion option if political events were not to the Indonesian military's liking. It was yet another example of *Komodo* intensifying its operations on all fronts. Shortly after the Lampung simulation, *Antara* reporters had cabled news from East Timor of the 'persecution' of Apodeti members. These reports, filed by Taolin and Dinuth in Kupang, were increasingly picked up by the foreign press, notably a report in late February of a planned *coup d'état* by the AFM and Fretilin, with arms provided by the governor.[45] At about the same time that Adam Malik made a speech, on 25 February, stating that Indonesia was finding it difficult to tolerate the situation in East Timor, *Komodo* operatives organized a repairing of 100km of road along the border, and initiated a military training programme in West Timor for young men from Apodeti leader Guilherme Gonçalves' region of Atsabe. One of Gonçalves' supporters was arrested by Portuguese soldiers on suspicion of being a recruiting agent for the Indonesians. Interviewed by an Australian reporter, he related how he had been told by Gonçalves in a 1 November meeting which was also attended by four Indonesians in civilian clothing that he must 'urge strong people from his tribe to go to Indonesia for training. They would then come back to Portuguese Timor to fight against parties opposing merger with Indonesia'.[46]

These events were the result of *Operasi Komodo* moving into a higher phase. Realizing the minimal support both for Apodeti and its integration option, Murtopo and his coterie appeared to have decided to build up an area of specific regional support for Apodeti near the border with Indonesian Timor, using military means if necessary. Such support would make Apodeti a stronger regional party, whose 'persecution' by or 'conflict' with other parties in East Timor could provide a justification for military incursions or annexation.

Meanwhile, Murtopo travelled to London to renew his contacts with the Portuguese. In a detached house in the north of the city, and with the necessary assistance provided by the British Foreign Office, he confidently expected further guarantees from the Portuguese delegation, such as Indonesian participation in the decolonization process, the withdrawal of radical army officers from East Timor and the creation of a joint Portuguese–Indonesian consultative body in Dili. These seemed reasonable demands after Costa Gomes' comments to him during their October meeting. To Murtopo's surprise, the Portuguese delegates were rather less flexible than expected, rejecting all three proposals and complaining of Tomodok's activities and the

Kupang broadcasts. Further, they urged the Indonesians to integrate through the power of persuasion of the Timorese, and threatened to internationalize the issue. All this was a far cry from the earlier 'nonsense' proclamations of Gonçalves and Costa Gomes, and it clearly reflected the influence of the Dili AFM administration, which was well represented at the meeting. It seemed that it would no longer be quite so easy for the Portuguese leadership to acquiesce in an Indonesian takeover. The secret talks ended with the usual complimentary written exchanges, but Murtopo returned to Jakarta feeling somewhat aggrieved. His frustrations were increased when, in mid-April, three *Komodo* operatives, under the guise of commercial travellers, returned from a visit to Dili and its governor with the news that Apodeti was a lost cause. With the UDT–Fretilin coalition successfully preparing itself for transitional power, and with Portugal unwilling to seriously back the integration option, *Komodo* was clearly in need of new political directions.

The right to independence

Sections of the leadership of the Timorese Democratic Union were similarly embarking on a re-think. UDT had started out as the most popular party, with support in most levels of Timorese society, but now it was declining, and for some of its leaders it was becoming indistinguishable from its Fretilin opposition. Whilst leaders such as Domingos d'Oliviera and Mario Carrascalao had been very active in supporting the coalition, others had been decidedly lukewarm and wary. Most notable amongst these was Lopez da Cruz, President of UDT, who had helped found the party. During a visit to Dili, *Komodo* operatives (and most notably Sugianto) struck a responsive chord with da Cruz, and his fellow leader Augusto Mousinho, by stressing the leftward trend of coalition politics and the international isolation that would be experienced by a radical independent state in the region.

When Sugianto reported to Murtopo, the deputy head of BAKIN seized the chance to switch strategy; UDT could be won over, the coalition could be split and Indonesia would have the support of two of the three parties in any transitional government. Consequently, the visits of UDT leaders to Jakarta became more frequent,[47] and by the end of April Sugianto was able to report that da Cruz had succumbed to the arguments for integration, and that Mousinho would follow him.

Thus, whilst for public consumption Suharto was claiming that 'Indonesia has no plans to take over East Timor',[48] *Komodo*-sponsored disillusionment with the coalition was gaining ground amongst other UDT leaders, as Fretilin strengthened its position.

Once again, the reasons for Fretilin's success lay in its rural-based programme. Throughout the coalition period, the literacy campaign had been introduced into an increasing number of regions. In addition, Fretilin members spent much of their time travelling to *sucos*, presenting their programme for independence. UDT also did this, but to a lesser extent, and, more importantly,

Fretilin had learnt to express itself in terms which had a more immediate meaning and relevance to the average Timorese, through using the local Tetum idiom. Fretilin members successfully elevated a culture despised by the Portuguese into a new language of independence. Nothing illustrates this better than Fretilin's use of the word *maubere*. Originally a word used by one of the poorest hill-peoples, the Mambai, to mean friend, it was appropriated by the Portuguese to denigrate the Timorese peasantry — *maubere*, the backward, primitive people from the interior. Fretilin took this word and made it a symbol of what the movement represented. In the words of an anthropologist working with the Mambai during this period: 'The phrase "*mau bere* — my brother" became a pervasive refrain, a call for Timorese unity, for to be a *mau bere* was to be a son of Timor'.[49] The use of this term, and its feminine *bi-bere*, was a shorthand for the reassertion of Timorese culture and the struggle against poverty and colonial subordination. So successful had they become that a contemporary commentator noted that they were the conventional form of address in mid-1975.

Similarly, Fretilin developed other indigenous forms — of music, poetry and dance — to express the ideas of independence. In this way, Fretilin leaders were able increasingly to express their ideas, not just for independence but for economic and social development, in ways that accorded with everyday imagery. Resulting from their work in the countryside since autumn 1974, this was the major reason for their transition from a formally populist to a genuinely popular party in the wet season of 1974–5.

This popularity expressed itself concretely in elections held from March onwards. Under the guidance of majors Mota and Jonatas, the Decolonization Commission proposed to hold elections for *suco liurai* in a number of *concelhos* (regions). The stated aims were to introduce the population to European electoral procedures, and to remove unpopular *suco* heads appointed by the Portuguese.[50] In Jonatas' words:

> Teams were created — comprising officer, sergeant, Timorese interpreter — to explain the elections. Each team was accompanied by representatives of the political parties. Elections would then take place two weeks later. In the interim, parties could carry out propaganda.[51]

The elections were organized as they always had been in Timor, by the throwing of pebbles into baskets for each of the respective candidates. The process occurred in the districts of the selected *concelhos* and most thoroughly in the first *concelho* to vote, that of Lospalos. Although the elections were not for party candidates as such, Fretilin did exceptionally well, with a substantial majority of the elected *liurais* supporting their programme.[52]

Fretilin's popularity was further confirmed during the post-March visits of Australian delegations, one of trade unionists and church members, and the other from the Labour Party. The reports of both delegations stressed the widespread support for both the coalition and Fretilin, arguing that independence would be chosen by a majority in any referendum.[53]

Building upon the coalition structure, the Portuguese proposed discussions with the political parties on transforming the administration into a transitional government. As usual, Apodeti refused to attend, objecting to the presence of Fretilin and the non-negotiability of integration. The ensuing proposals highlighted the success of both the coalition and the administration since, for the first time, they unequivocally recognized the right to independence, calling for:

> immediate acceptance of and recognition by the Portuguese Government of the right of the people of Portuguese Timor to independence [and] the setting up in October 1975 of a transitional government with a number of portfolios to be decided on in due course. The formation, also in October 1975, of an *ad hoc* consultative assembly composed of members freely elected by the people through the local authorities. This assembly would discuss laws on political parties, on electoral law regulating the election of a Constituent Assembly and the distribution of portfolios to be held by the political organizations with the exception of those reserved for the Portuguese Government.[54]

In two days of discussion, portfolios were agreed, and it was proposed to enact the necessary electoral laws in time for elections to a National Constituent Assembly to be held in November 1976, with independence following the initial meeting of this assembly. With this agreement, independence was no more than three years away. Despite determined efforts by the Indonesian military to subvert the process, and despite a marked lack of support from AFM leaders in Lisbon, a coalition had emerged with increasing support in the countryside. Through its work in the villages, Fretilin had begun to build a movement whose policies were based on the needs of the rural sector and whose aims, unlike any previous movement, expressed national perspectives in the language and values of local culture. Under difficult circumstances, the parties and administration appeared to have succeeded in creating the conditions for independence.

Notes

1. Details of this event come from refugee interviews in Lisbon in February 1985. See also O'Dwyer, B., *Development News Digest*, No. 11, 1974, p. 5.
2. Information on this group comes largely from interviews with some of its members in Lisbon, undertaken in 1981 and 1985.
3. The Legislative Council was set up by the Colonial Act of 1930 (see Chapter 1, p. 12).
4. Provisional statutes of the Timorese Democratic Union published by its Organizing Committee in Dili, 1 August 1974.
5. Ibid.

6. See Ramos-Horta, 1984a; see also *Nacroma*, the official ASDT newspaper, Vol. 1, No. 1, 31 August 1974.

7. Interview with a founding member of ASDT, Justino Mota, Torres Vedras, 17 February 1985.

8. Manifesto of the Associacao Popular Democratica Timorense, Dili, 27 May 1974, presented as an appendix to Evans, 1975.

9. For details on these points, see Hoadley, 1977, pp. 133–42.

10. *Indonesia Current Affairs Translation Service*, Jakarta, June 1974.

11. From the text of a letter from Adam Malik in the possession of José Ramos-Horta, dated 17 June 1974, and reproduced in part in Ramos-Horta 1985.

12. Dunn, 1974, p. 18.

13. See Barreto, 1982. East Timor produced a high quality Arabica coffee, valued in Lisbon

14. OPSUS was originally a special intelligence unit of the army's Strategic Reserve Command (KOSTRAD), of which Suharto was commander before the 1965 coup. It played a behind-the-scenes role in settling the dispute with Malaysia in 1964, and after the coup became a special operations unit for President Suharto. It has been involved in the rigging of elections, the organizing of protests and mobilizing of mass movements. Most notably, it masterminded the 'Act of Free Choice' in West Papua New Guinea (West Irian) under the auspices of the UN.

15. Information on *Operasi Komodo* comes principally from two sources: from the leader of the KOTA party, José Martins, after he defected from the Indonesian team to the UN, in 1976. Martins was recruited by Taolin as an agent for BAKIN in 1975. For details, see José Martins' 'Affidavit' submitted to the UN Secretary-General, March 1976. The other major source of information on *Operasi Komodo* is McDonald, 1980, Chapter 9, pp. 189–215.

16. *Sinar Harapan* (Jakarta), 12 September 1974.

17. *Sydney Morning Herald*, 19 November 1974.

18. The Future of Portuguese Timor, Document BP/60, Department of Foreign Affairs, Canberra, 11 September 1974, cited in Dunn, 1983.

19. *Sydney Morning Herald*, 19 November 1974.

20. Malik made this statement on 29 November 1974.

21. Evans, 1975, p. 9.

22. Freney, Denis, *Tribune* (Australia), 26 November 1974.

23. See Ranck, 1975, p. 20.

24. See Ranck, 1977, p. 20.

25. The full texts of each of the party's political programmes is contained in an Appendix to Jolliffe, 1978.

26. *What is Fretilin?* published by the Campaign for Independent East Timor, Sydney, 1975.

27. Santos said this as part of his speech to a large crowd in Dili on 19 October 1974.

28. Estado — Maior General da Forcas Armadas, *Relatorio de Timor*, Lisbon 1977, pp. 33–4, cited in 1982. Barreto's work, together with McDonald's analysis of OPSUS accounts, is the main source for this description of the Lisbon meeting; see McDonald, 1980.

29. Commonwealth Parliamentary Debates, House of Representatives, Canberra, 25 February 1978, p. 643.

30. These facts were confirmed in discussions with Lemos Pires in Lisbon on 19 February 1985.

31. Commonwealth Parliamentary Debates, House of Representatives. Canberra, 25 February 1978, p. 643.

32. 'New-found Attractions of Timor', *Petroleum Economist*, March 1975.

33. See M. Richardson, *Far Eastern Economic Review*, 19 April 1984, where oil deposits between Timor and Australia are estimated at 5 million barrels, plus 50,000 billion cubic feet of natural gas reserves. Richardson estimates that, if correct, this puts the area among the top 25 oilfields in the world.

34. Jonatas had served previously in the Oecussi enclave.

35. Interview with Lemos Pires, 19 February 1985.

36. Interview with Major Jonatas, Lisbon, 15 February 1985.

37. The Decolonization Commission consisted of a number of committees for decolonization of areas such as education, the economy, administration, public health and social welfare.

38. Robin Osborne, '500-year Siesta Breaks Up', *Australian*, 26 February 1975.

39. Coalition Document, translated into English and published by the campaign for an Independent East Timor, Sydney, Australia, March 1978.

40. Interview with Major Jonatas, Lisbon, 15 February 1985.

41. Their fears appeared to have some foundation when, in March 1975, the UDT, naively hoping to outflank Fretilin through rhetoric, issued a policy statement containing a commitment to destroy monopolies, the class system and capitalism in Timorese society. See Jolliffe, 1975, p. 13.

42. When a delegation of Australian Trade Union Officials visited East Timor in March, great stress was placed on the slogan *Viva Colligacao* wherever they travelled.

43. Text cited in Hill, 1978, p. 146.

44. See, for example, 'Indonesia Plans Armed Takeover in Timor', Melbourne *Age*, 22 February 1975.

45. For example, *Indonesian Times*, 27 February, reported that Apodeti supporters were 'bearing the brunt of terror inflicted by the Leftists in efforts to create a "psychosis of fear"', see Jolliffe, 1978, p. 98.

46. Michael Richardson, 'Indonesia told Chief to Recruit Guerillas', Melbourne *Age*, 4 March 1975. The training of Apodeti members by Indonesia in West Timor is also recalled in José Martins' 'Affidavit', p. 4. This document, presented to the UN Secretary-General in May 1976, is reproduced in part in Jolliffe, 1978, pp. 282–9.

47. UDT leaders had first visited in September 1974, when Mousinho and d'Oliveira had stated 25 September that they would not oppose integration 'if the people wished it'.

48. *Angkatan Bersenjata*, 6 April 1978.

49. Traube, 1984.

50. See Hill, 1978.

51. Interview with Major Jonatas, 15 February 1985.

52. Estimates of the election results vary. Hill claims that '90 per cent of those elected were Fretilin members or supporters', whilst Jonatas claims that although Fretilin did well initially, by the time the results for all the contested villages in Lospalos were declared at the end of July, there was an equilibrium between UDT and Fretilin (see Hill, 1978, p. 123, and interview with Jonatas, 15 February 1985).

53. See J. S. Dunn, 1983, p. 153, and Jolliffe, 1975.

54. Text printed in US *Foreign Broadcasts Information Services*, Daily Reports, Asia and South Pacific, 7 May 1975.

4. From Coalition to Coup and Independence: The Indonesian Campaign against East Timor

Several UDT leaders were less than euphoric about the proposals for a transitional government and independence. They were worried by the strength of support for Fretilin in the countryside. Early in May, thousands of people had travelled to Dili to support a demonstration celebrating the anniversary of the founding of ASDT.

In implementing its programmes, Fretilin had on occasion come into conflict with local *liurai*. Towards the end of May, however, these conflicts intensified, as more Fretilin members participated in the rural programmes. Such incidents enabled da Cruz and Mousinho to persuade other UDT leaders to implement a decision whose enactment had been in the forefront of their strategy since their succumbing to *Komodo*'s persuasion in mid-March. On 27 May, UDT leaders announced that they were leaving the coalition. Their communiqué claimed: 'Fretilin has adopted a political line which could seriously jeopardize the independence of Timor–Dili in so far as it engenders the internal security and political stability of the geopolitical context of which we are part'. The style of the statement seemed rather different to UDT's usual pronouncements. Indeed, the phrase 'Timor–Dili' was quite alien. It had last surfaced in BAKIN documents before the April coup. It seemed that *Operasi Komodo* was finally having a definite effect on the course of events. Anxious to maintain their position, *Komodo* operatives worked in earnest. In early June, it was reported that 1500 people had fled the enclave of Oecussi in fear of a campaign orchestrated by AFM officers and Fretilin members. Indonesian troops subsequently entered Oecussi briefly to 'restore law and order'. Meanwhile, Suharto finally went public: 'East Timor is not viable', he declared at the beginning of July.

Fretilin and its groupings: the road to Macao

In June, Fretilin's campaigns had moved into a qualitatively new phase, with the introduction of what were called Revolutionary Brigades. These involved Fretilin groups living permanently in the villages in which they were implementing their literacy or health campaigns. These achieved some success, increased the movement's popularity and marked the high point of Fretilin's development as a political organization. It had built up its support carefully and skilfully, allying with other political groups at the national level wherever possible, and had succeeded in placing a folk culture despised by colonial rule at the centre of the political process. Having made such substantial gains in a very short period of time, Fretilin now reached a decision which was both surprising and uncharacteristic.

At the end of May, the Lisbon Decolonization Commission announced publicly what had been under discussion in Dili for some time — that a further conference on decolonization would be held in Macao in mid-June, with representatives from all the Timorese parties, the AFM and the Portuguese Government. It was a poorly kept secret that Indonesian representatives would also be in Macao, to be kept informed of those parts of the proceedings that were considered relevant to 'Indonesian interests'.[1] The object of the conference was to discuss at government level the agreements already reached in Dili. To the administration's considerable surprise, Fretilin declined to attend, and the Lisbon Government declared that the conference would go ahead without the colony's largest pro-independence party.

To explain that volte-face, we need to look further into the political composition of Fretilin. Its leadership shared important unifying characteristics. They were almost all of the same generation, having been born during or shortly after the Pacific War. They had all been educated at Catholic schools, and several of them had trained for the priesthood, indeed many Fretilin leaders remained throughout practising Catholics. Several of the most prominent leaders were sons of *liurai* or *suco* chiefs who retained links with their rural areas. All placed great stress on the values of education, racial equality and nationalism. Beyond these, however, their political perspectives diverged somewhat, and there seem to have been a number of distinct strands in the party.

The dominant trend in the founding ASDT group was markedly social democratic, and was represented by such leaders as journalist José Ramos-Horta, administrators Justino Mota and Alarico Fernandes, and former teacher Xavier do Amaral. As Horta was to write later in ASDT's paper, *Nacroma*, social democracy meant 'freedom of ideas and expression on the one hand and a mixed economy on the other'.[2] To the extent that this group had a model, it seems to have been that of 1960s/70s social democracy in Austria and Scandinavia. Despite the importance of this social-democratic trend, its policies (and perhaps even its basic ideas) were never really worked out in the Timorese context. In the months following ASDT's founding, so much time had to be spent on assessing internal and external support that these notions could never be developed with any rigour.

A second, subordinate trend in the ASDT period was represented by leaders such as the former sergeant and administrator, Nicolau Lobato, who combined a fervent anti-colonial nationalism with notions of economic self-reliance and political development based on the Angolan and Mozambican experiences. As ASDT became Fretilin and began to develop its economic policies, Lobato's ideas became more prominent, particularly with the ascendancy of the ex-army officers in Fretilin, who allied with him increasingly throughout 1975.

A third perspective did not really emerge until after the founding of Fretilin in September 1975. Based on the participation of those such as Vicente Sa'he and Mau Lear (Antonio Carvarinho) who had been formed politically as intellectuals involved in the April events in Lisbon, it was characterized by an attempt to use Marxist politics in a nationalist Timorese context. Its ideas were most evident in Fretilin's literacy campaign and in the areas of its programme devoted to education, health policies, economic reconstruction and social justice. The members of this group were primarily responsible for the successful programme developed by Fretilin in late 1974. They were often grouped together with younger Timorese, who had returned from their studies in Lisbon to assist in rural programmes and had been instrumental in the foundation of the Fretilin students union in early 1975. Yet their analyses and political presentation were more sophisticated than the general sloganizing approach adopted by this latter group. Whilst most Fretilin members could be grouped in this way, there were also those who either had close ties with the various groups or who remained outside them. Amongst the former were Abilio Araujo and Guilhermina dos Santos, former students, who remained in Lisbon during most of the post-April coup period working on economic and educational policies and forming a link between the groups who had studied in Lisbon in earlier periods. A similar case was Mari Alkatiri who, through his specialization in diplomatic contacts with Portugal's African colonies, linked Lobato's perspective with that of Mau Lear. Many members of the central committee, who had experienced some military training, such as Nicolau Lobato's brother, Rogerio, concentrated primarily on military and strategic issues, and their lack of a coherent perspective for East Timor's development kept them largely outside these intra-Fretilin groupings.

From its inception, Fretilin had presented a unified appearance despite a swing away from the social-democratic perspective towards the end of 1974 with several of ASDT's founding members being given rather minor positions in the posts allocated after September. Whilst the majority of the central committee of Fretilin had welcomed the coalition, there was some opposition from the nationalist–Marxist group of Mau Lear and Sa'he, who considered that Fretilin could build itself independently through its distinctive political approach, and that this would be hampered by an alliance with a declining UDT. As the coalition became increasingly difficult to maintain this view became more widespread. Hence by mid-May 1975, it seemed that the decline in social-democratic influence was matched by a strengthening of the nationalist–Marxist perspective which had in turn been assisted by the successes of the rural programmes and the Portuguese decision to bring independence forward. This trend was quickened by the break-up of the coalition. This effectively severed the remaining links between Fretilin's social-democratic grouping and those of similar persuasion in UDT, links which had been instrumental in the coalition's creation in January. Indeed, UDT may well have withdrawn from the coalition in the hope of persuading Fretilin to drop its 'left-wing.' Support for this is provided by reports of meetings, in June 1975, between Lemos Pires and selected Fretilin and UDT leaders which discussed expelling 'the left' from the colony.[3]

It was in this context that Fretilin decided not to go to Macao. The reasons given were unconvincing, however: that Apodeti would be attending and that the Portuguese had already agreed to independence. Since Apodeti was no longer a serious threat, and since the independence programme had only been agreed in Dili and needed discussion at the Portuguese governmental level, there was clearly more to this decision than was immediately apparent. Indeed, it underscored the ascendancy of the nationalist-Marxist perspective to a majority position. The work of this group in the countryside had contributed greatly to Fretilin's success, and their policy formulation and presentation had won considerable support. However, in alliance with the group of Lisbon returnees, other aspects of their perspective now came into play, which seemed less relevant. Their view of Fretilin as the 'sole representative' of the Timorese people, and their equation of it with a 'liberation front' along Portuguese–African lines, led them to denigrate negotiations with other parties. Similary, their strident critiques of colonialism and neo-colonialism led them to view all Portuguese officials, nationally or locally, as set in the same immutable imperialist mould. These notions led them to dismiss Macao as largely irrelevant to the more urgent tasks of developing the 'Revolutionary Brigade' programmes in the countryside and opposing attendance on the grounds that there only remained to discuss with Portugal the arrangements for the granting of independence.[4]

These views prevailed over the social-democratic arguments, assisted by the absence abroad on diplomatic missions of leaders such as Lobato, Xavier do Amaral and Ramos-Horta, who might have been able to arrange a compromise between the two groupings.

The results of Fretilin's absence from Macao readily became apparent as the summit got underway on 26 June. Apodeti was able to present itself internationally as a viable party; UDT was free to criticize Fretilin in an international press arena; and the Indonesians were able to make political capital out of Fretilin's intransigence. A communiqué issued on 28 June referred to self-determination and not independence as a right, and the framework put forward by the Decolonization Commission in Dili was qualified in order to restrict the democratic process in the period up to the Popular Assembly elections in October 1976.[5] The absence of Fretilin meant that the frustrated members of the Portuguese Dili administration had little to show concretely in the way of readily feasible independence alternatives to the national government's theme of 'integration happening normally' (Costa Gomes' phrase). But, finally, and perhaps most importantly, the Macao episode confirmed UDT leaders' views of the correctness of da Cruz and Mousinho's portrayal of Fretilin, and of East Timor, in its regional context.

Komodo operatives now did all they could to confirm the worst suspicions of UDT leaders. In July, they implanted rumours of a planned Fretilin coup and of arms entering East Timor from China. Increasingly alarmed that a 'radicalized' Fretilin would provoke Indonesian intervention, and particularly so after Suharto's 'non-viability' statement of early July, UDT leaders Domingos d'Oliviera and Joao Carrascalao requested a meeting with Ali Murtopo to clarify Indonesia's position.[6] Murtopo took a hard line, arguing that Fretilin was now a communist movement, that it was planning a coup in the middle of August and that, if it succeeded, Indonesia would intervene. Lopez da Cruz also attended the meeting but said little. By this time he was fully committed to integration. After the meeting, d'Oliviera and Carrascalao returned to Dili, via Den Pasar, Bali, where they were contacted by a BAKIN agent posing as a Malaysian diplomat, who assured them of his government's support if they could prevent a left-wing regime coming to power in East Timor. Arriving back in Dili on 6 August, UDT leaders encountered rumours that Fretilin troops, describing themselves as communists, were manning road-blocks in the countryside. Joao Carrascalao confided his thoughts to an AFM officer, Major Bassento, who later claimed that:

> he had been deeply influenced by what he had been told in Indonesia . . . He told me they were convinced there would be no independence for East Timor under Fretilin and they were doubtful there would be independence even under UDT . . . They were very conscious of the need not to offend Indonesia. Carrascalao was also convinced that a communist-influenced East Timor could not survive next to Indonesia.[7]

On 9 and 10 August, UDT members organized demonstrations calling for the expulsion of 'communists' from the country. As reports began to reach Dili of the killing of Fretilin members in the Same area, armed UDT supporters came out on to the streets of Dili. By the morning of 11 August, they had occupied the police headquarters. What UDT was to term its 'show of force' was underway.

A coup and its allies

The UDT's coup attempt has been fully documented by several commentators.[8] What is less well known is the role of Indonesian intelligence agencies in the weeks of the coup. To look at this, however, we need to recount briefly the major events.

On the evening of the tenth, UDT leaders arrested the Portuguese police chief, Brigadier Maggioli Gouveia, and threatened to kill him if the police force did not join the coup. In a move that was probably pre-arranged, since Gouveia soon came out directly in support of UDT, 90 per cent of the police came over to UDT with their arms. UDT forces then took control of the key institutions of Dili — the airport, the communications centre, the water station and the main intersections. They surrounded the military barracks but, significantly, did not enter it, neither did they take over the arsenal. On 11 August, Joao Carrascalao cabled the outside world that UDT had occupied Dili to prevent a communist massacre. In a rather surprising move, he requested assistance from the US base in Guam.

Taken aback by UDT's action, Lemos Pires called together his advisers in the early morning of 11 August and agreed to try negotiating with both UDT and Fretilin. Since most Fretilin central committee members were either working in the countryside or had left Dili quietly on the evening of the tenth in the foreknowledge of the coup attempt, this proved no easy task and was not achieved until the twelfth, when a courier returned with a set of fifteen conditions for negotiation, signed by Nicolau Lobato. These stressed the need for Portugal to assume responsibility, provide a safe conduct for negotiators, disarm UDT and ensure the release of its prisoners. Meanwhile UDT, spurning the governor's overtures, issued its demands on the 13th, which were for the expulsion of 'communists' in both the administration and in Fretilin from East Timor, and a meeting with the moderate members of Fretilin to build a new independence movement. Caught between two incompatible sets of demands and arguing that he was bound by the AFM rule of non-interference in the decolonization process, Lemos Pires claimed that he was effectively stymied.

Meanwhile, UDT arrested Fretilin members in Dili, and moved against centres of Fretilin support in areas such as Baucau, Same, Maubisse and Ainaro, from which news came later of executions.[9] On 17 August, majors Jonatas and Mota left Dili for Darwin, ostensibly to report to Lisbon, but largely for their own protection. As 'communists', their departure had been demanded repeatedly by UDT, whose leaders saw their flight as a considerable victory. As the two majors arrived in Australia, the central committee of Fretilin called for armed support against UDT in the knowledge that its chief military negotiator Rogerio Lobato, himself a lieutenant, had almost persuaded units of the army to join them. On the 19th, two important army garrisons in Aileu and Taibesse declared their support for Fretilin. On the 20th, a Timorese corporal named Ponciano, capitalizing on the Portuguese having given him custody of the keys to the Dili barracks and arsenal, opened them to Fretilin supporters in the army, and used the arms to move against UDT. During the ensuing battle for the capital, Lemos Pires and his staff, incapable of controlling the situation, withdrew to a Dili suburb and then to the nearby island of Atauro. On the same day, 26 August, Indonesian troops made an amphibious landing in Dili harbour to evacuate their consulate. By 27 August, Dili was completely under Fretilin's control, and in the first week of September, regional areas of UDT support surrendered. After a westward flight and brief encounters with Fretilin troops in the towns of Liquica, Maubara, Atabae and Balibo, the bulk of UDT's troops were trapped at Batugade on the border with Indonesian Timor. On 24 September, a force of 500 soldiers crossed this border, with 2500 refugees and 19 Portuguese troops captured on their retreat. As they crossed, a condition of their entry was the signing of a petition calling for the integration of East Timor into the Indonesian Republic.

This petition was presented to Suharto as a collective plea from the people of East Timor. In reality, it had been drawn up by Lopez da Cruz with the assistance of *Komodo* operative, Colonel Sugiyanto, in the middle of August.

This event underscored the Indonesian military's role in the events of the coup. Throughout, *Komodo* had maintained a constant covert presence.

Shortly after the seizure of the Dili police station, Carrascalao had turned on his former colleague, Lopez da Cruz, and placed him under house arrest, since several UDT leaders had been worried that da Cruz was now so pro-integrationist that he would call directly for Indonesian intervention. This was the last thing the UDT leaders wanted since their coup was designed to create what they considered to be more secure conditions for independence, by purging the country of left-wing influence. Da Cruz, however, had managed to contact the Indonesian consul who, with the help of Apodeti supporters, arranged for his escape to Kupang.

This *Komodo* exploit symbolized BAKIN's reaction to the coup attempt. Initially confident that the coup would produce a prolonged conflict whose chaos could provide a justification for intervention, *Komodo* operatives were forced to retreat and rethink their strategy as Fretilin rapidly defeated UDT, and as sections of the Indonesian military baulked at actions which could not be justified adequately in the international arena. Thus, in the first week of the coup attempt, Gonçalves' trainees were prepared for deployment across the border to establish bases near Dili, but this never materialized. In the second week of the conflict, Yoga Sugama discussed it with foreign diplomats, most notably the American ambassador, stressing that UDT was, in fact, a socialist movement, and that, whatever the outcome of the civil war, East Timor would eventually have a left-wing government. Intervention, therefore, seemed desirable. Indonesian newspapers repeated these assertions, some even going so far as to claim that Fretilin and UDT were indistinguishable.[10]

Whilst this propaganda was disseminated, prime supporters and movers of *Komodo*, such as Minister of Defence Panggabean, Deputy Chief of the Armed Forces Surono and Murtopo himself, spent several cabinet meetings trying to convince Suharto of the merits of intervention. The president remained unconvinced of the need for immediate action, primarily for reasons outlined by Richard Woolcott, the Australian ambassador in one of his regular calls to Canberra:[11]

> Receiving reports from his senior advisers twice daily, the President is at present firm in his attitude that Indonesia should not intervene militarily in Portuguese Timor at this stage. Concern about Australia's reaction, the Non-Aligned meeting in Lima, the forthcoming session of the General Assembly, and his wish to concentrate his resources on *Repelita II* (the national economic plan) are all factors in his present attitude.[12]

This sounded very statesmanlike, but American reaction probably weighed heaviest in Suharto's decision. As Woolcott later wrote, the Indonesian Government was informed by the US ambassador, regarding East Timor, that it 'should be aware that if United States equipment were used, this could call into effect sections of the Foreign Assistance Act and could place the United States military assistance programme in jeopardy.'[13] This was the last thing

Suharto wanted, particularly when sections of his armed forces were undergoing modernization, and he clearly had to find some way around this problem before an invasion could take place.

BAKIN's attempt to prolong the conflict was perhaps most clearly illustrated in its treatment of a Portuguese diplomatic mission with 'special instructions' for Governor Pires which had been dispatched from Lisbon shortly after the beginning of the coup, on 13 August. After being held up in Jakarta by Indonesian officials on the grounds that he did not have a visa, the leader of the mission, Major Soares, arrived in Bali on the 15th to catch a flight to Kupang, and thence to Dili. Soares was held in Bali by immigration officials until his scheduled flight had left and then waited until the 17th before being informed by these officials that he could not travel further under any circumstances. In this situation, he decided, rather feebly, to return to Lisbon, and it was not until 20 August that another governmental official was able to travel to Dili.

As the conflict was fought out in the capital in the following week, it became clear that no delaying tactics could seriously influence the outcome. The Indonesians had overestimated UDT strength, just as they had miscalculated the extent of Apodeti's influence. From now on, the takeover of East Timor would be organized outside the country's borders, fronted by the most committed Timorese integrationists — Guilherme Gonçalves of Apodeti, José Martins of Kota, and Lopez da Cruz of UDT. As we have seen, da Cruz had been sprung from Dili by the Consul, Martins had crossed the border with UDT and Gonçalves had been airlifted from his home ground by helicopter across the border on 12 September. Most of the people who crossed the border in mid-September were hostile to integration, but without food or shelter and with Fretilin forces closing on them they had no real alternative but to sign the integration proposal. They were then sent off to camps where they were to remain in appalling conditions.[14] Kept there, they provided proof to the world outside Indonesia of its propaganda that 'the mass support of three Timorese parties (Apodeti, UDT and the Kota party of José Martins) were calling for Indonesian forces to intervene against a single party which had itself seized power by force'. As a UDT leader later stated: 'It was the last thing we wanted, but we really had no alternative but to agree'.[15]

At the other end of the scale, Lemos Pires argued that he and his entourage really had no choice either. Bound by AFM policy not to intervene militarily in colonial conflicts, and having to safeguard his personnel, he calculated that a withdrawal to nearby Atauro could achieve both these and a safer position from which to negotiate. As he later put it:

> On 11 August, I could have confronted UDT, and imprisoned them; however, most of the military were Timorese, and I had only two Portuguese parachute platoons at my disposal. So, I had only 300 troops, and if I had used them against UDT, the Indonesians would have claimed that I was supporting Fretilin. If I had imprisoned UDT leaders, the Indonesians would have reacted. If I had assisted UDT, Fretilin would have begun a

guerrilla war, and we would have started it. I went to Atauro because I could have been taken hostage, and I could remain in East Timorese territory. We could still talk to all parties concerned.

Until the last, Pires was still trying to forge a coalition by splitting UDT from its right and Fretilin from its left: 'We had talks on 17 August, and a declaration was signed by UDT and the Timorese (Fretilin) sergeants to join an "anti-communist movement", but Fretilin broke this coalition'.[16]

In Lemos Pires' own terms he was right, he could have made no real choice that would seriously have affected the outcome. He could only operate within narrow limits which his government had imposed. Aside from a relatively feeble attempt to send a rather low-ranking delegation, Lisbon had stood aside. To quote Pires: 'After the UDT coup, I requested my government to either give me the power to make an agreement, or send me a political leader, but the government did nothing'.[17] Indeed, Lisbon did nothing because, as Costa Gomes and his envoy Soares, were reported to have said during the conflict, they 'wanted the army out of Timor, and would probably now accept a UDT government',[18] a move which they knew would be used by Indonesia as a justification for intervention. The highest echelons of the Portuguese AFM government thus remained constant in their acquiescence to Indonesia right up until the last days of Portugal's colonial presence.

It was ironic that a movement which had overthrown a right-wing dictatorship in its home country should end up succumbing so early to the requests of an even more brutal and authoritarian military regime. Yet perhaps it was a fitting end to its 450 years of colonial rule. For all leaders of Portugal, there had always been one rule for its corporate élite and another for its incorporated and disenfranchized colonies.

Fretilin's administration

During the entire period of the coup attempt, and in the preparations for it, both Australian and American intelligence agencies followed events on a detailed daily basis.[19] Their monitoring reports were passed regularly to the relevant government departments in both countries. Whilst they claimed officially that they had only limited knowledge of what was taking place and could do little to influence events, it often seemed that they knew more of what was happening then most of the participants in the conflict. In the case of Australia, the reasons were clear, even at this stage. But why the United States? Why was the world's leading imperial power so interested in what was occurring in one of Portugal's distant and smallest colonies? Apart from the economic and political importance to it of Indonesia, which Richard Nixon had called 'the greatest prize in the South East Asia region',[20] East Timor had itself an important significance in American global strategy.[21] To the north of the island are the Ombai–Wetar straits, containing extremely deep channels through which nuclear armed submarines can travel undetected in their passage from the Pacific to the Indian Ocean. Should this route have been in any way threatened or denied, a total of at least eight days would have to be added to a concealed journey between the two oceans via the alternative Lombok or Sunda straits. The Ombai–Wetar straits were thus considered crucial to American strategy, vital in any potential conflict with its then southward expanding rival, the Soviet Union. Consequently, the American administration was anxious to effect a secure conclusion, in every sense of the word, to the conflict in East Timor. As early as 16 August, John Newsom, the newly arrived American Ambassador to Jakarta, hoped that if Indonesia invaded East Timor they would do so 'effectively, quickly, and not use our equipment'.[22] Whatever the outcome, the United States Government had to protect its strategic position, and the best way to do this was to play down any damaging reports of Indonesian involvement in East Timor. Thus, by mid-August, the American embassy in Jakarta was instructed by the State Department 'to cut down its reporting on Timor'.[23] This request could almost have been adopted as a slogan by the governments of Europe and Australia, as well as the United States. Publicly feigning disbelief and ignorance of events in a remote island, their decisions were actually taken on the basis of a detailed knowledge of events in an area which was more crucial to them than they were ever to admit openly. Nothing illustrates this better than their response to events as they unfolded dramatically in the months following the retreat of the UDT and its co-option by Indonesian military intelligence.

Initially, most foreign governments were taken aback at the speed with which Fretilin had defeated the coup attempt, and the strength of its support. Several had been influenced by a confidential report written after an extended visit to East Timor in July by Gordon Duggan, Head of Chancery to Jakarta's British Ambassador, Sir John Archibald Ford. Duggan concluded that: 'The people of Portuguese Timor are in no condition to exercise the right of self-determination'. Consequently, he recommended integration and, in a characteristically British diplomatic turn of phrase, echoed Newsom's sentiments: 'If it comes to the crunch and there is a row in the United Nations, we should keep our heads down and avoid siding against the Indonesian Government'.[24]

Faced with a Fretilin administration in *de facto* control, governments were rapidly forced to take the situation more seriously. From the outset, the Fretilin administration seemed popular and reasonably efficient. This was confirmed initially by two delegations visiting in mid-October, one from the Australian Labour Party (ALP) and the other from the Australian Council for Overseas Aid (ACFOA). Travelling from Dili to Baucau, Viqueque and Suai, the ALP concluded:

> Our tour around the island confirmed the claims by Fretilin that they are virtually in full control of the situation . . . Wherever we went, the Fretilin troops appeared to be well-disciplined; they were treating their prisoners well and appeared to have the overwhelming support of the local population.[25]

ACFOA, travelling more extensively and reporting more thoroughly, concluded that: 'Fretilin has strong support in the areas under its control, which include all of East Timor, except the Oecussi enclave and . . . an area in the northwest, extending from the border south of Maliana, across east of the town of Batugadé to the coast'.[26] Commenting favourably on the continuing implementation of Fretilin's policies on health, education, nursery care and agriculture, ACFOA highlighted the support for these as the decisive factors in their maintenance during increasingly difficult administrative circumstances.

One member of the ACFOA delegation, the former Australian Consul to East Timor, James Dunn, focused specifically on this support:

> Whatever the shortcomings of the Fretilin administration, it clearly enjoyed widespread support from the population, including many hitherto UDT supporters. In October, Australian relief workers visited most parts of Timor and, without exception, they reported that there was no evidence of any insecurity or any hostility towards Fretilin. Indeed, Fretilin leaders were welcomed warmly and spontaneously in all main centres by crowds of Timorese. In my long association with Portuguese Timor, which goes back fourteen years, I had never before witnessed such demonstrations of spontaneous warmth and support from the indigenous population. The Fretilin administration was not without its critics, but opposition appeared to be confined to expressions of dissatisfaction rather than hostility.[27]

Such support remained constant during October and November; it was crucial in keeping the country going since, with the departure of the Portuguese and the flight of the UDT, around 80 per cent of the administrative strata had been lost. In fact, East Timor was left with no trained doctors or engineers to rebuild its infrastructure after the August fighting. Although the International Committee of the Red Cross (ICRC) travelled extensively throughout the country, it and other groups, such as the ACFOA, required administrative back-up, which they received soon after a rapid Fretilin reorganization.

Fretilin's commissions, run collectively by army personnel, central committee members and professional advisers in areas such as agriculture, education and nursery provision, became the organizational core of reconstruction in the regions. The work of the economic commission was particularly crucial. The rice crop had been lost in several areas as a result of the conflict and particularly in the fertile areas around Maliana in the west. Trading networks thus had to be rebuilt and a system of food distribution organized as quickly as possible. The coffee crop had to be harvested and exported to provide revenue for food imports, the labour for the harvesting being provided through an expansion of the work-force in the public sector. These aims were realized by the end of October, a remarkable achievement when one considers that there was next to no technical expertise and that essential commodities such as money were locked away in the Banco Nacional Ultramino, which Fretilin central committee members were reluctant to break into, anxious not to prejudice a Portuguese return.

The coffee crop was finally exported on 15 November, when a barge carrying seed from an Australian aid group returned from a trip to Dili. The $Aus40,000 received from the sale of the Arabica was deposited in a bank in Darwin. (Unwilling to release it without the two founding signatories' permission, the money remains there to this day. One of the signatories was Ramos-Horta, the other was killed in 1976.)

After August, Fretilin inherited a large number of prisoners taken during the coup attempt. Consequently, much of the work of the Commission for Justice was taken up with organizing their trials. Of the 2000 prisoners held in various detention centres, only a small number had been tried by mid-November.[28] Most of these were lower-level members, since Fretilin argued that those who had helped in the planning and organization of the coup should be tried by the colonial administration. Throughout their detention, the treatment of the prisoners was supervised by the ICRC and they were visited by foreign journalists and delegations. The ALP delegation visited Dili prison in mid-October:

> Following discussions with the Central Committee, we then inspected the jail near the army headquarters in Dili where about eighty prisoners were held. These were mainly UDT prisoners but also included some Fretilin supporters who had been jailed for breaches of discipline, and some civil officers . . . The jail was crowded but the prisoners generally looked to be in good condition and were being fed the same food rations as everyone else in Dili.[29]

Although this account described only Dili prison, it was probably a fairly typical picture. With the ICRC allowed free access to all prisons during the post-coup period, news of maltreatment would have surfaced quickly if it had occurred.

One of the most striking features of the Fretilin administration was the degree to which unity was restored after the differences over Macau and the governor's attempts to use these to reconstruct the coalition with the UDT. This unified appearance was undoubtedly facilitated by Fretilin's new structure, since the commissions minimized conflicts between potential factions by including each group in the commissions' leadership. This was particularly important for members of the army, or 'Falintil'[30] as Fretilin's troops came to be known, whose role in the coup attempt and particularly that of the pro-Fretilin sergeants in the Portuguese Army, had given them a greater say in the running of Fretilin. Their influence increased as the conflict with the Indonesians intensified in November and December. Along with this went an ascendancy of the Lobato group, which had always had closer ties with the military. Gradually, their notions began to prevail over other perspectives. Consequently, Fretilin perceptibly became more nationalist, with less stress placed on the value of foreign diplomacy, aspects which, of course, were strengthened by the unfolding of events in the post-coup months and the role of the army in these events. Indeed, by early October it was clear that military matters would soon become paramount.

Indonesia's border strategy

Frustrated in their attempts to provoke intervention through internal conflict, *Komodo* leaders now turned to more direct military solutions. The Fretilin administration had to be removed as quickly as possible, before it was able to establish itself as a credible alternative. This was to be achieved either through a progressive erosion of the territory by attacks from Indonesian-controlled enclaves or, if all else failed, by outright invasion. On the international front, overseas opinion had to be carefully prepared to accept either outcome. The myth of the civil war continuing after August was perpetuated by *Komodo* precisely for this reason. This myth, based on border incursions by platoons of Indonesian troops, was created by Indonesian news agencies and reproduced in the foreign press.

As always, the US Central Intelligence Agency (CIA) seemed to know most accurately what was occurring on the ground. As early as 4 September, it reported that: 'Communications intelligence indicates that two Indonesian special forces groups, consisting of about 100 men each, entered Portuguese Timor on the evening of September 3–4'.[31] Again, on the 17th, it was reported that Indonesia had sent in 650 'Timorese irregular troops', on the 19th more Indonesian troops, and on the 26th that: 'Vastly increased Indonesian involvement is now proposed; special forces troops armed with weapons that cannot be traced to Jakarta will be used. Malaysia has reportedly agreed in principle to supply such weapons'.[32] The CIA report stated the aims of this operation briefly: 'Jakarta is now sending guerilla units into the Portuguese half of the island in order to engage Fretilin forces, encourage pro-Indonesian elements, and provoke incidents that would provide the Indonesians with an excuse to invade should they decide to do so'.[33]

A Timorese from the southern border area described the results of these incursions:

> In the border region of the Suai district where I was living, Indonesian troops had started coming across the border and fighting in September. They used bazookas and hand grenades, and burnt down houses. They came to the towns — Tilumor, for example — and shot people. There were Fretilin soldiers who were shot dead in these encounters . . . They came across the border at night, and then went back to Indonesian territory . . . I even recollect an incident when fighting took place in this border area before the beginning of September.[34]

Meanwhile, for overseas consumption, the Indonesian press was reporting these engagements as a resurgence of the conflict between Fretilin and parties opposed to it. The usual medium of these myths was the government press agency, *Antara*, with dailies such as *Sinar Harapan* regularly proclaiming military successes by Apodeti and UDT. The most spectacular orchestration came towards the end of September, when *Antara* reported that Fretilin forces had killed seven villagers in Indonesian Timor in a cross-border attack. Speaking to the press agency, Defence Minister Panggabean fumed: 'We will smash anyone at all who trespasses across Indonesia's borders'.[35] The army-sponsored parliament similarly vented its wrath. It 'expressed appreciation for the UDT and Apodeti, which had still been able to restrain themselves in the cauldron of war and had not committed acts outside the bounds of humanitarianism'.[36] The National Youth Committee of Indonesia claimed that its members were 'ready and await the command of the President for settling the question at the border with Portuguese Timor'.[37] With such national fervour ably fermented by BAKIN, and faithfully reported by its press agency, how could one doubt the validity, in the parliament's phrase, of this 'act of terrorism'? Consequently, the foreign press reported faithfully a border incursion which never occurred.

Such orchestration was crucial to Indonesia's campaign, since it justified a substantial increase in troops crossing the border at the beginning of October. This increase in troop deployment was vital. Fretilin had put up extremely stiff resistance throughout September, and the 'pro-Indonesian guerrillas' had found no support whatsoever amongst the population. Furthermore, it seemed that Fretilin might soon enter into negotiations with the Portuguese Government, and this could enhance its status internationally.[38] Finally, a successful outcome was needed even more urgently as a result of President Suharto's public commitment to integration in July. Convinced by Murtopo, Sugama and other BAKIN generals that military intervention could now be completed in a short campaign, Suharto nevertheless remained anxious that international reaction should not prejudice the annexation. Since the Wonosobo meeting, Suharto had subscribed, in Woolcott's words, to 'the settled Indonesian policy to incorporate Timor', and his differences with the BAKIN generals had been over the timing of military action and its possible international repercussions.[39]

Indonesia's increased troop deployment soon produced results. The last village to fall in the UDT retreat was the border-post of Batugadé. To preserve the myth of a continuing civil war, Indonesian soldiers disguised as UDT troops attacked Batugadé on the 7th. The village was 're-taken by UDT' on 8 October, when Colonel Dading and a platoon of Indonesian commandos set up headquarters for their forthcoming campaign. Whilst American intelligence provided the detailed background information to this attack within three days of its occurrence — 'The troops . . . may have come from an amphibious task force which ferried some 400 marines and other troops and vehicles to Atapupu on October 2' — Indonesia's foreign minister was still being reported in the world's press as claiming: 'We have never asked East Timor to join Indonesia, neither have we any objection to their formation of an independent nation'.[40]

Meanwhile, Dading was preparing to move eastward on a front stretching from Batugadé to Lebos, in the south, with the objective of setting up bases east of the border. As the CIA noted, this time before the event:

> The plan calls for the setting up of small military bases just inside
> Portuguese Timor. Indonesia's strategy is to nibble away at the Fretilin
> from these enclaves. The first of these enclaves is to be established on
> October 14, when Indonesian units are to attack the town of Maliana. The
> troops participating in the operation will wear uniforms without insignia
> and are to carry older, Soviet-made weapons, so as not to be identified as
> Indonesian regulars.[41]

In the initial phases of Dading's attack, UDT troops were sent back to the
border, after protesting at the brutality of Indonesian troops towards the
population. Although the village of Balibo and the regional centre of Maliana
were soon captured by the Indonesians, other villages targeted as base areas,
such as Lebos, remained stubbornly under Fretilin control. A week after the
initial phases of the border campaign, CIA coverage recorded that: 'The
Indonesian military operation launched last week in Portuguese Timor has got
bogged down. Field commanders apparently underestimated their logistic
problems and the strength of Fretilin forces operating near the border'.[42] As a
result, Indonesian troops were to advance no further west. The conflict
degenerated into a stalemate, with Fretilin troops blocking movement out of
Maliana. A typical day in this war was described by a visiting journalist:

> An attempted breakout (of Maliana) by the Indonesian-led forces sparked
> the 49th day flare-up. The attack was made by moonlight in the direction of
> the now unoccupied college. Fretilin units entered the fray to make a
> three-pronged counter-offensive. It was all foot-fighting, and they used only
> the Nato G-3 issue and the Mauser. Small groups of them, acting
> independently and using any and all vegetation for cover, are an invisible
> target for blundering shell and mortar . . . Indonesia is expending hundreds
> of shells and mortar around the clock . . . Fretilin continues to attack
> because, in the words of one soldier, 'they are there and the land is ours'.[43]

In the initial move to take Maliana, five journalists (two Australian, two
British and one New Zealander) were killed by Dading's troops in the village of
Balibo. The events surrounding their deaths illustrate the lengths to which
foreign governments were prepared to go to perpetuate *Komodo*'s myths in the
post-coup period.[44]

On 16 October, troops from the *Kopassandha* division and KKO marines
entered Balibo as the Fretilin garrison withdrew. The journalists, who had
travelled to the border area to film some military action, were lodged in a house
on which they had painted an Australian flag to advertise their non-combatant
status. As Indonesian troops approached, they came out of the house and
began to film the distant advance. Without warning, one was shot dead and
another wounded as they tried to escape a hail of bullets. After another had
been struck by a knife, the four left alive were shot with their faces to the wall of

the house they had been occupying. Their bodies were then placed in a neighbouring house, and their murders were reported to headquarters in Batugadé, and thence to Jakarta. Later that day, Dading and BAKIN agent Louis Taolin flew to Balibo and arranged for the bodies of the journalists to be dressed in Portuguese uniforms, propped behind machine guns and placed in front of the 'Australian's' sign. They were then photographed before being dumped in a nearby building, which was set on fire. Taolin and Dading returned to Batugadé, and the advance to Maliana continued.

On the very next day, the Indonesian daily paper *Kompas*, reported that UDT forces had 'discovered' the bodies of four Europeans at Balibo. This was to clear the way for Indonesia's subsequent claim that the journalists were killed in cross-fire between UDT and Fretilin forces. Meanwhile, on 20 and 21 October, in radio broadcasts from Kupang, Lopez da Cruz, through his BAKIN speechwriter, used the journalists' murders to illustrate the strength and determination of UDT forces:

> Those who are fighting against the communists are from UDT, Apodeti, KOTA and Trabalhista. We attacked with mortar, machine guns and various kinds of guns and aircraft all the peaks of Balibo. The Australian communists were supporting, and inside, Fretilin to fight against our forces showing their heroism to our traitors during the fights where they camped. How could they fight us, if as soon as our guns began crying, they all disappeared? Three Australians could run away so they want to tell the others we were anti-communist forces. We are not afraid of Fretilin, nor the Australian communists. You can send them to the border to play with us. We have also many friends in Asia.[45]

When a secretary from the Australian embassy travelled to Kupang to find out what had happened, some eight days after the murders, he was given an official version of events, in a letter signed by UDT, Apodeti and Kota leaders, that the journalists were probably killed in an attack on a house from which the UDT forces had been fired upon. They had thus been killed in cross-fire, and had themselves acted as combatants. Finally, on 12 November, BAKIN handed the remains of the journalists to the Australian embassy. Whilst it took the skills of a pathologist to verify that the ashes were human remains, the journalists' personal effects were remarkably intact, and showed no signs of having been near the fires which had burnt their bodies beyond recognition in the UDT counterattack.

If this attempted cover-up seemed rather thin, worse was to follow. Faced with demands for enquiries into the murders, the Australian and British governments claimed their by now usual ignorance of events. Australia's Foreign Minister, Senator Willesee, claimed on 29 October that no definite information was available. Two weeks after the murders, Whitlam followed this up by sending a polite message to Suharto asking for assistance in trying to discover what had happened in Balibo. It was not to be until April 1976 that the Australian Government sent a fact-finding mission to Balibo, by which time the Indonesians had prepared the ground; after all, they had by then been occupying the town for four and a half months. Similarly, the British Government concluded that 'in view of the circumstances then prevailing in Timor, Her Majesty's Government has no means of ascertaining the precise truth'.[46]

Both governments lied; the truth was known to them less than twenty-four hours after the murders. News of the killings was monitored by an electronic surveillance system operated by the Defence Signals Division of the Australian Government's Defence Department:

> After monitoring the battle for Balibo as it happened . . . the Shoal Bay DSD station sent recorded data immediately to DSD headquarters in Melbourne . . . That afternoon the analysed material went to the Defence Departments' Joint Intelligence Organisation in Canberra. Early in the evening a senior Defence Department official took a report over to Parliament House, to Defence Minister Bill Morrison. This was only twelve hours after the attack.[47]

This information was passed on to the intelligence networks of friendly governments, of which the most important were the USA and Britain. The contrast between these governments' private knowledge and public utterances in this episode was neatly expressed in a cable sent to Canberra by the Australian Ambassador shortly after the murders: 'Although we know it is not true, the formal position of the Indonesian Government is still that there is no Indonesian military intervention in East Timor'; questioning this 'formal position', he cautioned, 'would invite a hurt and angry reaction'.[48]

Independence and invasion

With their enclave strategy seemingly stymied and now contemplating a more effective but more open involvement, BAKIN leaders travelled to Rome, where Ali Murtopo once again met with Almeida Santos. The Lisbon Government had been receiving proposals regularly from both Lemos Pires on Atauro and Fretilin itself. It had always responded in the same manner: talks could only be held if all Timorese parties were present, that is if Fretilin would agree to be permanently outnumbered in discussion by parties who openly advocated integration with Indonesia. This policy had pleased Murtopo greatly and, by the time of the Rome meeting on 2 November he must have been even more delighted with some of Santos' recent statements: 'East Timor can count on the co-operation of the countries in its area of influence, or it must face a situation of suicidal isolation', or again: 'The highest Indonesian officials, starting with President Suharto himself, have asserted and re-asserted that they do not have in mind violent interventions'. The Rome talks specifically excluded all political parties, thereby according priority to Indonesia. They also excluded the UN, but then Santos had already ruled out an earlier suggestion by Lemos

Pires that the Portuguese Government could re-engage the decolonization process by applying for East Timor to be placed under UN trusteeship. The communiqué issued at the conclusion of the talks made no reference to Indonesian involvement, and called on the political parties in East Timor to end their armed conflict and open up discussions with the Portuguese Government. A more bizarre statement is hard to imagine; the former colonial power, having abandoned its colony and rejected all calls for serious discussions with the party now representing the majority interests of its colonial subjects, calls for an end to an armed conflict brought about by the very government with whom it is negotiating. The irony of Antunes' post-Rome statement that 'Indonesia is prepared to understand Portugal's position and proceed with contacts in order to solve the problems in East Timor' seemed to be lost on the Portuguese foreign minister.[49]

With Portugal so seemingly sympathetic and understanding, with the Australian Government turning reality on its head,[50] and with the United States feigning ignorance of an annexation in which it quietly acquiesced, BAKIN concluded that the moment was tactically opportune for a more determined and overt action.

Abandoning the strategy of establishing border bases, Indonesia mounted a combined land, air and sea attack on the town of Atabae, north of Maliana, in mid-November. The town was strategically placed for an eastward push towards Dili. It became the site of an intensive battle, lasting some two weeks, with off-shore bombardment constant during the night and daily aerial bombing. As Indonesia piled in more troops, the fall of Atabae became inevitable. On 24 November, Fretilin appealed to the UN Security Council for the withdrawal of Indonesian troops. Three days later, Lopez da Cruz declared that the 'combined anti-communist forces of UDT and Apodeti are on the road to Dili'. Atabae had fallen.[51]

The spectre of an Indonesian invasion which had haunted Dili for so long now seemed immediate. As a result, the Fretilin administration proclaimed independence unilaterally. Sensing that an independent state might have a more successful chance of appeal to the UN if it did not have to rely on its mentor in Lisbon, and persuaded by the intense feeling from the military front that, if soldiers were going to die, they would prefer to do so for a country which was actually theirs, the Fretilin administration transformed itself into the Democratic Republic of East Timor on 28 November. The leaders of the commissions were sworn in as ministers before a Dili crowd, the Portuguese flag was lowered and a new flag, red, black and yellow with a white star, was raised. As a newly drafted constitution was presented, Xavier do Amaral declared:

> Expressing the highest aspirations of the people of East Timor and to safeguard the most legitimate interests of national sovereignty, the Central Committee of Fretilin decrees by proclamation, unilaterally, the independence of East Timor, from 0.00 hours today, declaring the state of the Democratic Republic of East Timor, anti-colonialist and anti-imperialist.[52]

The decision to declare independence unilaterally had been taken after several weeks of intense and heated debate. With the fall of Atabae, however, independence took on a new urgency and immediacy. Ways had to be found to break through the diplomatic silence and indifference with which Indonesia's allies had shrouded its aggression. An independent appeal to the UN seemed the only way forward.

Having forced Fretilin into this position, BAKIN now used the declaration as a justification for what it confidently thought would be the final act in its long drawn-out takeover bid. In the border port of Atambua, a day after the Dili declaration of independence, a 'declaration of integration' was signed by the UDT–Apodeti coterie, overseen by BAKIN agent Louis Taolin, who with Colonel Sugianto had written the document. Soon after, Adam Malik arrived to make an address which he later coined his 'fighting cock' speech: 'Diplomacy is finished. The solution to the East Timor problem is now at the front line of battle'.[53]

The full-scale invasion of Dili, by sea and air, accompanying an advance from Atabae, was actually planned for the beginning of December but, at the last minute, it was called off. Aid workers, journalists and Fretilin members who had all left Dili by 4 December were somewhat surprised as they waited for news in Atauro and Darwin. The reason for the delay, as usual, came from the CIA: 'According to a reliable source, Indonesia will not initiate large-scale military action against Portuguese Timor until after President Ford completes his visit (to Jakarta) on December 7th'. Clearly Ford, accompanied by Kissinger on a visit which the US State Department dubbed 'the big wink', might have found the need to go public somewhat embarrassing.

On the morning of 8 December, Alarico Fernandes, Information Minister of the newly created Republic of East Timor, transmitted an urgent message:

> Indonesian forces have been landed in Dili by sea . . . They are flying over Dili dropping out paratroopers . . . A lot of people have been killed indiscriminately . . . Women and children are going to be killed by Indonesian forces . . . We are going to be killed . . . SOS . . . We call for your help. This is an urgent call.[54]

Meanwhile, President Ford was arriving in Hawaii. Asked for a reaction to the Indonesian invasion, he smiled and said: 'We'll talk about that later'. His press secretary, Ron Nessen, added: 'The President always deplores violence, wherever it occurs'.[55] Three days earlier, former Prime Minister Whitlam, asked what his government would do if an invasion occurred, replied: 'We would do absolutely nothing . . . Now, that's a blunt, truthful answer'.[56] It was probably the first truthful answer given in public by a minister in a government allied with Indonesia since the Lisbon coup in April 1974.

So began Indonesia's attempt to limit the development of a unique process in East Timor. A society which had retained the cohesion of its own institutions, but whose development had been retarded for centuries by colonial rule, had finally created a national basis for this development, but on its own terms. The framework in which an independent nation was being built had taken indigenous society and culture as reference points, and located the development of spheres such as education, health and politics within them. Symbolized in areas such as Fretilin's literacy campaign, or in the commitment to the cultural values of *maubere*, a new unity had been forged in Timorese society between and within its traditional and modern élites and its regions. In the process of working to create this unity, Fretilin had devised development strategies whose full implementation could have created the infrastructure for a successfully planned economy, based on the indigenous needs of the population. In every sense, economically, politically, socially and culturally, the foundations for a successful nation-state had been created. Furthermore, they had been created during phases of external threat and internal conflict, indicating immense capabilities for self-development which could have been even better expressed under more favourable conditions.

The emergence of these unifying tendencies at the national level coexisted with the regional cohesion which had been the hallmark of colonial society. Locally, despite all the incursions of Portuguese colonialism, the systems of exchange expressed in kinship, politics, religion and culture continued to reproduce themselves. Just as they provided the context towards which issues of development and independence had to be directed, so too did they establish a powerful basis for resistance to regional or foreign incursion.

Indonesia thus encountered a society with two predominant features: indigenous structures with long-established capacities for self-sustained regional reproduction, combined with newly established institutions and ideologies embodying nationalist aspirations for an independence which, although fleetingly, had been glimpsed by many and then denied.

These features, inconceivable in the Indonesian military's conception of economically underdeveloped Timor as 'primitive', and unimaginable in either the paternalist values of the colonial power or the assumed superiority of an Australian state, produced a sustained and powerful movement which could only be undermined by a pervasive and systematic attempt at social engineering. This attempt, and its impact on the people of East Timor is outlined in the following chapters. Constructed from first-hand reports and refugee testimonies, it recounts, as accurately as possible, East Timor's experiences and responses to Indonesia's brutal occupation.

Notes

1. For details of the Indonesian presence, see the *Far Eastern Economic Review*, 1 August 1975.

2. See *Nacroma*, 31 August 1974.

3. See Dunn, 1974, pp. 17–18. Lemos Pires later stated: 'If I could have separated, say, ten leaders from the others in Fretilin, and united them with the UDT, it might have worked', Lisbon interview, 9 February 1985.

4. Further evidence of this was provided in late June and July, when the Revolutionary Brigades strategy left only ten central committee members in Dili, to work on the committees of the Decolonization Commission, much to the anger of majors Jonatas and Mota (see Hill, 1978).

5. Furthermore, in the constitutional law passed in Lisbon to codify the results of the Macau summit, the Popular Assembly was charged with 'determining East Timor's future, rather than overseeing independence'.

6. The meeting with Murtopo was held in Jakarta on 2 August.

7. Jolliffe, 1978, pp. 117–18.

8. Most notably ibid., pp. 120–43.

9. For example, 39 people were said to have been executed in the Samé prison.

10. *Sinar Harapan* (Jakarta), 14 August 1975.

11. A number of these cables have been reprinted in Munster and Walsh (eds), Sydney, 1980.

12. Cable from Australian Ambassador Woolcott, to Canberra, 'Secret: Portuguese Timor', 18 August 1975, cited in Munster and Walsh (eds), 1980, p. 201.

13. Cable from Woolcott to Canberra, 'Secret: Portuguese Timor', 22 August 1975, cited in Munster and Walsh (eds), 1980, p. 204.

14. These conditions are most aptly described in J. S. Dunn's interviews with refugees in Lisbon in 1977 — see Dunn, 1977b.

15. J. S. Dunn, from an interview with a former UDT leader in Portugal, January 1977, cited in Dunn, 1977b, pp. 182–3.

16. Interview with Lemos Pires, Lisbon, 19 February 1985.

17. Ibid.

18. Barreto, 1982, p. 44.

19. The monitoring reports of the US CIA on the situation in East Timor, covering a period from 11 August 1975 to 13 February 1976, were published in an edited form in the *National Times*, Australia (see Van Atta and Toohey, 1982, 30 May and 6 June).

20. Richard Nixon, 'Asia after Vietnam', *Foreign Affairs*, 1967.

21. On this point, see also M. Richardson, 'Don't Anger Jakarta', *Age* (Melbourne) 3 August 1976.

22. Newsom's comment is cited in a Woolcott telegram to Whitlam's secretary, Alan Renouf, on 17 August (see Munster and Walsh (eds) 1980, p. 200).

23. Ibid., p. 200.

24. Quoted in a cable from Woolcott to Canberra, London, Moscow and Peking, from Jakarta, 21 July 1975, cited in ibid., p. 192.

25. Report on a visit to Portuguese East Timor by Senator Gietzelt and Ken Fry MP, 16–20 October 1975, p. 9.

26. Australian Council for Overseas Aid, 1975, Appendix I. The delegation travelled in East Timor between 16 October and 2 November.

27. Dunn, 1976, p. 7.

28. This information was received in an interview with a former deputy-secretary in the justice department of Fretilin's central committee, in Lisbon, 16 February 1985. It appears to be corroborated by the accounts available from foreign visitors during October and November.

29. Australian Council for Overseas Aid, 1975, p. 4.

30. FALINTIL (*Forcas Armadas de Libertacao Nacional de Timor Leste*).

31. Van Atta and Toohey, 1982, 30 May.

32. Van Atta and Toohey, 1982, 30 May and 6 June.

33. Van Atta and Toohey, 1982, 26 September.

34. Interview with a Timorese refugee, Neobere, in London, 11/12/13 May 1983.

35. *Antara*, 27 September, cited in *Indonesian Current Affairs Translation Service*, October 1975.

36. This statement was made by a representative of the Indonesian Democratic Party.

37. *Antara*, 29 September, cited in *Indonesian Current Affairs Translation Service*, October 1975.

38. The Fretilin administration called repeatedly for the return of the colonial administration to carry on and complete the process of decolonization. On 6 October, Lisbon responded by offering a venue for talks with the three parties. Given that UDT and Apodeti had by then become supporters of integration through military intervention, Fretilin understandably refused to meet with them, but agreed to send a delegation for talks with the Lisbon Decolonization Commission.

39. Munster and Walsh (eds), 1980, p. 19.

40. Van Atta and Toohey, 1982, 6–10 June. Malik made his statement to journalists in Jakarta; it is reported in Dunn, 1983, p. 229.

41. Van Atta and Toohey, ibid. and 1982, 11 October.

42. Van Atta and Toohey, 1982, June 6–10 and 24 October.

43. Roger East, 'East Timor Battle Ends in Stalemate on 49th Day', in *Independence or Death: East Timor's Border War*, eye-witness reports by Roger East, published by the *Campaign for an Independent East Timor*, Sydney, Australia, 1976.

44. The best analyses of these events are presented in Jolliffe, 1978, pp. 166–76, Dunn, 1983, pp. 233–52, H. McDonald, 'Death at Balibo', *National Times*, Australia, 7 July 1979.

45. Radio Kupang, 21 October 1975, recording made by Jill Jolliffe.

46. Reply from the Secretary for Foreign and Commonwealth Affairs to a question raised by the Right Hon. Geoffrey Edge, MP for Aldridge-Brownhills, 16 October 1976.

47. H. McDonlad, 'Death at Balibo', *National Times* (Australia), 7 July 1979.

48. Cable cited in *Canberra Times*, in an article by Bruce Juddery, 31 May 1976.

49. Antunes' and Santos' statements were reported in *O Seculo* (Lisbon), 5 November 1975.

50. Although the Whitlam Government had been replaced by the Fraser Government in December, Australian policy towards East Timor remained constant.

51. See Jolliffe, 1978, p. 207.

52. Cited in ibid., p. 212.

53. The *Canberra Times*, 3 December 1975.

54. Message received by a Darwin transmitter tuned to the Red Cross Radio in Dili hospital, 8 December 1975.

55. *The Boston Globe*, 8 November 1975.

56. *Sydney Morning Herald*, 5 December 1975.

5. Invasion, Resistance and the International Response

The attack on Dili, codenamed *Operasi Seroja* (or Lotus) began with a bombardment in the early hours of 8 December, followed by an aerial attack at 5 am, with soldiers of Indonesia's élite *Kopassandha* paratroopers being dropped on to the wharf area. The original plan had been to combine this assault with a rapid encirclement of Dili by troops mainly from the border area, but Fretilin's resistance had prevented this. The invasion force was led by General Murdani, with his subordinate, Colonel Dading. Ten thousand soldiers were deployed from Indonesia's *Brawijaya* and *Siliwangi* divisions from East and West Java respectively. The troops acted in the most savage fashion. The inhabitants of Dili were subjected to systematic killing, gratuitous violence and primitive plunder. In the words of Dili's former bishop, Mgr Costa Lopez: 'The soldiers who landed started killing everyone they could find. There were many dead bodies in the streets — all we could see were the soldiers killing, killing, killing'.[1] A letter sent from Dili to a Timorese relative in Darwin shortly after the invasion claimed that 2000 men, some 80 per cent of the male population of the capital, had been killed by mid-January. Initially, many killings took place in the wharf area. On 9 December:

> At 2 pm, 59 men, both Chinese and Timorese, were brought on to the wharf . . . These men were shot one by one, with the crowd, believed amounting to 500, being ordered to count. The victims were ordered to stand on the edge of the pier facing the sea, so that when they were shot their bodies fell into the water. Indonesian soldiers stood by and fired at the bodies in the water in the event that there was any sign of life.

Earlier in the day, at 9 am, a smaller group, many of them women with their children, had been executed in a similar way. An eye-witness testified: 'The Indonesians tore the crying children from their mothers and passed them back to the crowd. The women were then shot one by one, with the onlookers being ordered by the Indonesians to count'.[2] Another killing-ground was the area surrounding the Portuguese police barracks in the south of the capital:

> At about 12 noon, the green berets began to land, as I recall from battalions 501 and 502 (*Brawijaya* battalions). They advanced to where I was. They

ordered us all out of our homes, to gather in the street. We were taken to an open space, women, children, old people and men, including me. There was a military police barracks nearby but the Indonesians were afraid to enter so they ordered us in and told us to bring out the weapons and ammunition. Then they ordered us to gather together again. We didn't know why. There were about fifty of us then, all men, just picked up at random. All able-bodied men. In the middle, one of their men, an Indonesian soldier, was lying dead. Then the soldiers, there were three of them, started spraying us with bullets. Many died on the spot, some managed to run off, falling as they fled because they had been hit. As far as I know, only 3 or 4 out of the 50 men are still alive.[3]

There are many such testimonies: of entire families being shot for displaying Fretilin flags on their houses, of groups being shot for refusing to hand over their personal possessions, of grenades being rolled into packed houses, and of Fretilin sympathizers singled out for immediate execution. The scale of the killings is illustrated in the following testimony:

When the Indonesians arrived, we were all ordered to leave our houses. We were told it would be for three days, but after three days we were still not allowed back. After four days I went home to pick up some fruit and rice because I was hungry. There were bodies lying around everywhere. My sister-in-law told the Indonesians to bury the bodies or burn them, or else there would be a disaster.[4]

The Chinese population of Dili was singled out for selective killings. Five hundred were killed on the first day of the attack. An eye-witness described one such slaughter:

At the harbour were many dead bodies . . . we were told to tie the bodies to iron poles, attach bricks and throw the bodies in the sea. After we had thrown all the bodies in the sea, about twenty people were brought in, made to face the sea and shot dead. They were Chinese . . . more came later. After the killing stopped, we spent another one or two hours tying the people as before and throwing them in the sea.[5]

Such massacres were accompanied by extensive looting:

Shortly after the landing at Dili, most of the townspeople were ordered by the soldiers to go to a location near the airport. When they returned their houses had been thoroughly ransacked, and in some cases they were completely empty. Cars, radios, items of furniture, cutlery, even windows were taken to ships in the harbour. Most of the cars left in Dili were taken on board ships by Indonesian soldiers. Most of the tractors in the Dili area were taken away. Churches and the Seminary were also looted, and their books burnt.[6]

At one stage, it was reported that nineteen ships had been moored in Dili harbour to carry away the looted goods.[7]

On 10 December a further group of paratroopers landed in Baucau, and on 25 and 26 December 15,000 more troops were added to the existing 10,000. The aim of landing these forces was to move troops from towns such as Dili and Baucau into the interior, to which people had retreated prior to and during the invasion. As the Indonesians advanced, troop movements were supported by heavy naval and aerial bombardment, armed with incendiary bombs and toxic sprays. Their brutalities continued; it seems that entire villages were slaughtered for supporting Fretilin. In the villages of Remexio and Aileu, south of Dili, everyone over the age of three was shot, since 'they were infected with the seeds of Fretilin'.[8] In Maubara and Luiquica, on the northwest coast, the entire Chinese population was killed. Indonesian troops had been given orders to crush all opposition ruthlessly, and were told that they were fighting communists in the cause of *Jihad* (Holy War), just as they had done in Indonesia in 1965. The Timorese were portrayed as backward, primitive, almost sub-human. Motivated by such values, and by the promise of looting, nevertheless the Indonesians were poorly supported logistically. Training was inadequate and equipment inefficient. Paratroopers intended to block the retreat of Fretilin forces by landing behind them were parachuted on top of them, artillery jammed, and many shells failed to explode. Indonesian troops rapidly became demoralized. In one correspondent's words, there was 'no glory' to be had from the action. They were poorly paid and witnessed extensive corruption within their higher ranks. As many as 2000 died in the first four months of 1976. As troops began to refuse to go out on patrol and complained that they were not receiving enough food, it was reported that divisions were being rotated as quickly as possible in their duties.[9]

This stood in stark contrast to the position of the resistance movement. Having prepared for an Indonesian attack for some months prior to the invasion, Fretilin groups had set up base areas inland from the coastal zones, to which they retreated on or shortly after 7 December. As had traditionally been the case in East Timor in periods of conflict, most of the population also left the towns and villages, moving to the interior. Fretilin forces, comprising 2500 full-time regular troops from the former Portuguese Army, with 7000 part-time militia and 20,000 reservists, were reasonably well-equipped with weapons left behind by the Portuguese. Centred on the base areas, which in the early stages were supplied with food stocks accumulated and grown locally, Fretilin continued with their programmes developed during 1974–5. The most successful were the literacy and health programmes. By mid-June, for example, an inter-regional East Timorese medical organization had been set up. For two weeks at the end of May, Fretilin held a nationwide plenary conference, with representatives from each of the country's regions. Its radio continued to broadcast throughout the island.

The strength of the independence movement in the interior severely restricted the Indonesian Army's ability to make any headway. Throughout the early months of the invasion, Indonesian control was confined to major towns and villages, such as Dili, Baucau, Aileu and Same, and the areas surrounding them. Assisted by aerial and naval bombardment from ships blockading the coast, Indonesian troops attempted to move inland from the coastal areas to join up with troops parachuted further inland. Throughout 1976, this strategy failed. As they moved inland, they encountered stiff resistance, and were forced to withdraw. The units that were dropped in the interior usually had to be pulled out again fairly quickly, as they were surrounded by Fretilin troops. A good example of this was the town of Suai on the south coast, near the border; although only three kilometres from the sea, it took 3000 Indonesian soldiers four months to capture it.[10] During the last weeks of the dry season and the onset of the rains, Fretilin began to recapture villages held by the Indonesians, such as Alas in the south and Remexio, 15km south of Dili.

The strength of Fretilin's control was exemplified by the nature of the visits organized by the military. Responding to 'Timorese determination' to join Indonesia, Adam Malik, addressing a meeting in which soldiers 'armed with automatic weapons mingled with the crowd', spent one and a half hours in Dili and five minutes at the airport in Bacau.[11] In July, Indonesia's Interior Minister, General Amir Machmud, led a delegation on a one-day tour of five towns. A journalist accompanying the group reported that calls at Baucau and the island of Atauro were scrapped from the itinerary at the last minute 'because of cloudy weather'. There were reports later that Fretilin had mortared Baucau on the morning of the proposed visit.[12] As the military continued their restrictions on all foreigners and West Timorese entering East Timor[13], Suharto was forced to admit in August that Fretilin still possessed some strength 'here and there'.[14]

Frustrated by their inability to make any headway militarily, Indonesian troops stepped up their terrorization of the local population. Villages were destroyed and their surviving populations moved into strategic camps. Atrocities became widespread as did the use of chemical weapons. In mid-May, 67 boys were shot in Suai. In early August in the area around Zumalai, six villages were burnt and hundreds of their inhabitants executed;[15] and so it continued. Even the newly appointed governor, former Apodeti member Arnaldo Araujo, wrote to Suharto condemning the widespread killing.[16]

In a doomed attempt, a number of ex-UDT members staged a coup in Dili in early April, which seems to have been savagely repressed.[17] Some weeks earlier their erstwhile leader, Lopez da Cruz, ensconced in the Indonesian administration, claimed that 60,000 Timorese had been killed. He described the massacres as 'revenge for Fretilin's cruelty when it was in power'.[18] Da Cruz's figures were confirmed later in a report by a visiting group of Indonesian relief workers, who estimated that at least 10 per cent of the population had been killed: 'We found this figure rather high, but when I asked two religious fathers in Dili, they replied that according to their estimate, the figure of people killed may reach 100,000.[19]

Military myths

The contrast between this reality of the war and Indonesia's military accounts of it could not have been more stark. Until the end of March, the Indonesian Government denied that it had any troops whatsoever in East Timor, rather they were Indonesian 'volunteers' sent to assist the struggles of the indigenous parties, UDT, Apodeti, Kota and Trabhalista, against Fretilin. Indonesia had agreed only reluctantly to this assistance after these parties had signed a petition for integration just before the invasion. This myth was perpetuated even after the new governor, Arnaldo Araujo, issued a decree on 3 February banning all political parties.

Perhaps most notable, however, was the military's account of the UN attempt to control Indonesia's actions. On 23 December, the UN Security Council passed a motion calling for Indonesian withdrawal and a genuine act of self-determination. The secretary-general was requested to open negotiations between Indonesia and Fretilin. This task was entrusted to a special representative, Winspeare Guiccardi. The outcome of his mission, as portrayed by the Indonesian military, was clear. As stated by General Panggabean: 'The fact that the United Nations envoy was unable to meet Fretilin forces in Timor proved that the whole of East Timor is now controlled by the Provisional Government'.[20] On 18 January, Guiccardi made a short visit to Dili and Baucau but was unable to visit Fretilin areas. He then travelled to Darwin to try and make contact with Fretilin radio via a local transmitter. On 25 January, this transmitter was seized by Australia's Postal and Telecommunications Department, on the direct instructions of Prime Minister Fraser, since it was being operated 'unlicensed'. Shortly before its seizure, Guiccardi was informed by Fretilin leaders that he could fly to a number of airstrips or travel to Betano on the south coast. This information was intercepted by Indonesian intelligence which then duly bombed these areas, making any landings impossible. When Guiccardi suggested that he might transmit to East Timor using the radio of a Portuguese Corvette in waters which were still formally administered by the colonial power, Adam Malik replied tersely that the ship risked being sunk if it entered East Timor's territorial waters. Subsequently, Guiccardi was forced to return to the UN, his mission aborted.

In a document prepared for Guiccardi's visit, the Indonesian military issued strict guidelines to its battalion commanders and administrative officials in Dili. These guidelines became a model for subsequent foreign delegations' visits. The document read:

> All members of the armed forces stationed in the towns will continue to carry out their duties, but must nevertheless wear civilian dress so that it should appear to the delegation that they are unarmed civilians. All sites occupied by the armed forces or already abandoned by them must show no indication (weapons, munitions, notices) which might betray their presence or movement through such localities. Roads must be cleaned and free of military equipment.

Listing the towns and villages which the UN delegation would visit, the document advised:

> It is extremely important to make sure that the delegation does not spend the night in any of these places, and, if members of the delegation should desire to do so, the Provisional Government must firmly oppose the idea, finding any pretext . . . advancing as justification the very bad state of the roads, bad weather conditions for flying, or the reluctance of the communities living in those areas to meet the delegation because of the bad treatment they have received at the hands of Fretilin.

A series of model answers was provided to a range of possible questions. In answer to the question. 'What treatment is given to prisoners of war, and how many are there?', the following was suggested:

> Indicate some building that might serve as a prison, which must be guarded by sentries whose weapons are primed not to fire. Select some sensible people, particularly among the armed forces, to play the role of prisoners of war who have already surrendered to our troops and are being well-treated. To ensure realism, rations should be improved and those playing the part of prisoners must fulfil their role scrupulously.

Concluding, the document required that: 'Banners of protest against UN interference should be prepared, such as the following [in English in the original] — "United Nations hands off Timor Timur is Timor! We are already integrated with Indonesia! United Nations we do not want your intervention here!"[21]

Encouraged by the failure of Guiccardi's visit and allied support in the transmitter case, Indonesia's foreign minister reached new depths of cynicism. Of the journalists killed in September, he told a press conference in Jakarta attended by Australian correspondents: 'Let us forget them and we will erect a monument to them'.[22]

The most brazen of Indonesian moves, however, was undoubtedly the 'Act of Integration' staged in Dili on 31 May. The Ministers of the Provisional Government, appointed with Arnaldo Araujo on 18 December, convened a Regional People's Assembly in a former sports hall in Dili. Journalists were flown in from Jakarta for a three-hour visit to witness a short ceremony, conducted in Portuguese without translation, in which 28 delegates signed a petition requesting Suharto to grant integration. The tightest restrictions were placed on the visiting journalists. A correspondent from the Indonesian magazine, *Tempo*, commented: 'We were not allowed to leave the building. As soon as we took a step down the stairs officials in civilian clothes told us to go back. We were not even allowed to speak to assembly members in the vicinity'.[23] Another observer noted: 'No one had a chance even to shake hands with council members, and executive members of the Provisional Government refused to answer press questions, climbing immediately into their new Volvo cars'.[24] Information on the process of election of the 28 members was provided by an eye-witness, who testified later: 'Anyone nominated would have to be screened by the first assistant (intelligence officer). His past would be checked; if he was from Fretilin or UDT, he couldn't become a member. Most of the candidates were proposed by Apodeti people, then they would be chosen by Indonesian officers'.[25] These procedures notwithstanding, Malik's successor was able to claim, some years later, that 'East Timor's desire for integration was carried out legally'.[26]

Throughout these events, the crudeness and transparency of Indonesian propaganda was readily apparent. It bore no relation to the reality of the military's increasingly stymied annexation and the brutalities it had occasioned. Yet, the Indonesian perspective was constantly taken at face value in the foreign-affairs centres of countries such as Australia and the United States. Indeed, Indonesian pronouncements were adopted as axioms for foreign-policy formulation. Australian Minister for Foreign Affairs, Andrew Peacock, stated: 'The government regretted that further efforts were not made by the United Nations to play a more decisive role'.[27] In a similar vein, General Morais e Silva, Portuguese presidential envoy to Indonesia, claimed in August that there was no longer any dispute between the two countries.[28] Throughout the year US Government representatives repeated the myths — that over-zealous troops had been brutal in isolated incidents, that Fretilin had provoked intervention and that the numbers of deaths were exaggerated.

Why were these states so accommodating? Why were they prepared to accept so readily Indonesian interpretations despite the rejection of these by a majority of the world's governments? Why condone such levels of brutality? The answers to these questions are given in three events, all occurring within a few months during the first year of the Indonesian invasion.

At the beginning of August, Pentagon officials and members of the US Government met Malcolm Fraser in Washington and cautioned him against allowing any deterioration of his government's relations with Indonesia. American 'security interests' required the continuing 'good will' of the Suharto Government.[29] Paramount in these interests was the use of the Ombai–Wetar straits for deep-sea submarine passage. Concerned that new Law of the Sea proposals then under discussion at the UN could exclude underwater transit rights, Pentagon officials realized that these could only be maintained through bilateral arrangements with the Indonesian military. The maintenance of 'good will' was essential if the US was to maintain its capability to move undetected between the Indian and Pacific oceans. As a US maritime military strategist noted at the time:

It would certainly be an inconvenience to the superpower if their SSBN [nuclear-armed submarines] were denied unimpeded underwater passage through international straits inside territorial waters, having to surface according to the prevailing interpretation of innocent passage, and had to meet safety, pollution and other standards which could be applied for political reasons. For the US, however, the number of straits through which she needed passage in order to reach Soviet targets and for which she could not count on Allied permission was confined essentially to Gibraltar and the Indonesian straits, Lombok and Ombai–Wetar. There she had working arrangements for satisfactory SSBN transit, although they depended on favourable political reactions.[30]

As in the pre-invasion period, these strategic interests, central to the American Government's global nuclear strategy, were the most important influence in its policies towards the Indonesian invasion, which Australia should ensure it accommodated.

Accordingly, Fraser travelled to Jakarta for a four-day official visit, and in a speech to the Indonsian Parliament on 11 October, gave tacit recognition to Indonesia's occupation. In a subsequent press conference, he concluded that 'Australia now acknowledged the merger, for purely humanitarian reasons'.[31] Fraser visited Jakarta in the company of J. B. Reid, Director of Broken Hill Proprietary Company (BHP). Oil interests in Australia had lobbied strongly during 1975 in support of Indonesia's actions in the hope of ensuring their maritime presence in the Timor Sea. They needed to secure their position by the fairly rapid agreement of an Indonesian–Australian maritime boundary free from any unwelcome constraint by a Portuguese or East Timorese Government claiming control over its maritime areas. BHP was a prime example of such a company, having recently obtained a controlling share in the Woodside–Burmah Company, which had been drilling on and offshore in East Timor prior to the UDT coup. Some days after Fraser departed, the Indonesian Government circulated photocopies of cables received from its ambassador in Canberra. These summarized one of the regular meetings of the Australia–Indonesia Business Committee (AIBC), on 15 October, attended by representatives of all of Australia's largest companies, officials from departments such as foreign affairs and overseas trade, in addition, of course, to the AIBC's former president, J. B. Reid. The cable quoted AIBC as having made 'strong representation' for some time to the Australian Government to give tacit recognition of Indonesian integration.[32] As with the American strategic interest, this specific Australian interest should not be underestimated. It has been calculated that the sea-bed between East Timor and Australia contains oil deposits amounting to 5 billion barrels, together with 50,000 billion cubic feet of natural gas. This places the area among the foremost 25 oilfields in the world. The oil lobby quickly produced more concrete results. Shortly after Fraser's return, Foreign Minister Peacock similarly stated that Australia soon would have to recognize integration, but not, this time, for 'humanitarian reasons' but, rather, in recognition of 'the regional environment'. He concluded: 'It means that we must take into account Indonesia's view that East Timor is now part of Indonesia and that this situation is not likely to change'.[33] Just over a year later, in January 1978, the Fraser Government awarded *de facto* recognition to Indonesia's annexation.

The third event of 1976 occurred in Indonesia itself. In March 1975, the state-owned oil company, Pertamina, had been unable to meet its short-term debts. Since the late 1960s, the company had invested in enterprises outside the petroleum sector, in massive projects which often did little more than provide windfalls for members of the military élite. The extent of its consumption can be illustrated in a relatively minor example: Lieutenant General Ibnu Sutowo, the Director of Pertamina, signed four contracts with foreign companies in November 1969, in which officials were given 'presents' estimated to value US$60 million. During 1975, the government had to borrow US$1500 million to pay Pertamina's short-term debts and, as a result of the collapse of the oil company, the planned annual surplus on the budget proved unattainable — and this at the very moment when most oil-producing states were rapidly increasing their surpluses as a result of OPEC price increases. As it became clear throughout 1975 that Pertamina's demise was proving to be one of the worst corporate crashes in Indonesia, the main aid-donor body, the Inter-Governmental Group on Indonesia (IGGC), with a membership comprising representatives from most of the world's industrialized states, postponed its bi-annual meeting from April to May, in order to consider what policies it should adopt towards Pertamina's corruption-induced bankruptcy. The response was soon forthcoming: members rapidly agreed on the need to increase aid to meet the crisis. The IGGI agreed to supply US$920 million for 1975–6, an increase on the US$850 million given in 1974–5. In addition to this governmental aid, foreign banking syndicates such as Morgan Guaranty and the Tokyo Bank provided loans totalling just over US$1bn during 1976.

The way in which financial institutions and governments in the industrialized states reacted so immediately and co-operated so willingly in the operation to rescue Pertamina and reduce its debt burden on the military government is indicative of the tremendous importance which they attached to economic relations with the regime. The wealth of mineral provision in Indonesia's outer islands, the potential for development of its vast internal market and the revenue to be obtained from petroleum all combined to produce, in one commentator's phrase, 'foreign banks falling over themselves to get a firm foothold'.[34]

These three events, each one highlighting the strategic and economic importance of Indonesia for industrial nations such as the United States and Australia, go some way to explain the accommodating and acquiescent positions taken by these governments in their attempts to match Indonesian military propaganda with the starkly conflicting reality of the war in East Timor.

Undoubtedly, many government officials would have preferred the candour of one US State Department spokesman, admitting that 'we are more or less condoning Indonesian actions',[35] but the centrality of Indonesia in their political and economic strategies dictated otherwise; a more gradual, evolutionary approach was required since, outside such confined circles as those of IGGI members, Indonesian actions were alienating important sections of international opinion. Six months after the invasion, for example, Indonesia had little support in the neighbouring states of Southeast Asia, and even less support amongst African and Latin American governments. Furthermore, press coverage of the invasion had been universally hostile. Consequently, governments such as those of Australia and the US tried to make Indonesia's actions more palatable.

This was no easy task. In his October address to the Indonesian parliament, Fraser concluded that whilst it was important to look to the future, Australia also wanted to help alleviate the suffering in East Timor. Three days later, in a not unusual occurrence, Fretilin's Minister for External Affairs, Alarico Fernandes, reported in a radio message that Indonesian troops had burnt alive six people in a camp near Ermera. Broadcasting this news from East Timor had been much more difficult than usual, however, since the receiver picking up these messages had been confiscated by the Australian Government on 27 September, and the telecommunications centre relaying this information had been ordered to stop distribution of messages from Fretilin on 18 November. Hence, the prime minister's scope for helping the 'alleviation of suffering' in East Timor was restricted by his own government's action in preventing the dissemination of news of any such suffering. Perhaps silencing any news which could undermine the Indonesian government's portrayal of events was the only way Fraser could conceive of making the East Timor situation more palatable.

Notes

1. 'Interview with Former Bishop of East Timor', *Tapol Bulletin*, No. 59, London, September 1983.

2. Dunn, 1977.

3. Interview with Timorese refugee, Carlo Alfonso, in Perth, conducted by Carmel Budiardjo, 18 September 1982.

4. See testimony in Amnesty International, 1985.

5. Ibid.

6. Dunn, 1977b.

7. Fretilin radio message, 29 December 1975.

8. Dunn, 1977b.

9. A. Goldstone, 'No Glory in the Timor Secret War', *Guardian* (London), 21 April 1976.

10. Information provided in April by an Indonesian opposition source in Singapore, and subsequently described on Fretilin's Radio Maubere later that month.

11. M. Richardson, 'Under the Double Talk, Timor Suffers', The Melbourne *Age*, 10 January 1978.

12. See D. Jenkins, 'Countdown to Birth of a Province', *Far Eastern Economic Review*, 9 July 1976.

13. Details of these restrictions are contained in letters from Dili published in the Australian *Timor Information Service* on 18 August.

14. 'Indonesia admits Fretilin still active' *The Times* (London), 26 August 1976.

15. Information on all these points was supplied by radio messages monitored in Darwin.

16. J. Jolliffe, 'Indonesia Accused of Timor Looting', *Guardian* (London), 17 November 1979.

17. See *O Seculo* (Lisbon), 24 February 1977.

18. The report was first published in the BBC's *Summary of World Broadcasts*. It was publicized widely, and most notably in the *International Herald Tribune*, 8 March 1978.

19. 'Priests Confirm East Timorese Decimated', *Tribune* (Australia), 1 December 1979.

20. 'Portuguese Timor Under Pro-Indonesian Control', *The Times* (London), 13 February 1976.

21. This document, signed by the 'Secretary to the Provisional Government, Zeca Araujo', was held in secret for 12 years by an official in the East Timorese civil service, and was finally smuggled across the border into Indonesian Timor, hidden under the floor carpet of a car. It was subsequently published in part in *Timor Link* (London), No. 12/13, April 1988.

22. 'Australia's Rift with Indonesians over Timor Troubles US', *Washington Post*, 2 May 1976.

23. *O Tempo* (Jakarta), 12 June 1976.

24. H. McDonald, 'Staging the Rites of Integration', *Far Eastern Economic Review*, 17 June 1976.

25. Interview with Timorese refugee, Carlo Alfonso, in Perth, conducted by Carmel Budiardjo, 18 September 1982.

26. See Indonesian Foreign Minister, Mochtar Kusumatmaadja, cited in an *Agence France Presse* report from Hong Kong, 21 August 1985.

27. *Canberra Times*, 21 July 1976.

28. 'Lisbon Makes the Break', *Far Eastern Economic Review*, 6 August 1976.

29. M. Richardson, 'Don't Anger Jakarta', The *Age* (Melbourne), 3 August 1976.

30. R. E. Osgood, International Institute for Strategic Studies, London, 1976.

31. 'Canberra Accepts Jakarta Takeover of East Timor', *The Times* (London), 12 October 1976.

32. For details of the AIBCC calls, see 'Timor sold for Oil', *Tribune* (Australia), 27 October 1976.

33. Ironically, the article from which this quote from Peacock is taken was entitled, 'No Acceptance on Timor', *Canberra Times*, 21 October 1976.

34. 'Indonesia: Saved by Massive Rescue Operation' *The Times*, 18 February 1976.

35. A Kohen and R. Quance, New York, 1980.

6. The Indonesian Occupation: 'Encirclement and Annihilation'

The diplomatic cover shrouding events in East Timor since the Indonesian invasion was broken dramatically by eye-witness reports from Timorese who arrived in Lisbon at the end of 1976. The majority of these were members of the UDT group who had been held by the Indonesian military in camps in West Timor since the coup attempt of 1975, but some of them had lived in East Timor since the invasion. Their eye-witness accounts confirmed the brief details of radio messages and letters received in 1976. In interviews given to the former Australian Consul to East Timor, James Dunn, they gave details of the wharf killings and the Dili massacres, together with accounts of the use of torture and imprisonment.

They revealed that the killings were not confined only to East Timor, Dunn reported:

> A Timorese gave an account of an incident at Lamaknan, a location in Indonesian Timor near the border. This informant said that in June last year he had been in this area where Fretilin troops were active. The Indonesians set fire to the dwellings of East Timorese refugees who were camped there. When the refugees protested the Indonesians turned their guns on them. According to this informant who said he was a witness to the episode, the troops shot, he thought, 2000 of the Timorese, some on their knees, others with their hands raised. The victims he said, included women and children.[1]

From such interviews, Dunn concluded that:

> the military seizure of East Timor has been a bloody operation, in which atrocities of a disturbing nature have been committed against the civilian population. Indeed, these accounts of Indonesia's behaviour in East Timor suggest that the plight of these people may well constitute, relatively speaking, the most serious case of contravention of human rights facing the world at this time.[2]

Despite considerable Indonesian hostility to Dunn's findings, such as a governmental report that Indonesia could organize 130 million people to 'adopt an anti-Australian attitude if it so wished',[3] the military nevertheless gestured towards the validity of the evidence by admitting that some of their troops had 'got out of hand', but that the relevant units had been withdrawn and disciplined.[4] Although this justification contradicts directly all we know of the invasion, of its central planning and direction, it nevertheless reveals an important point — that several of the units fighting in East Timor had reacted in an increasingly brutal way during the first year of the invasion, as a result, partly, of the frustrations they had experienced when facing an enemy that was proving to be much more determined than they had ever imagined possible. By the end of 1976, there were no fewer than 40,000 Indonesian troops in East Timor, most of whom were rotated regularly. Yet, despite the size of this force, it was still making little headway. A relief workers' report summarized the situation:

> Indonesian forces occupy towns and villages containing about 150,000 people. But the bulk of the population and territory are not under direct Indonesian control. Beyond the main centres safety cannot be guaranteed because of harassment by Fretilin. Land communication is disrupted and the only means of communication is by helicopter or by sea around the coast.[5]

It seemed that apart from the élite *Kopassandha* and *Kostrad* troops, Indonesian army units had neither the training, commitment nor support to successfully defeat Fretilin forces in military engagements. A typical encounter in 1976 was later described by a Fretilin commander, recounting his first serious engagement with Indonesian troops in Bobanaro in March.

> The Indonesians protected their soldiers as they advanced with heavy artillery — rockets, mortars — and aerial bombardment. These caused little damage, since Fretilin's positions were protected physically. The Indonesians had two to three battalions, of about 3000 men. We tried to surround groups of them with squads of 18–20 Fretilin soldiers; these squads had back-up fire from five-men sections. After a few encounters, most of the Indonesians withdrew. Because we knew the terrain and were well-trained, we could defeat numerically superior forces. During 1976, we managed to defend successfully the frontier zone sector (in the west) with only 1800 men. The Indonesians occupied the main village, where they concentrated their troops, but they couldn't advance into the interior.[6]

Faced with military stalemates such as this, Indonesian troops took out their frustration on the local population in their controlled areas. Amongst many such incidents was the following, reported in July:

> In the second week of June a woman escaped from an Indonesian concentration camp in Aileu. She said that the attempt to take Lequica on 7 June had resulted in heavy Indonesian casualties, including two Indonesian officers. She said the enemy forced the captured population from Atsabe,

Quelicai, Ermera and Aileu to take part in the attack. Most of them died. The Indonesian officers were angry. They had been told Fretilin would not offer resistance to the attack. They punished the captured female population by forcing them to do heavy work in the ricefields, completely naked, in the role of buffaloes.[7]

Such violent forms of retribution persuaded these and more of the population to flee Indonesian areas. When the Indonesian troops entered Aileu in February 1976, it contained 5000 people; when a group of Indonesian relief workers visited it in September 1976, only 1000 remained — they were told that the remainder had moved to the mountains.

Fretilin's administration of its areas

In areas outside Indonesian control Fretilin maintained its administrative role, caring for the welfare of the Timorese population and organizing the defence of villages against Indonesian incursions. A priest who lived in the central eastern zone until his surrender in March 1979, gave a general description:

Fretilin built up a line of defence around the village perimeter and warned the population prior to an Indonesian attack. The civilian population then moved into the mountains, leaving the villages empty. The food situation in the mountain areas was satisfactory until mid-1977. New crops were sown and harvested. Fretilin set up their own administrative divisions. Schools functioned in each zone. Fretilin formed a health service with medical workers. They manufactured pills, liquid medicines and antibiotics, using medicinal plants.[8]

A more detailed picture of production and distribution in Fretilin areas is provided by a nurse who, although based in Suai in the southwest, transported medical equipment in the coastal areas and the central and eastern zones in 1976 and 1977:

At first, when we retreated into the hills, we had no idea how long the struggle would last. When we left the towns in Covalima (the southwestern region) we each took food with us. But as the struggle continued for a long time, we started producing food. We grew maize, rice, cassava and potatoes. In our particular region we were very restricted in the types of food we could grow, so in order to obtain rice we were in contact with other regions where rice could be grown. We developed a system of exchanging crops with other regions. This happened also with coffee, which we could grow because we were high up in the mountains. We were able to transport our coffee to areas occupied by the enemy and exchange it with other groups there.

The nurse gave details of pharmacological production:

We had two centres for manufacturing medicines, Lacluta and Matabea. What we usually did was to dry potatoes and maize. We then ground them into very fine powder, collected curative roots, leaves and herbs, boiled them to obtain the contents, which we then mixed and used for various types of medicines. Then we mixed these mixtures with the powder and manufactured the various kinds of medicines we needed. In this way, we made pills.[9]

With regard to political organization, a priest who lived in Soibada until early 1979 described a system which, although a shadow of the pre-invasion period, still retained its essential participatory democratic features:

There are political commissioners, and each commissioner has assistants. Many times they held meetings with the people for political clarification on the evolution of the struggle . . . There is a political education school where they train political assistants. There were also other types of meetings of the people with the political assistants and sometimes without them, to programme the way of life and solve all the problems of the camps, from latrines to housing the pigs and other animals . . . That is how things worked. They were conscious of what they were fighting for — independence. If they hadn't cared, then everything would have been finished. That meant the population was able to organize things easily.[10]

The defence of the camps and villages in Fretilin areas was simple, yet highly successful. A former Fretilin regional secretary commented:

The Indonesians bombed the fields in the populated areas in 1976. Subjected to their continued bombardment, the people moved into the mountainous areas, where Fretilin organized them into encampments in zones where they could be protected. They were organized in small groups, where they lived in my region until 1978. Since these zones were still subjected to bombing, the population was placed in this central area, with Fretilin troops controlling the periphery, periodically attacking Indonesian areas to capture weapons and gain more strategic positions.[11]

Ideological and military campaigns

By the end of the wet season in April 1977, the Indonesian military faced an all too apparent stalemate. With no advances on the ground for six months and with the brutalities enacted by frustrated troops producing a stream of increasingly adverse international publicity, rapid action was needed. The government mobilized on two fronts: it tried to organize more favourable publicity and, perhaps most importantly, it tried to improve its fighting capacity, to prepare for a more systematic, extensive campaign against Fretilin-held zones. In both these areas, the support provided by the governments of the industrialized countries was to prove indispensable.

On the publicity front, Indonesian officials reacted angrily and aggressively to refugee reports. Malik asked: 'Fifty thousand people or perhaps 80,000 people might have been killed during the war in East Timor. So what? . . . It was war . . . Then what is the big fuss?'[12] Moves were made to minimize the effects of the most influential refugee accounts, based on J. S. Dunn's interviews. The US government proved very co-operative, agreeing to Indonesian proposals for the hearing of Dunn's evidence in a way that would reduce its influence. Dunn was scheduled originally to appear before the Congressional Sub-committee on International Organization. However, under pressure from both the American State Department and the Australian Department of Foreign Affairs, it was decided to include the Asian Pacific Sub-committee in the hearings, since this committee's concern was to foster the relationship between the United States and Indonesia, to whom most of its members were very sympathetic. Dunn's testimony was thus less successful than might otherwise have been the case. Dunn himself was subjected to extremely aggressive and hostile questioning. Take, for example, William Goodling, member from Pennsylvania:

> Mr Dunn, I don't like to be a poor host, but if I would say I am happy that you are here, I would not be telling the truth . . . I am sorry to see you here under these conditions and I wish you had not been invited because of the political implications.[13]

The impact of Dunn's testimony was further lessened by the Australian Government's insistence that Dunn, despite being a diplomat, was doing everything in a 'private capacity', as *The Times* of London duly reported. When a British journalist headlined an article, based on an interview with Dunn, 'Indonesia Accused of Mass Murder in East Timor', he was subsequently called in to the Foreign Office and requested 'not to rock the boat'.[14]

Along with the attempt to discredit eye-witness accounts of Indonesian atrocities came the organization of brief orchestrated visits to Indonesian-held areas. The first such visit occurred between 11 and 13 April, arranged for Republican Congress member Goodling and Democratic member Meyner, both of whom had already participated in the hearings on Dunn's testimony. The members stayed in Dili with very brief trips to Baucau, Remexio and Bobonaro. The areas surrounding all these towns and villages were bombed heavily before the visit. Indeed, in Baucau the military conducted a two-week offensive south of the town prior to the delegation's arrival. At no stage did the members ask any critical questions, and at no time before, during or after their visit did they make any attempt to pursue the option of contacting officials in Fretilin-held areas. Congresswoman Meyner seemed particularly impressed by a women's refuge she visited in Dili. As refugees later testified, the refuge was created by Indonesian officials specifically for her visit. A few days before her arrival, large amounts of clothing, bedding and furniture were moved into a house commandeered for the purpose. It was duly filled with Timorese women who vacated the premises after Mrs Meyner's visit, at the same time as the removal of the blankets and furniture. Mrs Meyner found nothing exceptional in the refuge's spokeswoman addressing her in Bahasa Indonesia, a language then quite alien to the Dili population. 'Union with Indonesia makes good sense and the people want it,' she asserted confidently.[15]

The only other foreign delegation to visit East Timor in 1977 contained some rather more discerning members, notably Australian journalist Richard Carleton. Evading his Indonesian escorts, Carleton managed to obtain eye-witness accounts of the wharf killings and visited the site of the October 1975 murder of the Australian and British journalists. His commentary subverted the objectives of Indonesian design:

> The helicopters supplied to transport me were under instructions to fly above 3000 feet, beyond the range of small-arms fire . . . Everywhere the Indonesians took me they had three guards always within earshot and two concentric circles of 'civil defense' troops surrounding me. For my television cameras, I tried to recreate the events surrounding their (the journalists) deaths. Apparently my presentation was too graphic for the authorities. We were flown out with the excuse that the blue skies looked threatening . . . In Fatomaca and Lospalos I heard some small-arms fire, but my Indonesian escorts were quick to point out that this was the local people hunting.[16]

It was to be some time before further visits were arranged; not only as a result of Carleton's exposures but, more importantly, because the Indonesian military was beginning to move on its second front — the preparation of a sustained and heavy military campaign against Fretilin zones, made possible by a substantial array of new weaponry.

In February, the Malaysian Government provided the Indonesian military with four ex-Royal Australian Airforce Sabre jets as a source of spare parts for its own Sabres. In the early months of 1977, the Indonesian navy ordered missile-firing patrol-boats from the Netherlands, Taiwan, South Korea, the United States and Australia to replace its ageing Soviet vessels, together with submarines from West Germany.[17] The aim of this rapid procurement was clear — to reinforce the naval blockade of East Timor, and to enhance aerial capability to strafe and bomb Fretilin areas. In February, it was reported that the Indonesian air force had received thirteen Bronco OV-10F aircraft from the Rockwell International Corporation, with the aid of an official US government foreign military sales credit. The Bronco was ideally suited for use in East Timor, designed particularly for counter-insurgency operations in difficult terrain under varying climatic conditions. By the beginning of February at least six of these 13 Broncos were operating in East Timor.[18] Transported to Dili in May and June, the Broncos were used to pinpoint Fretilin positions in July, notably in the Baucau area. At about the same time, Suharto promised an 'amnesty to remnants of armed bands of Fretilin in East Timor who surrender to Indonesian armed forces by 31 December'. With an additional 10,000 troops poised to enter combat at the end of August, the military embarked upon what soon came to be known popularly as its 'final solution'.[19]

Encirclement

Beginning in September 1977, attacks were launched against Fretilin areas in the western, central and southern areas of East Timor. Saturation bombing by Bronco jets aimed to prepare these areas for military advances. Most notably, forested areas were bombed in an attempt to defoliate ground cover and chemical sprays were used to destroy crops and livestock. Many of the captured population were herded into camps, whilst others were deported to the offshore island of Atauro. In coastal zones, aerial bombardment was accompanied by the use of naval artillery. In October, Catholic sources in East Timor reported that the key objectives of the military campaign were 'encirclement' and 'annihilation', a surrounding of the population in an area, followed by their transportation to newly-created strategic camps and the killing of Fretilin members and sympathizers. In one action in early 1978, for example, the entire civilian population of the village of Arsabai, near the Indonesian border, was killed for supporting Fretilin.[20] A letter sent to a relative in a refugee camp in Lisbon described the results of the bombing of the village of Zumalai, on the south coast:

> Many elements of the population were killed under inhuman conditions of bombardment and starvation . . . The waters of the river were filled with blood and bodies. Husbands, fathers, brothers and abandoned wives, sons and brothers all in the same agony survived who knows how.[21]

Such descriptions were verified by a photo-journalist who managed to cross the border from Indonesian Timor briefly in September: 'The Indonesians are systematically wiping out the populations of villages known or suspected to be Fretilin supporters'.[22] A father wrote to his son in Australia: 'A continuously increasing violent war rages in Timor. The group of villages in which I lived has been completely destroyed'.[23] 'Pray for us', pleaded another writer, 'that God will quickly send away this scourge of war. The mountains shake with bombardment, the earth talks with the blood of the people who die miserably'.[24] Reports detailed the use of chemical sprays in the early phase of the 1977 campaign:

> In some places, a day or two after a bombing raid, maggots (*ular kecil*) would emerge and destroy the crops. Another experience was that after bombing raids, a large number of people would get violent attacks of diarrhoea and vomiting from the drinking water. This happened in Zumalai, Matabea and many other places.

And on the strategic camps into which the encircled and captured population were herded:

> The Portuguese had a system of *postos*, which were the places where local officers and churches were situated. So people were driven back to these posts because it was easier for the troops to keep them under surveillance in

these places. In some places, the people were settled around four posts, sometimes around six posts, and had to stay altogether there. They lived in a state of constant fear, because they knew that they couldn't leave — if they were to leave and be caught by the soldiers, they would be shot dead.[25]

As the bombing campaign intensified, the Australian Government lent its support by affording *de jure* recognition to Indonesia's annexation in mid-December, whilst the US Government, seemingly influenced by reports in the press of 'Indonesia running out of inventory',[26] announced the proposed sale of 16 F-5 jets to the Indonesian air force, in mid-January 1978, to be followed by 16 A-4 bombers in August. In similar vein, the British Aerospace Corporation announced in April that it had signed a contract with the Indonesian Government to supply eight Hawk ground-attack trainer aircraft. Both F-5s and Hawks were ideal for 'counter-insurgency' operations in forested, mountainous terrain, as were 12 Alouette helicopters promised by the French Government. The results of this rush to provide the Indonesian regime with the inventory necessary to intensify its campaigns in East Timor cannot be underestimated. Indeed, they appear, quite simply, to have heralded the move out of military stalemate. They provided the essential underpinning for the future successes of the campaigns of encirclement and annihilation.

Throughout 1978, these campaigns centred alternately on particular regions. The initial attacks focused on the areas bordering Indonesian Timor and then moved to the north-central region in April, in areas south of Dili such as Remexio nd Turiscai. The offensive against the north-central area continued on a very heavy scale until the end of August. From the north-central area, Indonesian forces tried to move eastwards, attacking villages such as Laclubar and Soibada in the centre of the country in June. In July, the focus of encirclement campaigns was the south coast, with marine landings directed towards villages such as Barique, Viqueque, Uatolari and Iliomar. Fighting then switched to the eastern sector, with Indonesian troops moving eastwards from a line between Baucau and Viqueque. The most brutal encirclement occurred at the end of this campaign, in the Mount Matebian area, southeast of Quelicai.

In each campaign, a similar strategy was pursued: days of heavy bombardment and strafing of villages in areas outside Indonesian control were followed by large-scale artillery attacks, culminating in the deployment of troops against villages, forcing their inhabitants into increasingly more confined areas until they were completely surrounded. After encirclement, came annihilation — executions, imprisonment, deportation to islands such as Atauro and the relocation of the population in camps away from its original village.

The full horror of these campaigns was testified by eye-witness accounts. A priest from Dili wrote as follows:

After September the war was intensified. Military aircraft were in action all day long. Hundreds of human beings die daily, and their bodies are left as food for the vultures. If bullets don't kill us we die from epidemic disease; villages are completely destroyed . . . The barbarities, the cruelties, the looting, the shooting of people without any justification are now part of everyday life in Timor.[27]

A refugee who testified to a Senate Inquiry on East Timor in 1983 gave the following account of the bombing campaign in 1978:

It was necessary to leave the villages in the daytime to hide from the aeroplanes that would drop bombs. The land would shake because of the bombs dropping, there was noise all the time and the bombs would make huge holes in the ground. So in the mornings at first light we would move back into the hills leaving behind the old and the sick who could run no more . . . The bombs dropped everyday. Aeroplanes flew from 8am till midday and then again in the afternoon. Firstly an aeroplane came to check if there was any smoke, a couple of minutes later the bomber would come and drop bombs, wiping out whole villages.[28]

A refugee who surrendered in December 1978 wrote:

When they attack any zone, in general their air and naval forces work together; sometimes the bombardment is every hour (at one hour intervals); at other times it is non-stop from morning to night and other times it is continuous for days . . . For example at the base of Mount Matebian they dropped about 600–700 bombs daily during the months of October and November 1978 when the majority of the population were still in the mountains. They had four bombing airplanes, each carrying 16 bombs. These planes bombed eight times every day.[29]

Detailing events in Natabora, in the south, a refugee described how:

Three aircraft — I think they were Skyhawks — bombed the region, killing thousands of people. In particular, women, children and old people were killed, people who couldn't run for cover. They were killed in large numbers. All we could do was pray for God's protection. The planes came in low and sprayed the ground with bullets, with their machine guns killing many people.[30]

Bombing was followed by a campaign of encirclement in which the population was surrounded by concentric circles of troops, with Timorese youths and men forced to march in front of them. A former Fretilin commander described this process:

The Indonesian troops advanced in groups, organized into long lines, burning crops and villages behind them. Their advance was simultaneous with naval and aerial bombardment. They captured the majority of the population, but many people died from bombardment and illness.[31]

After encirclement, Indonesian soldiers exacted terrible retributions. There are many reported instances of which the following are but a few: on 23 November 1978, 500 people who had assembled at the foot of the Vadaboro mountain, in the Matebian range, in the belief that they were surrendering were executed by Indonesian soldiers; shortly afterwards, in Taipo, 300 people were killed in a similar way; elderly people were burnt alive in their houses, women and men were tied together and shot, and children were executed in front of their parents. The reports continue into 1979: 97 people executed in Lospalos between April and May; 118 people killed on the southern slopes of Mount Matebian between 15 and 17 April. And these are merely a few incidents for which there are detailed accounts. Given that the numbers killed in each of the reported incidents ran into the tens and hundreds, it can be assumed that many thousands were slaughtered during this period.

'A population uprooted'

Those who survived encirclement were transported to camps located initially at the sites of former Portuguese *postos*, as described in an earlier refugee account. From these *posto* camps people were transported to newly-created resettlement camps. The American agency, USAID, estimated that some eight months after encirclement there were 300,000 living in such camps, which were to become the foundations for the Indonesian military's attempts to restructure Timorese society during the coming years.[32] For the moment, however, they were sites of utter despair; their inhabitants were prevented from travelling beyond the camp boundaries, and as a result they could neither cultivate nor harvest food; dependent on the military for basic medical supplies and foodstuffs, they received little or nothing and starvation became widespread. Everywhere they were subjected to a harsh military control:

> In the hamlets [stated a refugee] the people were not free. They had no food or other supplies, so life was very difficult indeed. They were issued with identity cards. They were not able to live on what they had and when they tried to leave the hamlets, so as to get extra earnings, they would be killed by the army if they were discovered.[33]

Most of the population captured in the May–August encirclement campaigns in the areas south of Dili were herded into a strategic camp in Remexio, some 14km south of the capital. In early September, the military organized a trip to Remexio for a group of selected journalists and diplomats from Australia, the United States, Japan, India, New Zealand, Bangladesh, South Korea, Egypt and Iraq — 'so they can check whether the integration of the territory into Indonesia was the wish of the East Timorese people or a mere fabrication', said Adam Malik's successor, Foreign Minister Mochtar Kusumatmaadja, with the unfavourable international coverage clearly uppermost in his mind.[34] What the visitors observed, in a very short visit to a camp which the military claimed was populated with victims of Fretilin's policies, was typical of the conditions then prevailing in East Timor's strategic settlements:

> In Remexio as in most other towns [wrote a reporter travelling with the diplomats] the people are stunned, sullen and dispirited. Emaciated as a result of deprivation and hardship, they are struggling to make sense of the nightmarish interlude in which as much as half the population was uprooted . . . The townspeople are undernourished and desperately in need of medical attention. Many have recently come down from the hills where they lived on tapioca and leaves — and berries so poisonous they have to be cooked six times before they can be eaten. Tuberculosis is a major problem and with so many people sleeping on the damp ground at night there is a danger of pneumonia. The children are so undernourished that one ambassador said that they reminded him of victims of an African famine. Remexio is a singularly depressing place. It is not, however, by any means unique. Timorese officials say there are 14 similar 'transit camps' in the province, many of them worse than Remexio. 'This is nothing', said one official. 'At Suai things are much worse and there are many more people. There is an urgent need for humanitarian aid'. As the 4164 inhabitants of the camp clapped and shouted *Merdeka* (freedom), with soldiers moving in lines behind them, the military's message was spelt out: 'I have never seen poverty like this in any other part of Indonesia', said an apparently shocked Mochtar.[35]

Images subsequently conveyed by the diplomats to national and international forums would thus portray an Indonesian regime burdened by the immense problems of its newly acquired province, problems produced by the futile resistance of a population misled by its independence movement's erroneous tactic of 'migrating' to the interior to avoid the allegedly brutal actions of Indonesian troops. Such problems needed rapid solutions. Asked whether his government would accept foreign aid earmarked for East Timor, Mochtar said 'Yes, if it is given with no strings attached'.[36]

The object of the exercise had thus been achieved, and here we have the ultimate irony: the victims of the encirclement and annihilation campaigns are presented as the results of the policies of those who, in reality, are trying to protect them from these campaigns.

Not surprisingly a number of governments responded, channelling aid to the strategic camps through the Indonesian Red Cross organization in late 1978 and 1979. 'I am definitely not promising a miracle', said Suharto when he granted East Timor development aid during an overnight visit to Dili in July. The president was hardly understating his case. As we shall see, most of this aid never reached the camps and the situation deteriorated rapidly throughout 1979. At the end of October 1978, a population census was undertaken by the Assistant for Defence and Security in East Timor. It gave a total of 329,271. Since we know from the last population census carried out under the Portuguese administration that the pre-invasion population was 688,771 in 1974, and that at least 100,000 had been killed during the post-invasion years it can be estimated that approximately 259,000 were living in areas outside Indonesian control, even as late as October 1978, which gives us some idea of the continuing strength of the resistance. However an even more revealing conclusion is reached with regard to the 329,271 figure if one compares it with another set of figures produced by the military in December 1978, claiming that 372,921 people were now refugees living in camps. Even allowing for a substantial movement of people into the camps during the period between October and December as the encirclement campaigns took their heaviest toll, it is clear from these statistics, however inadequate, that a majority of the East Timorese people were no longer living in their own villages but were now located overwhelmingly in camps controlled by the military.[37]

Notes

1. Dunn, 1977, p. 5.

2. J. S. Dunn, ibid., p. 12.

3. H. McDonald, 'Indonesian Troops Out of Hand in E. Timor', *Age* (Melbourne), 28 January 1977.

4. 'Malik Raps Australian Envoy's Coming Testimony to Congress' *Antara* Radio, Jakarta, 15 March 1977 (7.47, GMT).

5. M. Richardson, 'Fretilin's Alive and Kicking', Melbourne *Age*, 8 December 1976.

6. Fretilin Commander, Antonio Barbossa, interviewed by the author in Lisbon, 16 February 1985.

7. Radio message received in Darwin, 10 July 1977 and reported in *Timor Information Service*, Nos 20/21, October 1977, Walker Press, Fitzroy, Australia, p. 17.

8. Interview with Timorese refugee, Father Luis, Lisbon, 19 February 1985.

9. Interview with Timorese refugee, Neobere, 11–13 May 1983, London. Conducted by the author and Carmel Budiardjo.

10. Interview with Father Leoneto de Rego, Lisbon, published in translation in *S.E. Asia Record*, Vol. 1, No. 30, 1979.

11. Interview with Antonio Barbossa, Lisbon, 16 February 1983.

12. *Sydney Morning Herald*, 5 April 1977.

13. 'Human Rights in East Timor and the Question of the Use of US Equipment by the Indonesian Armed Forces', US Government Printing Office, Washington, 23 March 1977, p. 43.

14. This incident occurred after the journalist had published his article in *The Times*, 1 February 1977.

15. 'Congressmen [sic] Back Takeover of Timor', Melbourne *Age*, 18 April 1977.

16. Compiled from two articles by Richard Carleton: 'Brainwash Follows the Bloodbath', *Observer* (London), 31 July 1977 and *Age* (Melbourne), 10/11 August 1977.

17. See H. McDonald, *Age* (Melbourne), 2 February 1977, although Fretilin transmissions did not report their use until 13 May.

18. 'Big Build-up by Indonesian Navy', *Canberra Times*, 4 February 1977; see also *Sydney Morning Herald*, 15 February.

19. This phrase, used to describe the saturation bombing campaigns of 1977–8, to the best of my knowledge was used first by the Australian Liberal MP, Michael Hodgman, in a statement released on 31 August.

20. Radio broadcast received in Darwin on 4 February 1978.

21. Letter in the possession of Jill Jolliffe, Lisbon.

22. Denis Reichle, '75,000 Timor Deaths Blamed on Indonesia', *Australian*, 8–9 October 1977.

23. *Canberra Times*, 14 February 1978.

24. 'A Letter from East Timor Marked "X"', published some time after its receipt in Lisbon, in *Northern Territory News*, 28 July 1978.

25. Interview with East Timorese refugee, Neobere, 9–11 May, 1983.

26. 'Indonesia Running Out of Inventory', *International Herald Tribune*, 5 December 1977.

27. Letter cited in *Asia Bureau Australia Newsletter*, Parkville, Australia, June 1979.

28. *In camera* testimony to the Australian Senate Inquiry, August 1983, cited in Budiardjo and Liong, 1984 p. 32–3.

29. 'Report of this Sad Babylon Captivity', pp. 1–2, compiled by an East Timorese in late 1981. From documents collected in Indonesia in March 1982.

30. Interview with Timorese refugee, Christiano Costa, *Tapol*, London, No. 87, June 1988.

31. Interview with Timorese refugee, Antonio Barbossa, Lisbon, 16 February 1983. These atrocities are documented in Australian Council for Overseas Aid, 1982 (based on interviews with Timorese and documents received from East Timor and Indonesia during 1982).

32. US Agency for International Development (USAID), 'East Timor — Indonesia — Displaced Persons', Situation Report No. 1, 9 October 1979.

33. Interview with Timorese Refugee, Neobere, 9–11 May 1983.

34. 'Timor Faced a Viet War', *Sun* (Australia), 7 September 1978.

35. D. Jenkins, 'Timor's Arithmetic of Despair', *Far Eastern Economic Review*, 29 September 1978.

36. T. K. Peagan, 'Misery in Remexio', *San Francisco Chronicle*, 13 September 1978.

37. For a detailed discussion of these figures, see 'East Timor: How Many People are Missing?' *Timor Information Service*, No. 28, February 1980. On the extent of Indonesian control it is worth noting that Guilherme Gonçalves, former Apodeti member and chairman of the East Timor Regional Peoples Assembly, stated in response to a question on East Timor's participation in the new Five-Year Plan, *Repelita* II in the Indonesian Weekly, *Tempo* (Jakarta), that: 'At present, people can only work in places where our army has a concentration of forces, such as Dili, Same or Maliana,' 8 July 1978.

7. 'As Bad as Biafra': Population Resettlement and Starvation

A letter received from Dili in June, in the wake of 'encirclement and annihiliation', told of people 'slowly dying in the villages of Remexio, Turiscai, Maubara, Betano and Suro'.[1] Timorese church sources claimed that three hundred people were dying each month in the town of Ermera during the period up to June 1979.[2] When a priest visited the village of Maubisse on 8 March, he discovered that, according to records contained in the prayer book, 5021 of a 1976 population of 9607 had been killed.[3] During this period a saying current amongst the population ran, 'the more refugees, the more corpses'.[4] Those who were not transported to camps were either imprisoned or disappeared. Indonesian soldiers had their own way of describing disappearances. They called them *mandi laut* (gone for a swim); it was discovered some years later that many people who had been captured were taken by helicopter and dumped into the sea with weights on their feet. As in earlier phases of fighting, Indonesian soldiers were ordered to eliminate Fretilin members and their families. A priest testified that: 'No-one who had links with Fretilin is safe; at any time people can be taken without their family knowing, and put somewhere else; put in prison camps, or sometimes they just disappear'.[5] Letters described how 'many widows of the recently disappeared walk around in a very disturbed state, as thin as skeletons'.[6]

Resettlement

For most Timorese, the focus of their lives became the strategic camps into which they were herded prior to their being transported to new 'resettlement villages' in sites created away from their original homes. Located close to roads or at intersections, the new villages comprised groups of huts and houses in an area guarded by troops, with restricted entry and exit. The population was placed in the centre of the village in huts constructed of grass or palm leaves, whilst the outer areas were occupied by the military, local militia and camp administrators, living in houses with galvanized iron roofs. Village sites were chosen by the military primarily for strategic reasons. People were rehoused in zones far from areas of resistance, and any potential re-emergence of resistance based on traditional units such as the clan, hamlet or village was undermined by an attempted separation of groups from each of these units in the villages of a particular region. This often resulted in villages being built in lowland areas which traditionally had been avoided by Timorese, since they were infected with malaria, had poor water supplies and a much hotter climate than the mountain areas.

Each village was subjected to a rigorous system of internal control. Alongside the military, there were members of the Indonesian police force and teams of 'babinsas' (*Badan pembinaan desa* — village guidance bodies) whose job was to 're-orientate' the village's inhabitants. 'The babinsas are everywhere. They are the ones who have to know about everything happening in the villages and settlements. Everything has to be reported to them.'[7] All movement in and out of the villages was controlled, with individuals being allowed to travel outside only if they had been granted a *surat jalan* (travel pass). During the night, groups from the village's population were forced to guard the perimeter under the watchful eyes of the military.[8]

Since no cultivation took place within the village's confines, the captive population was allowed to tend gardens at short distances from the camp. Initially these were 1500m, but were reduced progressively to 500 and even 300m. Either as a form of sanction, or as a result of security measures, this garden-tending outside the village was often curtailed by the military, despite the need for food inside the villages. As Mgr Costa Lopes, Apostolic Administrator of Dili until his dismissal in May 1983, noted:

> If the Indonesians were to allow Timorese people to move around freely and live where they like, there would be no shortage of food. Of course, food production is influenced by such factors as the climate. But the problem is that people are forced to live in the settlements and are not allowed to travel outside . . . This is the main reason why people cannot grow enough food.[9]

In the resettlement villages [wrote a refugee]

> the people die of hunger because their fields are reduced to kitchen gardens. They have to work the same ground all the time, and it becomes exhausted. Sometimes there is no time to tend crops because there is too much forced labour.[10]

A former East Timorese worker for the Catholic Relief Services confirmed Costa Lopes' views:

> The main problem in the camps is famine. The areas where people are allowed to go are very restricted, whether they are growing or harvesting crops. Most families can only have 100–200 square metres of ground, which is clearly insufficient to feed a family throughout the year. They have to fall back on collecting wild fruit, roots and leaves, these also in insufficient quantities because the army forbids them to go far from the camp.[11]

Subsequently, it was hardly surprising that the foreign delegations which visited East Timor in the years after the villages were set up commented on the seeming irrationality of an agricultural sector which managed to combine population concentration, unworked fields and food shortages in its domestic economy. From the viewpoint of meeting the basic agricultural needs of the indigenous population, this situation, of course, was irrational. Such, however, was not the military's perspective. They had very different designs for the agricultural sector, perspectives which were highly rational in their own terms. Restricting the use of labour for domestic cultivation, the military began increasingly to try and direct it into forced work, on road building, house construction, timber logging and the cultivation of crops for export — sugar, coffee, even rice itself. The aims of this exercise were clear — having forcibly altered traditional patterns of settlement, the military planned to use the controlled population concentrations produced by resettlement as a basis for a massive economic and social transformation of East Timorese society. The economic aspects of these plans were introduced initially by Indonesia's official news agency, *Antara*, in February 1979. Ten of East Timor's 13 districts were to give priority to projects building up 'model plantations', in which crops would be planted for export. This was to be East Timor's contribution to *Pelita III*, the Indonesian Five-Year Development Plan begun in April 1979. The plantations were to 'set examples of modern agricultural methods for the local population.[12] Livestock ranches were also planned. Outlining *Pelita*'s proposals, the Indonesian weekly, *Tempo*, commented: 'The system of developing plantations should also be linked up with efforts to resettle the population, so that people are not so spread out as they are at the moment'.[13] This linking is illustrated in descriptions of the Lospalos area, brought out by refugees in June 1986. They claimed that around the village of Lospalos there were eight resettlement camps, whose inhabitants came from different regions. Close to the camps were vegetable gardens and a sugar plantation, linked by an asphalt road, to transport crops for export to Java. The camps' inhabitants were allowed to cultivate their own gardens on land close to the village but they also had to work on the plantation and gardens run by the military.[14]

The links between resettlement and military-organized cultivation in areas close to camps were strengthened during the 1980s by the creation of further model villages and 'development villages' by the military. These became an integral part of the economic transformation engineered by the military in East Timor.[15] (We return to this in chapter 9.)

Resistance quelled

After the encirclement and annihilation campaign, the Indonesian military felt able to present a much more confident face to foreign governments and international opinion. Certainly, the invasion had been brutal and, as a result of the conflict, many had died. The population had been traumatized but, according to the government in Jakarta, this had ended and the tasks of economic and social reconstruction were underway, expedited with supplies of foreign aid. Above all, the military stressed, the independence movement had been crushed. As proof of this, the army abolished the East Timor military command in April 1980, transferring control to the army's Eastern Indonesian *KOREM* zone headquarters in Bali. It seemed that Fretilin areas had been unable to survive encirclement and annihilation.

One of the most important achievements of the independence movement had been its ability to build an organization which, although unified through common political policies and adherence to common cultural values, nevertheless retained a strong emphasis on regional autonomy and local culture. Indentifying with the values of Mauberism or focusing on nationalist issues in literacy campaigns, for example, in no way weakened one's kinship or tribal affiliation as a Makassae or a Mambai. Traditional kinship alliances and political structures continued to be reproduced during the post-invasion period, just as they had been under Portuguese rule throughout the twentieth century. This existence of traditional structures within a nationalist political framework explains much of the early success of the resistance to Indonesian occupation during the period 1976–7. Basing its organization on political, ecomomic and military links between regions, Fretilin leaders were able to co-ordinate strategies based on powerful and cohesive local units. This co-ordination was exemplified in the success of the resistance during the dry season of 1976, by such events as the central committee meetings of May and the inter-regionally organized East Timorese Red Cross.

However, as the Indonesian army began to chalk up successes in maintaining troop concentrations in strategically located villages during late 1976 and early 1977, co-ordination between Fretilin groups became much more difficult, except in neighbouring sectors. Twelve months into the occupation, communications were confined to radio, except in local areas. This weakened Fretilin's national framework and gave much greater control to regional committees and commanders. In several areas, organization came to rely more on traditional links and, as a result, on traditional relationships and authority. This had both benefits and disadvantages. Whilst the capacities of regions to resist were maintained and even enhanced by time-honoured military networks based on kinship ties in the village and clan, the reversion to these ties, last used during the Japanese invasion, gave greater emphasis to commanders' status and role in the local rather than the national framework. With areas having different strategic needs in their varying campaigns against Indonesian forces, local political affiliations at times jarred with national political organization, and this generated bases for conflict.

The first of these conflicts emerged in November 1976, in the central-eastern zone, focused on a local *liurai* from Quelicai, Aquiles Soares, who had a strong traditional following but was also an important figure from the group of Timorese sergeants in the AFM who had played an important role in defending the border areas before the Indonesian invasion. Politically conservative, yet a fervent nationalist, Soares and a group of sergeants around him had clashed with the majority at the May central committee meeting over the role of political representatives in overseeing the military campaign. This difference over strategy was reinforced by national policy requirements for Soares' zone, which requested food from his zone for other regions and a movement of people to areas which the central committee considered could be defended more successfully. As a local *liurai*, responding to requests from areas in his zone, Soares used his support in the traditional networks to organize a movement to replace more nationalist-oriented leaders in his region. There is some evidence to suggest that, in this, he contacted Indonesian commanders to the north and south of his zone. Subsequently he was arrested by neighbouring Fretilin commanders and imprisoned in Quelicai and transferred to Ossu, where he and three others of his group were tried and executed near Vermasse.[16]

A case similar to Soares' was that of Fretilin's president, Xavier do Amaral, who was arrested for 'high treason' by Fretilin's central committee on 14 September 1977. Appalled by the atrocities committed by Indonesian troops, Xavier had increasingly retreated into his traditional area of Turiscai and, as with Aquiles Soares, strengthened his local network to the detriment of national policies, building up an alternative power structure based on local kinship alliances. To protect his region from Indonesian brutalities, he negotiated local troop withdrawals and ceasefires, most of which were detrimental to neighbouring zones. Throughout the first 18 months of the invasion, Xavier had been convinced that negotiations should be undertaken to reduce the level of fighting, and that ultimately, a settlement would have to be reached which, at whatever cost, would put an end to Indonesian military barbarities. In this, he clashed with all other groups on the central committee. Despite his isolation nationally, however, Xavier's popularity in areas such as Turiscai and Manatuto enabled him to retreat into an isolation which was broken periodically by attempts to reassert his control over national politics. This isolation in no way undermined the ability of his central sector to contain Indonesian attacks, but it did limit national co-ordination and restricted the possibilities of Fretilin implementing its political and economic policies in Xavier's zone. As his refusals to carry out such policies increased, he was detained by local commanders and was moved from one Fretilin unit to another for 12 months until he was captured by Indonesian troops in the prolonged battle for Remexio on 30 August 1978.

Despite the effects of such actions on Fretilin's ability to co-ordinate resistance at a national level, the strengths of local bases combined with the continuing popularity of its policies ensured support in most regions. With the onset of the bombing campaign, however, each zone — and even regions within zones — were forced to rely on their local resources. In areas where Indonesian attacks were strongest and regional populations faced destruction, most notably in the north-central sector, the ferocity of the onslaught produced proposals for surrender and negotiation which were rejected by other areas. In the Remexio area, this led to the surrender of Alarico Fernandes, Fretilin's Minister of Information, together with four other central committee members on 3 December. Fernandes surrendered with Fretilin's radio equipment, breaking their communication link with northern Australia. It also seems that this group gave information on the location of Fretilin commanders to the Indonesian military after the failure of a plan by Fernandes, named Operation Skylight, to remove other Fretilin leaders. This information undoubtedly assisted the military in the strategy they were pursuing during clean-up operations in early 1979. In each area that was encircled, Fretilin troops were chased across their zones into neighbouring regions, where many were surrounded and captured. On 1 January, Nicolau Lobato, Fretilin's president since Xavier do Amaral's detention, was killed after a six-hour gun battle in the Maubesse mountain range, south of Turiscai, through which he had travelled in the hope of regrouping Fretilin troops in the north-central sector after their encirclement. In February 1979, Mau Lear and Vicente Sa'he, respectively Vice-President and Prime Minister of Fretilin, died after long chases by Indonesian troops. Mau Lear was executed near the River Dolar, in February, and Vicente Sa'he prevailed on his comrades to leave him after being wounded in the leg. Most members of Fretilin who were captured or surrendered suffered a similar fate, although some were held in detention for several months before being killed, despite President Suharto's amnesty promise of August 1977, announced in thousands of leaflets dropped over East Timor throughout 1978.

It thus appeared that resistance to the invasion finally had been quelled. Portugal, still formally in control of East Timor as its colonial power, could thus advise its delegates to the UN 'not to actively solicit support for the self-determination of East Timor',[17] whilst the United States could now more openly offer to supply a further 16 A4 fighters,[18] and the Australian Government could negotiate its sea-bed boundary agreements with renewed confidence in the future.

Estimates of the many thousands of deaths resulting from Indonesia's occupation were dismissed, even though they had been substantiated by varying sources, from the ICRC to the Catholic Church. The governments of the industrialized countries sought to minimize them to the greatest extent possible. For example, referring to allegations of genocide in East Timor, a US State Department report of 1978 noted that 'most of the human losses in East Timor appear to have occurred prior to Indonesia's intervention'.[19] Such myths were soon to be shattered.

At the end of the dry season, in October 1979, a correspondent was allowed to travel outside Dili to see how aid disbursed by the Australian Government was being distributed. For the Indonesian military, the visit went terribly wrong. Despite intelligence service bans on transmission, the Jakarta correspondent of the *Sydney Morning Herald* successfully dispatched pictures of East Timorese suffering from severe malnutrition in the camps of Laga and Hatolia. They were published on the front pages of all the major Australian daily papers. An ICRC delegate, surveying the Hatolia camp where 80 per cent of its 8000 inhabitants were suffering from malnutrition, was reported as concluding that it was 'as bad as Biafra and potentially as serious as Kampuchea', whilst the head of the Catholic Relief Services was said to have commented that the problem was 'greater than anything I have seen in fourteen years of relief work in Asia'. 'The problem has not surfaced overnight', concluded the Jakarta correspondent.[20] Certainly, it had not. Almost 12 months after the Remexio visit, and with aid received from many donor nations, nothing had been done by the military to alleviate the starvation in the strategic camps since the end of encirclement and annihilation. Most of the aid had been appropriated and sold profitably, with a small amount used for bribing the population into submission.

> The Indonesian armed forces impede the medical and food aid which is needed by the people. Foodstuffs, which should be handed over to the people, are sold by the local military command, and often medicines are also sold in the shops at high prices,

wrote a group of East Timorese.[21] The Indonesian military tried to limit foreign entry as much as possible after the Rodgers visit, lest more damage be done to its already tarnished image. 'All this talk of starvation drives the Indonesian government up the wall', confided a senior US official.[22] Accordingly, the military produced a 'revised' population estimate. Contrary to the data provided in the October 1978 survey, officials now claimed that a census undertaken in mid-1979 estimated the population to be 522,433, a mere 130,778 less than the Portuguese census figure of 653,211 in 1974. Interviewed in Jakarta on the famine conditions in East Timor, Foreign Minister Mochtar concluded that 'within its limited means Indonesia had done what it could'.[23]

Notes

1. Letter received by Fr Pat Walsh of the *Australian Council for Overseas Aid* (ACFOA), July 1979.
2. From an eye-witness account presented in the *Asia Bureau Newsletter*, June 1979.
3. 'East Timor: Some Experiences and Thoughts', *Inter-Nos, Journal of the Society of Jesuits, Indonesia*, Year XXIII/1979, No. 2, April–June 1979 (translated from *Bahasa Indonesia*).
4. *Asia Bureau Newsletter*, June 1979.
5. Part of an interview with Fr Leoneto, cited in *Amnesty International*, 1985.
6. Letter received from Dili by ACFOA, August 1979, and written on 14 July.
7. 'Interview with Former Bishop of East Timor', *Tapol Bulletin* (London), No. 59, 1983, p. 6.
8. *Indonesian Army Manual for East Timor*, Part 3: 'How to Protect the Community from the Influences of GPK Propaganda', translated under the aegis of Amnesty International, London, 1983.
9. Mgr M. da Costa Lopes, interviewed in London, September 1983. The interview was published in *Tapol Bulletin* (London), No. 59, 1983.
10. José Guterres: Testimony to UN Sub-Commission, Geneva, 1987.
11. Antonio Tavares interviewed by Jean-Pierre Carry, Lisbon, 1988.
12. See *Antara*, 23 February 1979.

13. 'It's Peaceful Now, But Barren', *Tempo* (Jakarta), 3 November 1979 (translated from *Bahasa Indonesia*).

14. This information was carried by refugees to Lisbon in August 1986, and published subsequently in *Tapol Bulletin* (London), No. 77, September 1986.

15. *Daily Telegraph*, 17 March 1989.

16. Information on these points comes from refugee interviews carried out in Lisbon by the author in 1979 and 1985.

17. J. Jolliffe, 'Portugal's "Do Nothing at UN"', *Canberra Times*, 23 October 1979.

18. 'US Jets Slated for Indonesia', *Washington Post*, 16 June 1979.

19. *Country Reports on Human Rights Practices*, US Department of State, Washington, 3 February, 1978.

20. P. Rodgers, 'Food, Not Politics, Dictates the Fate of East Timor', *Sydney Morning Herald*, 31 October 1979.

21. 'Materials for Reflection on the Situation in East Timor', composed by a group of Timorese, 17 September 1980. The document was sent to Jakarta, and was published in Australian Council for Overseas Aid, 1982.

22. Kohen and Quance, 1980.

23. P. Rodgers, 'Indonesia Defends Efforts in Timor', *Sydney Morning Herald*, 3 November 1979.

8. Military Control: Imprisonment, Killings and Human Rights Abuses

'Now we know quite clearly that the Indonesian army intends to annihilate us', wrote a Timorese.[1] He was referring to the policies pursued by the military after encirclement, as a result of which, in the words of another eye-witness, 'East Timor is one big prison'.[2]

For many of those who were captured or surrendered in 1979, the consequence was immediate and brutal. They were either executed or murdered. Killings on an extensive and widespread scale, begun at this time, have continued throughout Indonesia's occupation. Indonesian troops have carried out the most wanton acts of brutality without recourse to any form of justice, however rough.

Disappearances

The first detailed accounts of Indonesian brutalities came in lists of people shot or disappearing after surrender, which were carried to Lisbon by refugees in early 1980. Similar accounts were given by East Timorese interviewed in Jakarta in 1982. Evidence of brutalities was also given secretly to members of East Timor's Regional People's Representative Assembly, the body set up by the military in 1976 to legitimize 'integration', who, as a group, wrote a report to Suharto in June 1981, stating that they were 'continually, with deep sorrow, receiving verbal as well as written reports or complaints from the people about torture, maltreatment, murders and other unimaginable cases'.[3]

Many of these early cases referred to disappearances, specifically in Dili, and gave general descriptions of the procedures involved.

The normal procedure is for a captured or surrendered person to be interrogated at the *Koramil* (the sub-district military command). If they were important people, they would be held for a few months. Then they would be sent to Dili for further interrogation and held in the San Tai Ho (a warehouse before the invasion) and possibly after that they are sent to the Comarca (Dili's main prison) and then after six months they completely disappear without a trace.[4]

An eye-witness living near the headquarters of the Indonesian army commandos (the *Resimen Para Kommando Angkatan Darat* or RPKAD) described the procedures for disappearance in Dili in April 1979:

> Every night they went out capturing people. . . The soldiers went out, dressed in sarongs, with their weapons hidden underneath. They'd go off to take people in. Then a few days later, we'd hear: so-and-so has disappeared . . . During that time, people were really afraid. Many, many people disappeared.[5]

> My brother-in-law was captured and taken to Dili [wrote a refugee]. The Deputy-Chief of the Secret Service allowed his wife and two daughters to visit him. On the third visit, however, they were told he was unavailable because he was being interrogated by the then Defence Minister, General Yusuf. The following day they were told that he had been taken away. His whereabouts were never revealed, and today he continues to be 'disappeared'.[6]

During the initial killings of 1979–80, the military focused particularly on Fretilin supporters and the relatively more educated strata of East Timorese society — seminarians, nurses, public officials and teachers. 'The senior authorities would decide who was to be killed after interrogation. Most of the leaders, or the educated ones, those who were talented, were killed. Their wives would also be interrogated, tortured and killed'.[7]

Particular sites were designated as killing grounds, to which people would be taken in groups, and murdered. Quelicai was such a site chosen after the encirclement of Mount Matebian in late 1978. According to an eye-witness:

> When they want to liquidate someone, they say that they have gone to continue their studies or that they have left for Jakarta or Lisbon, or that they were called urgently to Quelicai . . . To speak of Quelicai makes our hearts thump and our hair stand on end, for Quelicai means certain death for those called there.[8]

A similar site was the Areia Branca beach, east of Dili, where people were killed in groups and their bodies left to the sea, tied to rocks or else dropped from helicopters. The waters in this area were referred to by the local population as 'the sea of blood' in 1980.

In many cases, the numbers killed in groups were often considerable. Many refugees have described an incident in Lacluta, southeast of Dili, in September 1981, in which at least 400 people were killed, mostly women and children. An eye-witness to this event, providing information for a submission to the Australian Senate inquiry, stated:

> Indonesian soldiers took hold of the legs of small children and threw them around in the air a number of times and smashed their heads against a rock.

There was a woman who asked that one of the children be given to her after the mother had been killed. At that time, a soldier permitted the woman to take this small child, but a few minutes later he grabbed the child and killed him. The poor woman who asked for the child was not so wise, because she too was then killed. There was one other who asked for one of the children to be given to her . . . the army person did not want to hear her pleadings and in front of everyone destroyed the body of this small child, who had done no wrong. And then this soldier opened his mouth, showing his teeth with a smile, and said a sentence which was considered to be part of the wisdom of Java. He said: 'When you clean your field, don't you kill all the snakes, the small and large alike?'.[9]

A similar massacre was carried out in the strategic village of Kraras, near Viqueque, on the south coast, in which 200 people were burned alive in their homes. Most of those killed were sick or elderly, and the rest of the population fled to the slopes of the Bibileu mountain, on the west bank of the River Be Tuku, home region of most of those who had been resettled in Kraras. Indonesian troops then carried out a 'clean-sweep' operation around Bibileu, as a result of which 500 people were killed on the banks of the Be Tuku.[10]

Justifying such events, there has been a notion prevalent in the Indonesian military since the encirclement campaigns that the climate of terror produced by killings is functional for the maintenance of stability. A letter written in Bobonara in February 1984 illustrates this: 'In the month of February alone, more than fifty people were killed. But it is being said that the military plan to kill altogether 167 people in this zone. Only then, they say, will they be able to re-establish peace'.[11]

Such killings became institutionalized as the occupation proceeded. The following examples are but a few, selected from many documented cases. An eye-witness gave the following account of events at Manatuto, 45km east of Dili, on 13 July 1981:

On the first day that I arrived in Manatuto, the big shock and sadness for me was to see two civilian men carrying three heads of our brothers from the bush . . . Accompanying these men were Indonesian soldiers with a revolver and a knife. They took the heads to bury in the cemetery located seventy to eighty metres from the Manatuto church. The heads were in a bag which was thrown into a hole without covering them with a cloth or anything. Five other Timorese were killed ten days later. Indonesian soldiers ordered troops to behead the corpses.[12]

In July 1984, a priest wrote a detailed letter, recounting events during the previous six months. One of the many cited runs as follows:

From March 1984, many men and youths were imprisoned and killed. In the tribe Kota Boot, near Hua Ba, almost all men and youths disappeared. They were taken by Indonesian soldiers, killed and thrown on a fallow piece of land. There are eye-witnesses to what happened. The witnesses talk of the complete extermination of the population.[13]

A refugee describes how:

> I was captured by the Indonesians in March 1979 during the 'encirclement and annihilation' campaign. After our capture various people were taken to Laka-Dula, where soldiers from 1412, 1512 and 126 battalions killed unarmed Timorese. In October 1980 at Laka-Dula, 384 skulls were uncovered.[14]

In a campsite named Maupitili, near Lospalos, in August 1983, 30 Timorese were imprisoned and under interrogation named the organizers of the local Fretilin resistance. The population of the camp was then gathered together by the local commander, who paraded before them five leaders named by those interrogated. Eye-witnesses give the following account of what happened next:

> The terrified population did not yet suspect what would occur . . . A *nanggala* ['knife-wielding killer', the Timorese phrase for the *Kopassus* para-commando troops] with his knife put an end to the five. The Indonesian officer, forbidding the population to cry, threatened them, saying that if he learned of anyone else continuing to support the resistance, he would get the same fate. The population, quiet and with their heads lowered, was motionless.

In the same month of August, Indonesian troops, stationed in Viqueque, entered a village called Malim Luro, and:

> after plundering the population of all their belongings, firmly tied up men, women and children, numbering more than sixty people. They made them lie on the ground and then drove a bulldozer over them, and then used it to place a few centimetres of earth on top of the totally crushed corpses.[15]

In Bere-Coli, Baucau, between 12 and 15 April 1989, 20 people were shot dead by soldiers under the command of Colonel Prabowo, President Suharto's son-in-law.[16]

Imprisonment

The military's objective, so evident from these examples, of terrorizing the population into submission was also evidenced in their widespread use of imprisonment. From eye-witness accounts, the most frightening aspects of imprisonment were its arbitrary nature and its indeterminacy. People could be arrested for any reason, and at any time. There are cases of imprisonment for refusal to give troops food or for straying too far from a resettlement village, as well as the more formal cases of opposing the government. Once in prison, there was no means of knowing if the sentence was for a week, a month or life, and no trials were held until 1984, and then only for some of those held in Dili, who were known to such bodies as the ICRC. Furthermore, at any time during detention, prisoners could be taken by troops and killed, as in the following account from the Comarca prison in Dili during 1980–1:

> When the Indonesians want to kill any prisoner they generally always do it at night. The place preferred by the Indonesians for this is the lake of Tacitola, situated in the west part of the city of Dili. Other times prisoners are put in helicopters and dropped into the sea.[17]

After the encirclement campaigns, prisons were organized in every region of the country, each attached to military and police headquarters. On many occasions, private houses were commandeered for use as short-term prisons or interrogation centres. An East Timorese who worked for the Indonesian Red Cross wrote that:

> The Indonesians have prisons everywhere. For example, where there is a chief of police, he has a prison; where the red berets are, there is a prison; the military police have their prison, an infantry unit will have its prison, artillery units theirs; the District Command have one, the Secret Services have theirs.[18]

In Dili, all interrogations took place in large family houses, whose previous occupants had either fled or been imprisoned. No matter where they were held, prisoners provided labour for the military on such projects as tending rice fields, road-building and street cleaning. Many were forced into personal service to military officers, tending their gardens, house cleaning and carrying food and water, 'like beasts of burden', claimed a refugee.[19]

Fretilin members and their families who were captured during encirclement, and survived, were transferred to the island of Atauro, north of the Dili coast. Although Atauro was in use as a detention centre from 1977 (the first reports of this came in September of that year) it was not until 1980 that substantial numbers were transferred there. The initial groups came from Dili, in June and July, after the military had captured documents naming Fretilin sympathizers, who were rounded up with their families and shipped out. Between December 1980 and April 1981, many more people were transferred, mostly from the areas of Baucau, Liquica and Lospalos. A Timorese student, travelling to the east for a school holiday away from Dili, recorded in his diary the following entries for 2, 7 and 13 July:

> I saw a convoy of trucks coming from Viqueque, full of poor and oppressed people who were destined for exile to the island of Atauro. In the trucks one could see also that there were very old people who could not work anymore and also children and the sick . . . When I was going to Baguia, I saw

another convoy of trucks passing in front of the Baucau church. This convoy came from Viqueque and they brought people from Uato-Lari, Ossu, Lacluta, and also people of Viqueque, of the zones of Baucau. The trucks were going in the direction of Laga, because it was in Laga that the people were put in boats like animals to be exiled . . . When I was returning from Uato-Carabau, and passing near Laga I saw a sea of people under trees and old houses, accompanied by *hansips* (civil guards) and Indonesians, waiting to be exiled.[20]

Between June and September 1981, a total of 3400 people was moved to Atauro from districts throughout the country, with 700 added from the Ainaro district in August 1982. By this time, there were 6800 prisoners on the island. The reasons for their detention are stated briefly in a document published in 1982 for use by the army in East Timor. Under the title of 'How do the *Babinsa* (the army village guidance body) or *TPD* (the village guidance team) expose/dismantle GPK support networks?' (GPK is the military acronym for Fretilin), the document states: 'Evacuate to Atauro or other designated places those in the GPK support network who are still in the settlement and the relatives of GPK not yet evacuated. In this way, we can cut the ties between the support networks and the Nurep' (the military term for those acting as contacts between Fretilin and its networks in the villages.[21] This aim, of using imprisonment as a means of breaking Fretilin's organization, is stated most explicitly in a report by an Australian embassy official after a visit to Atauro in September 1982:

Atauro is an integral part of the strategy being followed by the Indonesian authorities in an attempt to rid the province of remaining Fretilin, ie to remove Fretilin's possible base of support. Any family thought to have a relative 'in the mountains' is sent to Atauro. They are sent in family groups.[22]

These confidential documents are refreshingly frank, when compared with the usual reasons given by the military to visiting delegations. When an Australian parliamentary delegation visited Atauro camp in July 1983, its report noted without comment that: 'The authorities said that those brought to the island had either given themselves up or had been relocated for their own safety'.[23]

Describing conditions on Atauro in November 1981, an East Timorese wrote:

There is a general impression of sadness, hunger, distrust. The majority of the exiles (about two-thirds) are women and children — women of every age, a good number between the ages of 60–70 years. The exiles live in tents. Altogether there are forty-five tents; 45–70 people (ten to fifteen families) live in each tent. Everyone is hungry . . . they receive one small can of corn per week for each person; these cans of corn have to last for the meals of one week. To mix with corn, the exiles go in search of leaves, roots and whatever else can be found to eat. The general impression is that everyone lacks clothes. The people that were not warned came only with the clothes they were wearing at the moment they were captured and taken to Atauro. Some who brought more clothing are forced to sell or exchange it for food so that they can survive. The children are skeletal, badly fed and they suffer skin diseases caught since arriving on Atauro. There is an average of two deaths per day.[24]

Eighteen months later, a Portuguese television journalist visited Atauro. He described an encounter with inmates:

'They are trying to get rid of us', someone says. In the makeshift tent of the Indonesian Red Cross, I see a little boy fall and drop two tins of food containing a little maize and some pieces of fish; the food had been brought there by helicopter the day before. 'They are trying to get rid of us', repeats another voice just beind me. The atmosphere is quite dreadful, killing. I think to myself: all this misery is caused by hunger and despair. People look bewildered, the children never smile.[25]

Shortly after the journalist's visit, Governor Carrascalao promised that Atauro would be closed in the coming year, by speeding up the process of prisoner release. This had begun early in 1983, with the shipping out of 650 detainees who had been sent to a newly-created resettlement camp named Paragua, on the mainland. Further groups of prisoners, leaving between 1984 and 1986, either went to similar camps near the villages of Zumalai, Ainaro and Manatuto, or were reimprisoned in Dili's Comarca prison. There were no genuine releases, since resettlement camps were designed specifically for the Atauro inmates, who were subjected to constant military surveillance and not allowed to move beyond the camps' immediate confines. Families were split up, with the husband being forced to remain on Atauro and the wife and children being sent to a resettlement camp. By the end of 1986, which is the last year for which we have reliable information, 1174 prisoners remained on Atauro, although some evidence indicates that small groups have been moved to the mainland in the last few years. Despite the administration's promises, there has been neither closure nor release; and despite government claims of improving living conditions for the remaining prisoners, reports of malnutrition on the island are given regularly in refugee accounts.[26]

'Established procedures'

The use of torture is sanctioned officially throughout East Timor. Army documents outline a set of 'established procedures' in which one step follows another: preliminary interrogation, classification of suspects, main interrogation, decision to murder, imprison or release.[27] These steps could last for days or months. The severity of the tortures appears to have increased as the occupation developed. Beginning with beatings, burnings with cigarettes, and sexual abuse, the army and police progressed rapidly to electric-shock treatment, systematic cutting of the skin and crushing of limbs. The most barbaric examples proliferate through each year of the occupation.

> I do not have the courage to relate [said a young man from Dili prison on Atauro] as I do not want to remember moments that I passed. I took so many kicks and beatings that there was no part of my body where there were no marks of torture. They removed all my toe nails: this was a terrible torment. Many times I was tortured with electricity. Now here in Atauro I lead a life similar to other exiles; even if the life is very difficult, it is better than always being tortured.[28]

'I suffered the minimal torture', said a former Fretilin commander. 'In June 1980, in Dili, I experienced shocks to the head, my fingers were crushed under a chair on which someone stood, and I was beaten. Other tortures practised were cigarette burns and water immersion. Some inmates died directly from torture.'[29] In detention centres in Baucau, torture was similarly widespread:

> I was arrested by the military command in Baucau, KODIM 1628. They started interrogating me around midnight. On that first night, I was tortured. On the second night they started torturing me and that was when I lost my front teeth. They held me on the ground, face down, and trampled so hard on my head that my two front teeth fell out and a third was broken. I refused to tell them anything, so on the third night they used electric shocks and threats of all kinds.[30]

There are many other such cases. A woman who was imprisoned in San Tai Ho, a former warehouse in Dili, describes meeting her teenage sister in prison: 'Maria Gorete had cigarette burns on her arms and chest and had had electric shocks applied to her neck, ears and arms. We embraced and cried, and that night we shared a cell, sleeping in the same bed'.[31] Subsequently, her sister was taken to Baucau and, with her uncle, was shot behind the main church in the town.

In addition to the San Tai Ho warehouse, the Comarca prison in Dili was also used as a torture centre (INTEL is the acronym for Indonesian Intelligence):

> At about 8pm on 28 July 1979 [reported a refugee], after being arrested we were driven to the Comarca prison in Carcoli district. Near the prison we saw two columns of soldiers from the military police, armed with pistols and truncheons. One by one we had to walk between them, being violently beaten and shoved from one side to the other with sticks and punches. They ordered us to undress to our underpants, and they cut off our hair and removed our jewellery, money and other possessions. A few moments later I was taken away from the group by the INTEL commandant and six military

policemen. They put me with my back to the wall, stretched my arms out like a cross and began hitting me again. I received so many blows to my head and other sensitive parts of my body that even today I still ask myself how I managed to survive it at all. Blood began to trickle from my mouth, nose, ears, eyes and from my toes which had been crushed repeatedly under military boots. I couldn't do anything except call on the Lord Jesus. Then the INTEL commandant ordered me to open my mouth, and rammed into it the end of a long stick with which they had beaten me. He told me to bite it hard, and began to shake it as you would shake the branch of an orange tree to dislodge an orange. My head was spinning. He began to push and pull the stick hard, and I had to bite on it with all my strength to prevent it piercing my throat. I don't know how I managed to endure it at all. They wanted me to denounce other people whose names they gave me. They tortured me until well into the night, and then led me to a cell. Even in the cell, a military policeman saw my wedding ring and wanted to rip it off by force, but I resisted. For three days we were woken at 2am with buckets of cold water that they threw on us in the cells. An hour later some policemen burst into the cells, began to beat us up and made us go out into a yard where we were obliged to crawl and do physical exercises. While we did these, they beat us, especially on the joints and sensitive parts of the body. They used chair legs, broken benches, sticks, lengths of bamboo, and even stones. This pattern lasted for three days and nights.[32]

A Timorese who worked for the Indonesian Red Cross before fleeing Dili in 1987 recounted similar experiences in the Comarca prison.

I was beaten with rifle butts and sticks. I was then tied hand and foot and hung up by the feet; my head was plunged into a tank of cold water. After about two minutes I was hoisted up and interrogated. They repeated the procedure until I confessed.[33]

In addition to being used institutionally, torture has also become part and parcel of the daily intimidation experienced by the population, often for reasons quite unrelated to the military conflict. We have, for example, the case of three men arrested, detained for four months and tortured for not repaying money borrowed from the sub-district military commander of Venilale.[34] Also, the following, documented by a former member of the Indonesian Government's Department of Information in Dili:

Three students were forced by Red Berets to go into the bush and try to contact the resistance. They carried with them a document which was supposed to serve as a justification in case they were intercepted by any Indonesian battalion. The first day they were found by the 125 battalion which, ignoring the document, separated one student from the other two and proceeded to torture him using a knife. When they heard his screams, the other two tried to escape. One was shot, but the other managed to reach the village and informed the student's relatives. His father protested to the Red Berets, but only after three days did he manage to get authorization to go to the place where it had happened. He found the body of his son; his head had been severed from the body, and the sexual organs cut off and stuffed into the mouth. Back in the village he received orders not to divulge what had happened.[35]

Again, from an account of August 1985:

Three women who refused to dress in shorts and play volley-ball with soldiers were accused of being agents of Fretilin. They were taken away for interrogation by the military chief of intelligence in Viqueque. They were subjected to electrical torture and lighted cigarettes were used to burn their faces and sexual organs.[36]

As a former nurse, detained in the Comarca prison for two and a half years, put it: 'The methods of physical and mental torture which I witnessed were indescribable. The torturers competed with each other in their zeal to inflict torture'.[37]

Such examples constitute only a small number of the recorded cases of torture in East Timor since the end of encirclement, examples recalled by those who have been able to testify to the barbarity.

A terrorized population

Living with constant threats of capture, imprisonment, torture and disappearance, and under permanent surveillance, the population was forced into submission. This was assisted by regular and often arbitrary punishments, executed by soldiers almost at will. A refugee testified:

When I was 16 I was living in Bacau. I saw a Missionary Sister helping two men from Quelicai who were injured when some soldiers suspected them of being guerrillas. They were stoned to death in front of me and the nuns, by Indonesian soldiers from battalions 315 and 731.[38]

All aspects of local culture were suppressed, as the administration carried out its development plans. The values of Javanese society were introduced systematically into all the major institutions of East Timor to reorient what an armed forces newspaper termed 'A primitive and backward community such as exists in East Timor'.[39]

This determination by the military to control and resocialize produced an increasingly terrorized population. Nowhere was this more evident than in Dili to where, following encirclement, thousands were transferred from the surrounding areas. From an original population of 28,000, Dili's inhabitants swelled to a total of over 80,000 by 1985. Although some of these were civil servants from Java, persuaded by greatly increased salaries to take up official posts for short periods, most still came from the Dili region. As early as 1980, refugees in Lisbon described Dili as:

> A world of terror: police units forcibly break up small groups on the streets, residents are afraid of being arrested for listening to foreign broadcasts, mail is censored, the use of Portuguese is forbidden and the Timorese live in fear of being denounced as sympathizers of the guerrillas.[40]

The army's priority was to organize an informer network in the city with the aim of one member for each extended family. Although this was never fully realized, it did have some impact. Refugees have reported an increasingly restricted family life, in which discussions are confined to the most mundane topics and assumptions made, however unfounded, about its members' opinions and allegiances, all under the constant threat of military harassment and seizure.

> People are constantly scared of being picked up at any time by the military [said a resident of Dili in 1982]. Each evening the army truck goes around picking up people — ordering them to get into the car without reasons given . . . People are scared to live in Dili, but are not permitted to go back to the districts.[41]

Years of living under such conditions have exacted a terrible toll on the capital's population. Visiting Dili some six years after the end of encirclement, a delegation of German politicians remarked: 'The people never smile . . . (they) look stern, bitter, hostile and numb'.[42] Little had changed by the end of the 1980s. On a brief visit in 1989, a journalist concluded that 'many Timorese are afraid to speak to foreigners for fear of subsequent interrogation which may still involve physical as well as mental abuse'.[43]

After encirclement, in April 1979, the ICRC requested applications from those living in Dili who wished to leave the country. In two days, an Indonesian administration forced to comply with this request received 17,000 applications, only a handful of whom have since been allowed to leave. Referring to the population of Dili, a refugee arriving in Lisbon at the beginning of 1980 concluded: 'If every Timorese who wanted to leave was allowed to go, only the stones would be left'.[44]

Notes

1. The quote is from a document based on eye-witness accounts, Australian Council for Overseas Aid, 1982, Document 9, p. 9.

2. From a letter received from East Timor in 1980 (writer's name and details withheld).

3. 'Report of the East Timor First Level Regional People's Representative Assembly to the President of the Republic of Indonesia on questions connected with the implementation of government in East Timor' in Retboll (ed.), 1984, p. 50.

4. From interviews by Fr P. Walsh, in Jakarta, 15 March 1982, in Australian Council for Overseas Aid, 1982, pp. 26–9.

5. Interview with Timorese refugee, Carlos Alfonso, by Carmel Budiardjo, Perth, 18 September 1982.

6. Extract from testimony of Joao Maria dos Reis, UN Human Rights Commission, Geneva, February 1989.

7. Interview with Timorese in Jakarta, 14–15 March 1982, in Australian Council for Overseas Aid, 1982, pp. 26–32.

8. From a letter cited in Amnesty International, 1985, p. 22.

9. The then head of the Catholic Church in East Timor, Mgr Martinho da Costa Lopes, has said that eye-witness accounts of the Lacluta massacre indicate that as many as 500 people were killed. This particular quote was published in Melbourne *Age*, 14 May 1982 in 'Timor: Tales of Torture'.

10. This account has been constructed from many sources. The most systematic and detailed analysis of Kraras thus far is contained in *Tapol Bulletin*, No. 68, London, March 1985, p. 13.

11. Letter received in Lisbon in April 1984, currently in the possession of Jill Jolliffe.

12. Submission to the Australian Senate Enquiry on East Timor, cited in 'Timor: Tales of Torture', Melbourne *Age*, 14 May 1982.

13. A letter from a priest, dated 14 July 1984, and received in Lisbon.

14. East Timorese refugee, Estevao Cabral, interviewed in Lisbon, April 1988, by Jean-Pierre Catry (interview unpublished).

15. Both these cases, from Lospalos and Viqueque, were cited in a long report of 8000 words transmitted by Fretilin radio during February and March 1985. The report was subsequently published as a booklet by the Australian Coalition for East Timor.

16. This incident is cited in a document dispatched from Dili, arriving in Lisbon in June 1989. It is dated 15 April and was carried by a refugee.

17. From a document written by an East Timorese in late 1981 and published in Australian Council for Overseas Aid, 1982 p. 10/4.

18. This quote comes from the submission of José Guterres to the UN Human Rights Commission, Geneva, 1987.

19. On these points, and for an outline of living conditions in prisons, see Amnesty International, 1985, pp. 62–4.

20. 'Excerpts from a Diary', written by an East Timorese student, in Australian Council for Overseas Aid, 1982.

21. This document was captured by a Fretilin group in December 1981. It was verified as genuine by international scholars of *Bahasa Indonesia* and the military in 1983, under the auspices of Amnesty International.

22. 'Visit to East Timor: Mr D. J. Richardson', a report submitted by the Australian Department of Foreign Affairs to the Australian Senate Enquiry, June 1983, p. 4.

23. Australian Government Publishing Service, 1983, p. 177.

24. Letter from East Timor, November 1981, published in *Timor Information Service* (Victoria, Australia), No. 35, March/April 1982, p. 2. Author known, but name not for publication.

25. 'Where Have These 116 Timorese Gone?', *ABC Monthly*, Lisbon, April/May 1983. Written by Rui Araujo, after a short trip with a camera crew to East Timor. No similar visit, with television cameras, has since been allowed by the military, who have said on several occasions that the Araujo visit was a disaster for them.

26. This analysis of conditions on Atauro since 1983 is based on refugee interviews and on documents from church sources in East Timor. Much of the material used is contained in a document entitled 'Prisons Politiques a Timor-Leste', published by the Lisbon research group, *Em Timor-Leste a Paz e Possivel*, Lisbon, 1988.

27. See, for example, Instruction Manual No. PROTAP/01-B/VII/1982, 'Established Procedure for Interrogation of Prisoners', Military Region Command XVI Udayana, Military Resort Command 164 Wira Dharma, Dili, 8 July 1982.

28. 'Situation of those Exiled to the Island of Atauro', in Australian Council for Overseas Aid, 1982, pp. 8–12.

29. Interview with Antonio Barbossa, Lisbon, 16 February 1985.

30. Christiano Costa, East Timorese refugee, interviewed by Carmel Budiardjo in Geneva, and published subsequently in *Timor Link* (London), No. 14, July 1988.

31. This interview, carried out by Jill Jolliffe in Lisbon, is printed, in extract, in the *Toronto Globe and Mail*, 9 March 1988.

32. Timorese refugee, Andre Faria, interviewed in Lisbon by Jean-Pierre Catry, February 1986 (translation available from author).

33. This account comes from an interview undertaken by Jean-Pierre Catry, in Lisbon, March 1988. The interviewee was imprisoned in 1980, from where he was sent to Atauro before being released in 1984. He then worked for the Indonesian Red Cross until his departure in 1987. A transcript of the interview is available from the author.

34. The imprisonment of these three men dated from November 1986 to March 1987. See 'Allegations of Torture', published by Amnesty International, London, 21 May 1988.

35. This forms part of a testimony made before the UN Human Rights Commission by Joao Maria dos Reis, in February 1989. He reportedly received the information from an Indonesian administrator and subsequently confirmed it with the student's relatives. Dos Reis' testimony is published in *Timor Link* (London), No. 17, May 1989.

36. This account was written by two inhabitants of Klarerek Mutin Resettlement Village, who fled the village on 11 October 1986 and subsequently sent out their account via Indonesian Timor to Jakarta, from where it was dispatched to Lisbon, arriving in September 1987.

37. East Timorese refugee, Antonia Maris de Araujo, testimony to the UN Sub-Commission on Prevention of Discrimination and Protection of Minorities, April 1989. The testimony is published in *Tapol Bulletin* (London), No. 95, October 1989.

38. East Timorese refugee, Anselmo Aparicio, in a testimony given to the UN Sub-Commission on Prevention of Discrimination and Protection of Minorities, Geneva, 1988.

39. Anton Tabah, 'Binpolda, the Spearhead of the Police Force in East Timor', *Angkatan Bersenjata* (in translation), 24 October 1985.

40. James M. Markham, 'Refugees from East Timor Report Famine Situation', *New York Times*, 29 January 1980.

41. Interview with East Timorese resident of Dili, contained in Australian Council for Overseas Aid, 1982, pp. 26–9.

42. 'Alles wirkt wie unter Arrest', *Der Spiegel* (in translation), April 1985.

43. *Guardian* (London), 22 February 1989.

44. James M. Markham, 'Refugees from East Timor Report Famine Situation', *New York Times*, 29 January 1980.

9. Military Campaigns and the Indonesian Transformation of East Timor

With the population of East Timor under its control, the military declared its 'special operations' terminated, claiming that nothing could now prevent the inexorable incorporation of East Timor into the Indonesian archipelago as yet another subordinate outer island.

Consequently, when refugees reported continuing fighting in the eastern region some ten months after the end of encirclement, or when the Bishop of Dili, in an interview for West German radio in March 1980, spoke of military engagements in the Lospalos area, such reports were treated with considerable scepticism. Equally disregarded were letters from Dili which went further:

> I don't know how it's possible for them to do it, but those in the bush are giving strong resistance to tens of Indonesian battalions . . . There is sporadic fighting in all areas . . .

> The situation in the interior of the island is very stormy . . . during the New Year season Dili was placed under a state of military alert against all eventualities.[1]

With Indonesian information services constantly asserting that annexation was complete, there occurred a most astonishing event. On 10–11 June 1980, a three-pronged attack was made on Dili, lasting six hours. The engagement centred on a television relay station on the outskirts of the city, and the attackers were well armed with machine guns and an extensive supply of explosives. Surprised by the attack, Indonesian units were unable to mount any co-ordinated defence. This event gave substance to the reports of a renewed and revitalized independence movement. An attack of such strength and duration on the capital of a country whose territory was supposedly subdued could hardly be ignored. The military imposed their usual blackout, but it was too late; the news had already been dispatched and it appeared shortly in press coverage in the United States, Australia and Europe.

Reprisals in Dili were immediate. Indonesian soldiers evacuated the areas attacked and burnt their inhabitants' houses. Hundreds living on the hilly outskirts of the capital were resettled at Lahane, a camp near Dili. Many people were tortured, arrested and disappeared. A no-go zone was created around the city. More ominously, a week after the attack two warships docked in Dili harbour, unloading troops and tanks. Two months later, a Timorese official in Jakarta claimed that there were as many as 30,000 troops in East Timor. Clearly, 'the insurgency' was far from over. Encirclement and annihilation had failed in their objective of eradicating Fretilin. Amazingly, the independence movement had reasserted itself, and in the most forceful manner. How had this been possible?

Fretilin: defeat and re-emergence

Following the encirclement and annihilation campaigns, Fretilin's national framework had been broken. With the population in its areas being forced into Indonesian-controlled zones, Fretilin groups were chased, captured and killed, the last major pursuits occurring in the south-central and eastern areas in the early months of 1979. With the destruction of Fretilin's leadership, its support bases and its communications system, the Indonesian military confidently concluded that the resistance was finished. Yet during the latter part of 1979 and early 1980, refugees arriving in Lisbon and Darwin reported similar events — clashes between Indonesian troops and Timorese groups in the border area and, most frequently, in the east. The locations were specific — the regions of Ermera, Venilale, Baucau and, above all, Lospalos. It seemed that, despite the destruction of its organization, the resistance was continuing, but on a more local, isolated level, based firmly on an organization centred on traditional kinship ties and allegiances. Supported by hamlets not yet included in the strategic resettlement villages, groups were able to move around and be provided with food, shelter and local lines of communication. During 1979 and 1980 this reliance on traditional forms of organization was crucial for the maintenance of the resistance. Regionalist perspectives which had created problems for the maintenance of a successful national organization in earlier years now proved themselves an invaluable asset. Traditional resistance was reasserting itself under the most adverse conditions.

In this respect, the eastern areas were most important. Here, a group of Fretilin leaders had managed to evade capture, as they were chased from the Matebian encirclement. It contained the only surviving Fretilin central committee members — Xanana Gusmao, who was subsequently elected president in 1981, Mau Hunu, a founder-member of Fretilin, and Seraky, a political organizer from the eastern zone, who was subsequently killed by Indonesian troops in 1979 whilst trying to contact Fretilin groups in the central sector. In areas such as Lospalos, support was provided for this group from a network of hamlets and village organizations. Gradually, it was able to rebuild itself militarily, and by late 1979 had the capacity to mount ambushes on local groups of Indonesian troops.

This process of regrouping within a local network also occurred in the Baucau region, in the north-central sector in Ermera, and in Bazartete, from which the attack on Dili was launched in June 1980.[2] During this year, an increasing number of isolated engagements occurred in these areas, despite Fretilin nationally having lost approximately 90 per cent of its weaponry and 80 per cent of its troops. Throughout 1979 and 1980, the group in the eastern zone made several attempts to contact remaining groups in other parts of the territory, travelling as far west as Turiscai, Remexio and the border, in each case passing along established kinship networks, from one region to another. In October 1980, contact was finally established with groups in Kablake, in the border region, followed by further contacts in the central zone. With this limited communication between groups established, a national conference, similar to those held up to 1977, but with greatly reduced numbers, was organized in March 1981. At this, the remaining Fretilin groups developed a new strategy, organizing themselves into what they termed mobile units, moving around in the regions in which they were based, attacking Indonesian convoys with the aim of disrupting supply lines and capturing weapons.

Such a strategy relied heavily on local support to provide shelter and to cultivate and stockpile food. This was important in the first half of 1981, and enabled Fretilin units to carry out successful raids, capturing large quantities of arms. As 1981 progressed, however, this became more and more difficult as increasing numbers of the population were relocated into new settlements. With this, a new aspect of Fretilin's strategy came into effect: the creation of communication lines between the mobile units (who by now were able to grow, collect and stockpile their own food) and clandestine networks built up within the villages. The military's attempt to deprive the independence movement of its support bases was thus overcome by the creation of these networks, again making use of traditional structures, which continued to be reproduced in the resettlements, since the latter regrouped pre-existing villages from the same areas of origin. Developing their communications with these networks, Fretilin had rebuilt itself into a viable fighting force by the middle of 1981, organized into district groups, which were located in one of three military zones — the eastern, central and border regions.

This reconstruction of the independence movement and its renewed ability to confront the Indonesian army were quite remarkable. No other anti-colonial movement in recent years has been able to rebuild itself so strongly in such a short period of time under such difficult conditions. It attested not only to the capacity of East Timorese society to resist occupation and control, but also to the tremendous courage of surviving Fretilin members in turning once again to face the Indonesian military machine. It also showed their immense skills in reorganizing the resistance framework and in devising a new, highly successful military strategy for the movement in the 1980s.

Faced with this rapid and successful organization manifested directly in a growing number of attacks on troop convoys and military camps, the Indonesian command mobilized the resources it had steadily brought on to the island since the attack on Dili.

Operasi Keamanan: the 'final cleansing'

From 25 March to 1 April 1981 a series of exercises was conducted in Baucau, in which ten thousand troops were deployed to encircle and defend the town. The reasons for practising a new form of encirclement were never clarified at the time, and the military seemed unusually reluctant to give details of the operation, which were published only in the Indonesian daily, *Kompas*.[3] The reasons for this lack of publicity were clarified a month later, when the military began preparations for what it termed variously *Operasi Keamanan* (security), *Operasi Ganesha* (a figure in Hindu Javanese mythology) or, more ominously, *Operasi Kikis* (final cleansing). Priests aptly called it 'a mass mobilization of ordinary citizens to make war on each other'.[4] Specifically, *Operasi Keamanan* entailed the forcible recruitment of men, from the age of 8 to 50, to form human chains across the island from north to south, in the border and eastern regions. These chains then marched eastwards and westwards respectively, converging on the plains of Manatuto in the north-centre of the island. The objective was to flush Fretilin groups out of their support areas and chase them into an area where they could be surrounded and captured. This technique, known in Indonesia as *pagar betis* (fence of legs) had been used previously by the military in village campaigns in Indonesia.[5] It had also been tried briefly in the Natabora and Matebian areas in late 1978, but it had never been attempted on such a grandiose scale. In this case at the most conservative estimate 80,000 men were involved.

Those recruited for *Operasi Keamanan* were given no advanced warning. The army marched into villages, ordered together all men and boys and took them to the region from which the fence of legs was to begin. Once assembled, they were organized into small groups and forced to walk in front of units of soldiers, searching the countryside for Fretilin cadres. The groups advanced some 500m apart. Fretilin groups were faced with the choice either of surrendering or of engaging the Indonesians in combat through firing on their own people. Many, in fact, surrendered, but a remarkable process also occurred in which Fretilin groups were able to pass through the fence of legs unnoticed by the military, with the assistance of Timorese in the human chain who either hid them or led the military away from their encampments. By such means, many Fretilin groups evaded capture. The cost to the population as a whole, however, was considerable. Since they were forced to leave without any notice, they were unable to take with them supplies of food or clothing. Provided with the most meagre food rations, many died of starvation. A Timorese wrote the following extract in a dairy kept during *Operasi Keamanan*:

> One group of the forced patrol has spent the last five days without food and was only able to satisfy its hunger with leaves from the forest and water. Because they were incapable of going on any longer, they organized some of their number to meet the commander and demand food. And what did the commander reply? He shot his pistol into the air several times. And so without food and without any source of protection from the cold of the

mountains, or sleeping facilities, many people have been suffering from fatal diarrhoea. Those who are sick are left behind. They are left to die by the side of the path. And those who struggle on with great difficulty finally return to Dili or other districts walking all the way. The population thus return to their villages in a severely debilitated state.[6]

Another diarist, in Dili, wrote:

30th September 1981. Many groups of people, just skin and bones, arrived in Dili after returning from their forced patrol. Many people returning to Dili from Baucau met these groups walking along the road. Among them they could see young children who were no more than skin and bones.[7]

The full horror of *Operasi Keamanan* was later to be revealed by Timorese who had been forced to participate in it. One described how:

The Indonesians gave instructions to the village heads and the sub-district chiefs who told the population to join in. The 'fence' consisted of three lines. The front line consisted of Indonesian troops, then there was a line of people with more Indonesian troops, and behind them a third line consisting of Indonesian troops. The fence started in the extreme west of the country, went down south, then along the coast to the east, then up north and along the north coast to complete the circle. It was like a huge fence encircling the whole country which moved slowly forward, getting smaller and smaller . . . Each day we moved forward. The Indonesian plan was to push Fretilin forces back to the region of Aitana. The huge fence reached Aitana region at the end of July. It was here that a ghastly massacre occurred. Many people still under Fretilin's protection were slaughtered in cold blood. They murdered everyone, from tiny babies to the elderly, unarmed people who were not involved in the fighting but were there simply because they had stayed with Fretilin and wanted to live freely in the mountains . . . I was in a team of Timorese who had all fought previously in the bush. We were armed and used by the Indonesians to take part in the *pagar betis*. I was with the troops when they reached Aitana. But I did not go in with the first-line troops which attacked Fretilin forces surrounded in Aitana. We were behind. But when the attack was over and mopping-up operations were underway a week or two later, our team entered the area. It was a ghastly sight. There were a great many bodies, men, women, little children, strewn everywhere, unburied, along the river banks, on the mountain slopes. I would estimate about ten thousand people had been killed in the operation. There were so many decomposing bodies that the stench was unbearable and we couldn't stay in the area. The Indonesian soldiers showed no mercy to anyone.[8]

The conduct of *Operasi Keamanan* coincided with the harvesting and planting seasons and, as a result, very few crops were collected. Just as in the preceding year harvesting had been restricted by the forced movement of the population into the new resettlement villages, so too in 1981 severe food shortages were produced directly by military action. After travelling through the Baucau region in mid-June, a Timorese student described the food situation:

> In Laga, Quelicai, Vermasse, Laleia, it is the period of the rice and corn harvest. These crops are going to be wasted and be eaten by rats and other animals as there are no men to harvest them. This year and last year the people of Baguia went through terrible starvation because the *bapaks* (Indonesians) prohibited them from harvesting the rice and corn. The crops were destroyed and eaten by animals. This year, 1981–2, the starvation is going to be in all the areas mentioned above because people are forced to go into the bush and there is no one to prepare the land for cultivation. This time will be another extermination of the people.[9]

Returning in a state of starvation from the fence of legs the population thus had little food with which to survive the 1981–2 wet season. This pattern was repeated throughout the country, except in the highly fertile regions in the west, such as Bobanaro and Ermera.

In February 1982, church personnel gave their own estimates of food shortages based on information coming from parishes. They concluded that at least half the population was facing serious food shortages, particularly in the east. On a more detailed level, one of the few journalists allowed to visit in 1982 travelled undetected to the Lahane camp outside Dili and recorded the vital statistics of 22 children under the age of 12. Using the standards for malnutrition used by the World Health Organization, he found that 18 of the 22 children fell into the category of 'Chronically Malnourished', their food intake being so inadequate that their growth was seriously and perhaps irreversibly stunted. From his trip by jeep and helicopter to 15 towns and villages, covering eight districts, the journalist concluded that malnutrition was widespread. In Baucau, he experienced the following encounter:

> Staff member of Baucau district, Sinaga, an Indonesian, introduced Sister Osario Saurez, a Timorese nun who is principal of the Catholic primary school there. She listened as Sinaga described what a success Operation Security had been. 'Every time we go to a village now', he said, 'they are happy to see us.' 'Because of the political situation', Sister Suarez said quietly, 'because the people had to help the military for Operation Security, they were not able to plant the fields.' 'There is plenty of food here', Sinaga said insistently, and a little nervously. The nun continued to contradict him with a soft-spoken resolve that clearly astonished some of the officials present. 'We are very short of food, namely in Baguia, Quelicai and Laga. But even here the food is not sufficient, the health care is not sufficient. Last year it was better, this year it is worse because of Operation Security'.

In Aileu district, at a resettlement village newly named Saburia, respondents were in no position to give such confident replies to the journalist as he entered their houses in the company of a military intelligence major:

> Under the table lay a boy sweating and shaking in what his family said was a three-day-old malarial fever. Other children in the household had bloated bellies and emaciated limbs. Thomas Ferreria, the family spokesman, was asked through an interpreter about his family's condition. 'Tell him', Major Marsidik warned Ferreria in Indonesian, 'that it's OK here.' Ferreria did as he was told. 'So even though the crops are bad, you have enough food for the whole family?' he was asked in English. 'Tell him you have enough until the next rainy season', said Marsidik in Indonesian. 'We have enough until the next rainy season', Ferreria said.[10]

Aid: use and abuse

As news of the scale of the food shortages seeped out in 1982, the military was forced to take some action to avoid further adverse international reaction. The ICRC programme distributing food to some 34 villages and the emergency relief provided by the Catholic Relief Services (CRS), both begun in late 1979, had come to an end just before the start of *Operasi Keamanan*. Once the fence of legs was finished in September, the ICRC were once again permitted entry to undertake a further evaluation survey, in areas to which they were guided by the army. The results of this survey were devastating. The ICRC concluded that: 'According to official figures, the anticipated crop of 40,000–60,000 tons of maize and 30,000–40,000 tons of rice will not be harvested in 1982'.[11] Data provided by the ICRC on amounts of food distributed for use in an emergency situation in early 1981, when compared with the total food supplies available in the same villages after the 1981 crop should have been harvested, indicate the agricultural shortfall produced by the fence of legs operation. For example, in Alas in the south, the ICRC distributed 2166.8 kilograms, yet by the end of 1981 this village had in store only 770kgs. The equivalent figures for the village of Dilor, in the central region, were 3952 and 450kgs, and for Liquica, in the northwest, 12,040 and 1115kgs.

Faced with this situation, agencies such as the ICRC began to try and provide aid on a more systematic basis. In this they faced the same problem they had encountered in 1979–80, that much of the aid provided for the villages was simply not getting through. Refugee reports and letters described repeatedly how aid was being appropriated and sold. The military hoarded ICRC supplies and sold them in areas of scarcity, through local shops. Aid was given in very small amounts to families in the villages to reinforce their dependency on the military, and the withdrawal of food aid was used as a sanction to gain compliance. A Timorese who worked for the CRS gave this illustration:

Our job was to go to the village and count the number of families. Then we would report back and be given 10kg of food for each person plus medical supplies. We were supposed to distribute the food but were forced to surrender it to the *Koramil* district military post. They would not permit us to give out so much food at once because they said it would be given to Fretilin. They would only give out 5kg. They were supposed to give out 5 more later but they would only give out 5 more when new supplies were sent by CRS — the rest, we were told, they used themselves or sold or used as wages for building programmes.[12]

On the receiving end of aid, a Timorese commented:

At Maubisse in February 1979 an average of 150 people per day came for treatment to the poorly stocked government health centres, whilst at the same time there were medicines for sale in the Chinese shop (at prices) people cannot afford to pay.[13]

Similarly, in the capital: 'Aid supplies stored in the *godown* (warehouse) in Dili are being sold by the Indonesian army and Indonesian Red Cross direct to the people or to Timorese and Chinese merchants'.[14] A former UNICEF worker, commenting on aid abuse in the years of *Operasi Keamanan*:

The Indonesians use the best. A large amount of supplies is diverted into private commerce. If there are no medicines available in the hospitals, the doctor sends the patient out to buy them in the shop, to which they have been diverted. Since the people can scarcely afford to buy them, mortality — especially child mortality — is very high. Many deaths are due to lack of food or medicine. In Dili, for example, when a sick Timorese needs an operation, he has to pay a backhander of 150,000 rupiahs.[15]

One might have expected the representatives of the aid agencies to register complaints, however discreetly, at such a widespread abuse of aid provision. But this does not appear to have been the case. Of the two main agencies then operating in East Timor, the ICRC and the CRS, the former quietly withdrew when faced with difficulties, whilst the latter claimed that there were no serious problems. The ICRC has played only a minor role in food distribution since 1979, confining itself to visiting the prisons of Atauro and Dili and arranging family repatriation; the CRS, after providing short-term relief aid, has concentrated on a small number of specific local projects.

The ICRC relied heavily on the Indonesian Red Cross to carry out its programmes, most notably those concerned with the distribution of food and medicines. Indeed, the agreements signed between the ICRC and the Indonesian Government in 1979 stipulated that: 'The relief operation will be carried out in the field under the auspices of the Indonesian Red Cross with ICRC material and technical support'. This was rather an unusual procedure for the ICRC since its links with national Red Cross organizations are normally confined to general operational issues. In this case, however, not only these matters but detailed activities of all operations and all accounting procedures were entrusted to the Indonesian Red Cross. Even the auditors employed by the ICRC to check the financing of the operation did not visit Dili, confining their investigations to the checking of records at Indonesian Red Cross offices in Jakarta.[16] Distribution was thus organized by the Indonesian Red Cross, with its policy of co-operating closely with the army, its funding by the central government and its use of military personnel. Under such conditions it was hardly surprising that few complaints were made, either of misappropriation or of maldistribution.

The relief operations mounted by the CRS were also operated largely by Indonesian military personnel. At no stage did the CRS employ any non-Indonesian personnel in East Timor. The reasons for this had less to do with the CRS's tenuous position, as with the ICRC, than with the closeness of its perspectives to those of the military. Leading CRS officials in Jakarta, for example, were reported in June 1980 to have said: 'We have visited East Timor and saw no instances of violations of human rights'. Similarly, a journalist visiting East Timor in May 1982 was discussing the use to which grain sent from Jakarta was being put with an Indonesian colonel, A. P. Kalangi: 'We don't just give it away', he (Kalangi) added. 'If you give people something for nothing they get lazy.' To which CRS project director, Hans Meier-Eybers, added: 'Yes, and soon you have an island of beggars'. Later, in the village of Uatolari, the journalist encountered children whom he considered to be 'severely malnourished', to which Meier-Eybers retorted: 'They look like healthy kids to me. Sure, they're a little dirty, but that's all'. Asked if he thought the children malnourished, an accompanying Indonesian doctor replied: 'You can see for yourself. These children are all malnourished'.[17]

Such statements, set in ideologies contradicting the very reality which they purport to explain, illustrate in microcosm the place of the CRS in Indonesia. The CRS campaign received most of its funding from the USAID and, as one might expect, it meshed neatly with US foreign policy in East Timor. As CRS's assistant regional director for the Asian–Pacific region so aptly put it, as the relief programme got underway in East Timor: 'CRS is going where the government of Indonesia wants it to go and doing what the government of Indonesia wants it to do'.[18] An example of such a perspective was the CRS-sponsored agricultural project in the village resettlement of Raimata, west of Dili, in the basin of the River Loes, funded with US$5 million since 1981. It fitted neatly into the military's strategy of using a resettled population to cultivate cash crops on land previously farmed in common by a collection of hamlets. The CRS provided agricultural machinery, tractors, seeds and fertilizers, initially to 50–60 families who, in the CRS's phrase, were 'given title to the land'.[19] Since 1981, several hundred families have been added to the original 50–60. The crops cultivated are rice and peanuts, most of which are exported. After harvesting, the crops are taken to the state purchasing company, since farmers are not allowed to sell them to any other body. The tending of the crops has been interrupted regularly by military officials who have conscripted men for unpaid work on road-building, cleaning and, of course, for longer periods during *Operasi Keamanan*. At the end of 1982, 50 families were transferred from Atauro to Raimata where, according to someone who worked for the CRS on this project, they lived 'in an open prison'.[20]

Structural transformation: the military project

Despite the severity of food shortages in the wake of *Operasi Keamanan*, the cultivation of cash crops for export was extended by the military. Areas devoted to crops such as coffee, previously accounting for some 90 per cent of East Timor's exports, were increased and new crops such as cloves, coconuts, peanuts, cinnamon, sugar cane and rubber introduced. Plans were also laid to transform the fertile Maliana region into an area producing rice for export. These crops were to be grown in the environs of resettlement villages, with planting, tending and harvesting being done by workers drawn from the villages. Displaced from the traditional agricultural sector, with no hope of creating the conditions for cultivating their staple crops, the population of the villages had little choice but to comply. In military jargon, the village resettlements were 'model farms', organizing labour for cultivation and distributing crops provided from other regions or from Indonesia itself. Cultivation of cash crops outside the settlements occurred on areas termed 'plantations' by the military; actually, these comprised land traditionally cultivated by groups of hamlets, which was now simply handed over to local officials or supportive *suco* chiefs from other areas. The absence of tenancy in any formal sense in the traditional sector enabled the military to reallocate land on the assumption that it belonged to no one. 'Villagers are not given any guarantee of land tenure', stated the head of East Timor's Transmigration Department.[21] According to Indonesian government data, the creation of plantations soon resulted in a substantial increase in cash-crop cultivation. For example, the daily *Sinar Harapan* claimed in 1981 that plantation output almost doubled between 1977 and 1983, increasing from 18,584 tons to 30,766.01 tons.[22] These statements were probably unreliable, but they did give at least some indication of growth, and some indication of the military's priorities.

With the success of the plantations, the Indonesian Government increased its funding in the early 1980s and announced plans to open up more substantial areas for cash-crop cultivation in the five-year period, 1984–9, focusing mostly on coffee, areca nuts, kapok and tobacco, in addition to existing crops. During this period, according to government figures, the area devoted to plantations rose from 144,693 to 156,637 hectares, at a rate of 2.72 per cent per year. A typical model village, set up in October 1985, was Salele, near Suai. Each family received 0.25 hectares for a house and garden, plus 1 hectare for crops, and was required to cultivate coconuts for export.[23]

In 1986, in addition to model villages, the military also began to refer to 'model gardens' or 'development villages', a concept introduced by colonel Yunus Yosfiah, a commander of East Timor in the mid-1980s. These were smaller units of around 500 hectares, comprising ten families, run by *babinsas*, and concerned more with the cultivation of food for local consumption.

Transmigration

In addition to providing labour for cash-crop cultivation, resettlement villages in the more fertile regions, such as Ermera, Maliana and Bobonaro, in the west, were accorded a further task, that of receiving transmigrant farmers from areas in Indonesia itself. Transmigration was and is of major importance to the military government, which hopes to resettle 65 million people from Java to the outer islands by the early years of the twenty-first century. The reasons for such a massive transfer are both economic and military. 'Minority populations' are to be assimilated into national development plans because this will make them easier to control, and because the movement of the population to outer island areas will create pools of cheap labour for use by military-controlled companies. Farmers transmigrated from the island of Bali following East Timor's designation as an official area for resettlement in early 1980 were given land formerly used by East Timorese who had themselves been moved to other areas. An initial group of 50 transmigrants arrived in 1980. Their task was to train East Timorese farmers in the skills of irrigated farming. No matter that the Maliana region in which they were settled had a long tradition of highly fertile irrigated cultivation; their first migration was largely symbolic — farmers skilled in traditional methods would have to learn the techniques of modern farming if East Timor were to develop within the Indonesian orbit. With these farmers arriving in 1980 and with at least 800 more planned to move in the next four years, it appeared that Indonesians would increasingly be given land to farm, whilst Timorese would be displaced from their land, forced to become plantation workers in resettlement villages.

In reality, the number of Indonesian families transmigrating to East Timor turned out to be far less than the military had planned. By 1989 only about 500 families had settled from outside, 'shifting people from high-density to low-density areas',[24] with most settling in the border areas of Kovalima and Bobonaro. The exceptions to this have been the creation of transmigration sites near Viqueque in the east, for 100 families from the East Javanese Christian Church in Jember and, most recently, near Baucau. Despite its limited success, the Dili administration nevertheless retains hopes that, with the help of transmigrated families, East Timor's population will reach one million by the end of the century.[25]

As is the case with Indonesia's overall transmigration programme, the movement of families into East Timor is sponsored by the World Bank and its affiliated institutions. Similarly, the Bank supports transmigration from East Timor to areas of Indonesia such as Irian Jaya, West Kalimantan and Sumatra, thereby assisting the Indonesian government's attempted displacement of the problem of East Timor by the removal of those groups in its population who are unable or unwilling to play their part in the transmogrification of East Timor.

Military monopolies

Just as the military increased its control over cultivation and population movement, so did it reinforce its control over the distribution and exchange of crops. In the immediate aftermath of the invasion, a company was set up in Dili, calling itself P. T. Denok Hernandes International. Although headed nominally by two Indonesian Chinese in Dili, the company was owned by General Murdani and two of his colleagues who were to play a prominent role in the occupation, Generals Dading Kalbuadi and Sahala Rajagukguk. As one Indonesian commander put it, P. T. Denok was 'the only company that landed with the marines. They came together'.[26] Through Denok the military monopolized trading, but particularly the exporting of cash crops. Initially, the company moved into the cultivation and export of coffee, East Timor's most profitable commodity. It took over the running of plantations controlled formerly by the Portuguese state company, SAPT. The remaining smallholders, accounting for approximately 60 per cent of total output, were subjected to confiscation. One of the first areas attacked in strength by the military was the main coffee-growing area of Ermera. As early as June 1976, coffee was being exported by Denok through a company set up in Singapore in September 1978, P. T. Timorlaut International. As one of the world's finest coffees, Timor Arabica achieved high prices in the years up to encirclement in 1978, benefiting from a rapid price rise world-wide. One commentator claimed that if the same crop had been produced in 1977 as in 1975, its value would have increased six-fold during this period, from US$5 million to 30 million. Government statistics put the total revenue from coffee exports more conservatively at US$30 million between 1977 and 1983.

Denok monopolized coffee trading by a rigorous military control over buying, selling and transporting of coffee. All trading had to be carried on through Denok's official agents, stationed in each region, and the restrictions on population movement prevented Timorese from selling their coffee elsewhere. In case these policies proved inadequate, no producer was allowed to keep any more than 10kgs of coffee in her or his possession, and rigorous sanctions were imposed on anyone attempting to transport coffee. A driver who worked for P. T. Denok described the situation in March 1982, as follows:

> Anyone who is caught transporting crops to other districts, even in small amounts for private distribution among family, for example, in Dili, will be punished. If the amounts are small, 2–3 kilos, the crop will be confiscated by either P. T. Denok or by the military for P. T. Denok. If the amounts are large, the crop will be confiscated and the people carrying it will be put in jail.[27]

The prices at which P. T. Denok purchased the coffee from plantations were relatively low, lower than during the last years of Portuguese colonialism, according to refugees. The current governor of East Timor, Mario Carrascalao, a former member of the UDT, commented in June 1982: 'Before, one kilo of coffee would buy up to four kilos of rice. Now, one kilo of coffee can't buy one kilo of rice'. 'The price is considered far too low by the local people who grow it. P. T. Denok would sell it to local Chinese for local consumption with a 100–150 per cent mark up', claimed a Timorese who lived in Ermera until the end of 1981. In 1987, the price paid to local cultivators by P. T. Denok was 1250 rupiahs per kilo. When sold in Singapore by the company, the same coffee fetched 5000 rupiahs per kilo.

The wealth accruing from control over coffee enabled P. T. Denok to diversify into other areas, particularly after 1979. Indeed, by 1982, a refugee claimed that: 'The whole export economy is controlled by P. T. Denok'. Whether this was true or not, it seemed that Denok had moved into other areas by 1980. Indeed, by 1982 only 30 per cent of its wealth came from trading in coffee. By this time, it had moved to monopolize the sandalwood trade and to control the cultivation of new export crops, such as cummin, copra and cloves, through a subsidiary, P. T. Scent Indonesia. It had also moved into entertainment through P. T. Batara Indira, and into controlling the distribution of staple foods and household goods through another subsidiary, Toko Marina.[28] By such means, according to government data, Dili's entrepreneurial class has grown by 120 per cent annually since 1980.[29]

P. T. Denok used its wealth to recruit support from local *suco* chiefs, *liurai* and indigenous officials. By way of illustration is the case of the second governor of East Timor who succeeded Arnold Arraujo in 1978, Mario Gonçalves, a former UDT member. Before his dismissal in 1982, Gonçalves was in charge of a US$300,000 per annum slush fund, deducted from the government's tax on coffee exports, which he was supposed to distribute to district heads in the Indonesian administrative system. He was dismissed because 150,000 of this sum disappeared each year, according to Indonesian sources. When the present governor, Mario Carrascalao, took office, he had recently been granted a special concession, becoming the only East Timorese to receive back his expropriated plantation. He was also allowed to sell his Arabica coffee to P. T. Denok at a price almost three times as high as that paid to all other cultivators. Referring to the latter, just before Carrascalao took office, Indonesia's military commander commented: 'They aren't the owners, why should they protest?'

Gradually the dominance of P. T. Denok was challenged by other Indonesian companies, all owned by or closely involved with the military hierarchy. The best known of these companies had been set up in the 1950s in Indonesia by President Suharto's half-brother, Probosutedjo, the president's son, Sugit Suharto and an Arab–Indonesian family, Bakrie, after whom the company was named. In the mid-1980s, Bakrie Brothers tried to wrest control of the export of East Timor's cloves and coffee from P. T. Denok. A deal was subsequently agreed whereby Denok would purchase the crops from local producers and Bakrie Brothers would take charge of exporting through its more extensive international trading network.

In addition to owning P. T. Denok, Murdani, Dading and Rajagukguk also own a further company in East Timor, P. T. Astakona, which has access to substantial proportions of East Timor's budget through its handling of seed and fertilizer supplies to the rural sector. Other prominent companies involved in East Timor are P. T. Nusa Bhakti, owned by Suharto's wife, Tien, and P. T. Lianbau, owned by Suharto's son-in-law, Prabowo.

Before the Indonesian invasion, East Timor's economy contained a number of basic industries producing tools for agriculture, clothing, household goods, building materials and food processing. Under Indonesian control, these have all disappeared with one exception, that of 'traditional textiles'. As a government publication stressing the importance of 'plantation crops, livestock and fishery' (sic) puts it:

> For the moment, the production of other requirements of life cannot yet be undertaken except the production of traditional textiles. Other essential goods, like building materials, kitchen utensils, clothing and others are till now [sic] imported from other parts of Indonesia like Denpassar.[30]

Such enforced dependence on the Indonesian economy, implemented through the policies of resettlement and population control, undermined the pre-existing unity of the handicraft sectors just as it severed the economic ties linking agricultural units in the East Timorese economy. A system designed to meet basic economic needs through long-established and finely balanced relations between cultivation, processing and handicraft–artisan servicing was destroyed in the interests of what was ultimately a reckless profit-seeking military project.

Just as the higher echelons of the armed forces have gained from profiteering on a grand scale, so too is this matched by extensive curruption in the lower ranks. This takes many forms: levying local taxes, demanding money at military checkpoints, releasing prisoners in exchange for bribes, payments to avoid harassment and, perhaps most lucratively, payments for emigration papers: 'It costs anything up to four or five million rupiahs [US$3636–4545] to leave', claimed a refugee who left Dili in the mid-1980s. 'This is a lot of money for people in East Timor. It can take up to two years to get the relevant papers, but people who are rich can leave in a couple of months if they can pay immediately.'[31]

Re-education and control

Of all the data published internationally by the Indonesian military to substantiate its myth of progress in East Timor, the most striking appear to be those illustrating the growth in primary education. A publication in 1984, entitled 'East Timor Develops', claimed that 400 primary schools had been created since 1975, containing 98,850 pupils with 2446 teachers. The impression is given that there was little or no provision of primary education under Portuguese colonial rule, an illiteracy rate of 93 per cent in 1973 being cited as proof of this. No comparisons are drawn between the 1984 data and statistics from the Portuguese period, since the comparison is, of course, unfavourable.[32] In 1973, there were 463 primary schools in East Timor, most of them, as we have seen earlier, run by the Catholic Church. Despite this, the fact that the Indonesian military has highlighted the data on primary education indicates the importance it attaches to resocialization through the primary system. Existing schools have been used to introduce and inculcate children with Javanese and Indonesian military values and culture. The military government claims that: 'At the beginning of the integration, the government had to bring 410 teachers from Java and Sulawasi to make up for the lack of teaching staff in this province'.[33] This lack is explained by many teachers in Catholic schools either crossing the border with the UDT group in September 1975 or leaving their villages to move into the hills to avoid Indonesian attacks prior to encirclement in 1978–9. The teachers that did remain were offered the choice of teaching in Indonesian schools on wages treble their existing income or of remaining in Catholic schools which received no support whatsoever from the military. The only way Catholic schools survived was by receiving small sums from external Catholic development agencies, channelled through Catholic social institutes in Indonesia. Such schools have been subjected to military harassment and their funding agencies informed repeatedly that their programmes are obsolete and redundant. The only way agencies have ensured that their funds arrive and are actually used in primary schools is to permit Indonesian teachers to service the schools they are funding.

In all schools outside the Catholic system the use of both Tetum and Portuguese is banned. Javanese culture is introduced systematically and thoroughly through the exclusive use of *Bahasa Indonesia*. There is a strong emphasis on *Pancasila*, the national ideology of Indonesia, on the values of Javanese society and on military culture. A refugee described the inculcation of *Pancasila* in the following way: 'We had two months to learn the *Pancasila*. If you didn't know it, you had to run round the block or stand on a big wooden box for three hours. And tomorrow, you must know it'. Another refugee described a similar process: 'There is a lot of physical education, less academic work and considerable singing of songs — the Indonesian anthem, the *Pancasila* set to music which you must memorize, school songs and songs patriotic to Indonesia'.[34]

> We learnt Indonesian, we had lessons about Indonesian history, we had *Pendidikan Moral Pancasila* (PMP — Pancasila Moral Teaching) and we had to learn by heart the words, 'Freedom is the right of all nations', taken from Indonesia's Declaration of Independence [related a former secondary school pupil]. The only things I remember now are that it happened on 17 August and the names Sukarno and Hatta. We had to sing '*Indonesia Tanah-Airku*' ('My Fatherland Indonesia') and so on. We had to sing it every

Monday morning at a special flag ceremony. Every day we had to spend an hour singing Indonesian songs, and an hour learning PMP. We had to do physical jerks every morning and we all had to join *PRAMUKA* [the Indonesian Scouts Organization]. It was compulsory to go to *PRAMUKA* meetings every Monday, Thursday and Saturday afternoons. When things were tense and we would try not to go, father would say, 'You had better go, or you might get beaten up'. We were always afraid, so we went not because we wanted to go but because it was compulsory.[35]

Data released by the military in 1985 highlighted the priorities of the education system in East Timor. Of a total of 274,971 textbooks for use in elementary schools, no less than 200,670 were devoted to *Bahasa Indonesia* and PMP. Only 9292 dealt with the sciences.[36] Some 14 years after the invasion 92 per cent of the East Timorese population remained illiterate according to Governor Carrascalao.[37]

Visitors to East Timor have commented on what one journalist termed 'the oppression evident in daily life'.[38] This stems directly from the control the military have been able to exercise in their areas right down to the basic social unit, the family. In a military manual written in 1982, a section headed 'How to prevent contact between Fretilin and the Community', suggests the following strategy for resettlement villages:

Appoint reliable people as *ketuas* (elders) to help neighbourhood chiefs. Arrange it in such a way that each *ketua* takes responsibility for 10–15 families. Each *ketua* must be able to know exactly the activities of the families under his guidance; for example, when they go to their field, go to collect wood, go to another village, go to market and so on. Appoint an 'informer' in each group of 10–15 families led by one *ketua*. This informer should be able to follow, secretly, all the activities of these 10–15 families.[39]

The results of such an extensive system of control are described by a refugee, as follows: 'People are afraid — they are scared — they do not even trust their own family. People are becoming less willing to utter their disagreement and agreement'.[40] The armed forces daily, *Angkatan Bersenjata*, put the military perspective more directly:

Feeble mentality is still very evident among the Timorese, particularly among the older generation. Their feeble mentality results in unhealthy physical and economic conditions. These low social, economic and mental conditions are the source of many negative features because they result in extremely inappropriate thought processes and experiences. The *Binpolda* (the local military village guidance officers) have a very great role to play in building village society if this is to proceed in accord with the programmes that have been decided upon. All the more is this so in East Timor where society so greatly yearns to be guided and directed in all spheres of life. Guiding the people is a process of communication whereas communication means conveying ideas or concepts for the purpose of creating uniformity.[41]

In Lisbon, a refugee pointed out a courting couple to me in the street. 'What's the matter?' I asked. 'You couldn't do that in Dili', he replied. 'The soldiers wouldn't allow it.'[42]

Notes

1. Letters received in Lisbon, dated 8 March and 8 January, cited respectively in 'The Timor War Goes On', *Advertiser* (Adelaide), 22 May 1980, and in 'Reorganised Rebels fight back in E. Timor', *Guardian* (London), 8 March 1980.

2. A refugee who arrived in Lisbon in February 1981, having left Dili in September, claimed that Fretilin's Radio Maubere was broadcasting regularly in the Ermera district, daily from 5.30–6.30, and was listened to by many people. The signals were of a low frequency and could not be monitored in Dili. See 'Testimony from Timorese Refugees', February/March 1981, *Timor Newsletter* (Lisbon), Vol. 1. Nos. 4 and 5, March/April 1981.

3. See *Kompas* (Jakarta), 26 and 28 March 1981.

4. 'East Timor Religious Reflect on the Integration Experience', a document prepared by the Religious of East Timor for presentation to the Conference of Indonesian Major Religious Superiors (MASRI), Jakarta, November 1981.

5. In Bahasa Indonesia, *pagar betis* has come to mean a system of volunteer service for combating banditry in a village.

6. An interview with an East Timorese in Jakarta in March 1982, published in *Timor Information Service*, Clifton Hill, Victoria, Australia, No. 36, May/June 1982.

7. From a diary, sections of which are published in Australian Council for Overseas Aid, 1982, p. 9/8.

8. Christiano Costa, who escaped from East Timor in October 1987, interviewed by Carmel Budiardjo in Geneva, March 1988 (interview available from author).

9. From a report by a Timorese student, travelling in the Baucau region at the end of June and the beginning of July, published as 'Report About my Holiday' in Australian Council for Overseas Aid, 1982, p. 3/1.

10. These extracts are taken from Rod Nordland, 'Hunger: Under Indonesia, Timor Remains a Land of Misery', *Philadelphia Inquirer*, 28 May, 1982.

11. ICRC, 'East Timor Situation Report No. 7', 1.1.82–30.6.82, Geneva, March 1982, p. 1.

12. Interview with East Timorese, Jakarta, March 1982, in Australian Council for Overseas Aid, 1982, p. 26/30.

13. From an account published in *Asia Bureau Australia Newsletter*, No. 46, 1979.

14. Letter received from East Timor in 1979, and published in *Aid and East Timor*, Australian Council for Overseas Aid, Canberra, 1979, p. 16.

15. East Timorese refugee, Antonio Tavarres, interviewed by Jean-Pierre Catry, Lisbon, April 1988 (interview available from author).

16. On this point, see S. Nichterlein, *Food Aid to East Timor — the Arithmetic of Despair*, unpublished document, New York, 1980.

17. These quotes are taken from R. Nordland, 'Under Indonesia, Timor Remains a Land of Misery', *Philadelphia Inquirer*, 28 May 1982.

18. Interviews at the Catholic Relief Services (CRS) Office in Jakarta, 19 June 1980. Conducted by Fr P. Walsh, unpublished document.

19. Australian Government Publishing Service, 1983, Appendix 5, p. 102.

20. East Timorese refugee interviewed in Lisbon on 5 February 1985.

21. Basoeki Adisoekma, in *Kompas* (Jakarta), 4 December 1986.

22. *Sinar Harapan* (Jakarta), 29 March 1984.

23. *Pedoman Rakyat* (Jakarta), 1 December 1986.

24. Ibid.

25. *Mutiara* (Jakarta), 30 July–10 August 1986.

26. Barry Wain, 'Military Seen Behind Firm Controlling Timor's Coffee', *Asian Wall Street Journal*, 16 June 1982.

27. Interview with East Timorese refugee, Lisbon, 15 February 1985.

28. Barry Wain, 'Military Seen Behind Firm Controlling Timor's Coffee', *Asian Wall Street Journal*, 16 June 1982.

29. Ibid.

30. *East Timor Develops*, published by the Regional Government of East Timor Province, Dili, July 1984, p. 17.

31. Interview with East Timorese refugee, Rogerio A. P., conducted by Carmel Budiardjo in Lisbon and published in *Tapol Bulletin* (London), No. 84, December 1987. For the period in which he is describing events, in 1985, the exchange rate for the Indonesian rupiah against the US dollar was 1100 to 1.

32. *East Timor Develops*, published by the Regional Government of East Timor Province, Dili, July 1984, p. 17.

33. Ibid., p. 32.

34. Both these quotes are taken from material presented to the Australian Senate Inquiry on East Timor, conducted during 1983 (see *Senate Records*, unpublished p. 1702).

35. Interview with East Timorese refugee, Rogerio A. P., by Carmel Budiardjo and published in *Tapol Bulletin* (London), No. 82, August 1987.

36. These data are given in a report written by Rüdiger Seifert, following an official visit to East Timor in January 1986. The report is presented in summary form in *Die Welt*, 'Mit grossen Einsatz hilft Jakarta den Insulamen', 29 May 1986.

37. *Jakarta Post*, 5 August 1989.

38. 'Alles wirkt wie unter arrest', *Der Spiegel*, 29 April 1985.

39. 'Ways to Protect People from the Influences of GPK Propaganda'. *Instruction Manual Number JUKNIS/04–B/IV/1982*, Military Region Command (Korem) 164 Wira Dharma Intelligence Section. (Document captured on 30 December 1982.)

40. Interview conducted in Jakarta, March 1982, and cited in Australian Council for Overseas Aid, 1982, p. 26/45.

41. Anton Tabah, 'Binpolda, the Spearhead of the Police Force in East Timor', *Angkatan Bersenjata*, 24 October 1985.

42. Comments following an interview with an East Timorese refugee (name withheld), 16 February 1985.

10. 'Ascertaining the Facts': The Indonesian–Fretilin Ceasefire and the Visit of the Australian Delegation

Since 1975, the governments of the industrialized states have maintained that they have had insufficient information and access to be able to influence events in East Timor in any significant way. Refugee reports have been deemed unreliable and eye-witness accounts contradictory. Many have wished to recognize Indonesian integration, but when faced with the crudities of Indonesian Government pronouncements only a relatively small number have done so openly. It was difficult to support such justifications as the following, for example, issued after the invasion:

> Based on anti-colonialism and humanitarian principles, the Indonesian people had the moral obligation to protect the people of East Timor so that the decolonization process could be implemented in accordance with the ideals and wishes of the entire population of the territory.[1]

Or, some ten years later, that the invasion was 'a positive response to the people's movement in East Timor to set themselves free from the shackles of foreign colonization'.[2] Furthermore, events regarded as decisive by the Indonesian military were viewed with considerable scepticism internationally.

Take, for example, the elections held since the invasion, in which the people of East Timor were said to have exercised their right to self-determination in favour of integration. After the elections, Defence Minister General Mohammed Jusuf concluded: 'I am happy that the general election in East Timor proves to the outside world that the Indonesian Government has granted the people of East Timor their proper democratic rights'.[3] The reality of this event, however, was somewhat different. Indigenous parties were banned and only three parties, all Indonesian, were allowed to run candidates. These were the government party, *Golkar*, the Moslem party, *Partai Persatuan Pembangunan* and a Nationalist–Christian coalition party, *Partai Demokrasi Indonesia*. The latter two had been created by military-induced amalgamations of pre-existing parties. None of these parties had any roots inside East Timor itself, and the only party allowed to campaign in the pre-election period was *Golkar*. The presence of the other parties on election day was nothing more than a formality. Even the then governor, former UDT leader Lopez da Cruz, was moved to comment that: 'The only contest between the contestants was over who could decorate the polling booths most attractively'.[4]

Indonesian journalists covering the election reported that during polling there were three separate boxes, one for each party, into which votes had to be placed. Electoral booths were draped with curtains hanging to knee-height, so that officials standing outside the booths could observe in front of which box the voter was standing. Forced to vote by local military commanders, many Timorese devised passive resistance:

> People knew the policeman was checking everyone, watching where their feet were, so they were careful to place their feet in front of the *Golkar* box, but in fact they bent over and voted for one of the other parties.[5]

The number of votes cast in the election was 309,734, a total of 3227 more than the number of people registered to vote, according to government figures. No less than 99.5 per cent of the population voted for *Golkar*. Despite its distance from Jakarta and despite the difficulties of collecting ballot boxes in an inaccessible mountainous territory, East Timor was the first to declare its vote, well in advance of all other areas.

> During the General Elections [wrote an eye-witness] one of my fellow seminarians and myself were taken away during the night by secret agents. We were interrogated and threatened because we hadn't voted. On the day before the elections I had seen Indonesian soldiers giving orders to Timorese people, forcing them to vote for *Golkar*.[6]

A further set of elections held in 1987 produced similar results. The population were issued with voting cards, requiring them to return to where they had been placed in their initial resettlement camps: 'Because everyone entitled to vote had to leave home for several hours, they all had to lock up their houses and take their children to the polling booths', reported the Indonesian press.[7] Once again, more than 100 per cent of the registered population cast their vote, with some regions producing startling results: Aileu, for example, recorded 327.6 per cent. In Jakarta, the results from East Timor were once again the first to be published. *Golkar* was stage-managed to achieve 93.7 per cent, enabling Governor Carrascalao to conclude that, since the opposition had made some running, 'the international world can see that there was freedom for the East Timorese people to cast their votes'.[8] A novel feature of the election was the participation of Foreign Minister Mochtar as *Golkar*'s chief candidate for East Timor; his main contribution to the campaign was a road-show of rock groups, marching bands, Timorese horsemen, and Balinese dancers from a transmigration site. A high turnout, Mochtar concluded, would show 'that East Timor is part of the big family of the Republic of Indonesia'.[9]

Finding it difficult to support such conduct publicly, governments were forced to do the best they could under the circumstances, hence the 'inadequate information' thesis. This did not, of course, deter them from supplying military equipment: Bronco OV-10 bombers, F-16 fighter jets and helicopters from the

US; Hawk ground-attack planes and frigates from the UK; naval patrol boats from the Netherlands and Australia; submarines from West Germany; and helicopters from France. These were some of the more significant purchases made by the military after the initial failure of the campaign in 1976. Despite claims that such weaponry was intended solely for defence, each of these purchases was made with the Timor campaign in mind. Whether it was a question of reinforcing the naval blockade, of enhancing air-ground strike capacity in inaccessible terrain or of patrolling routes with highly manoeuvrable tanks, arms supplies from the industrialized states were strategically vital, as we have seen in the case of the encirclement and annihilation campaign of 1978–9. Information on such arms sales was kept to an absolute minimum, having to be teased from the relevant foreign and defence departments. By contrast, the 'inadequate information to comment' thesis was used constantly as a stock response to questions of present and future involvement by the governments of the industrialized countries. For example, following the fence of legs operation and the subsequent refugee accounts of its brutal results, the US State Department, testifying in congressional hearings on East Timor in September 1982, claimed in response to questions on human rights abuses that: 'There have been reports over a period of time going back quite a period of time and we have heard these reports, but none of these has been substantiated. We have nothing to corroborate them'.[10]

Similarly, the whole thrust of the Australian Government's policy after 1975 was its self-proclaimed ignorance of what was actually occurring in East Timor. It afforded *de facto* recognition of Indonesian annexation in January 1978, on the grounds that there was no evidence of any resistance from indigenous forces and that integration was, therefore, a *fait accompli*. When the ALP came to power in 1982, its policy committed it to support for an Indonesian withdrawal and an exercising of the right to self-determination. It thus seemed that the Australian position might change. Yet, several ministers in the new government, particularly Prime Minister Bob Hawke, opposed this since they saw it as a barrier to improving economic and political relations with the Suharto Government. Hence they used the 'inadequate information' argument as a means for delaying implementation of party policy, in the hope of a future reversal. When criticized subsequently, they reluctantly suggested that a delegation of politicians should visit East Timor and 'ascertain the facts'. Its conclusions could then become the ultimate arbiter for policy formation. Rather than relying on Timorese eye-witness accounts, the delegation would be able to assess for itself the situation on the ground. Policy could then be formulated on a more adequate basis.

Despite Hawkes' resistance, the idea of a delegation opened up tremendous possibilities. If sufficiently well organized and permitted even a limited freedom of movement, it could play an important role. The justification of inaction through inadequate knowledge would no longer be tenable if the reality of the conflict could be uncovered. For this reason it was a crucial event. It enabled the government of an industrialized state, with some ability to influence the Indonesian military, to enter East Timor, meet and discuss with both Indonesian and Fretilin forces and assess competing claims. Moreover, the situation in the territory at the time of the delegation's visit, in July and August 1983, was particularly favourable for the achievement of these objectives. A moment emerged in which the governments of the industrialized nations could ascertain seriously the reality of the conflict. To understand what happened during this delegation's visit, we need to place it in the context of the rather remarkable period in East Timor in late 1982, following the fence of legs operation.

Ceasefire

Just as in the aftermath of the encirclement and annihilation campaign, so too following the fence of legs operation did Fretilin forces experience a considerable resurgence. Despite the institutional restructuring, resocialization and control policies implemented by the Indonesian military, it appeared that once again the resistance had been able to re-group and re-establish contacts with networks in the resettlement villages. In the wet season period following the end of *Operasi Keamanan* in 1982, attacks were reported over an increasingly widespread area, from Lospalos in the east to Suai in the southwest and Bobonaro in the north. Even Dili was attacked again in November. A letter received in Lisbon in November described how:

> The country has been closed to all corners of the world so that we have heard nothing of what is being said about Timor. What is certain is that since August the Front [Fretilin] has been considerably active and is winning more territory.[11]

By the beginning of 1983, Fretilin's position seems to have been strengthened. A letter received in March concluded:

> The resistance forces in the bush number about 4000 — in possession of heavy armaments. Now they are well-equipped with arms captured from the Indonesian army. The effectiveness of the resistance forces makes it impossible for Indonesia to beat them.[12]

The military capability described here was evidenced in the Lospalos region at the end of March, when a fierce engagement occurred for several days as a result of which Indonesian troops were forced to retreat westwards at considerable cost in men and weaponry.

This resurgence of the resistance movement in the aftermath of *Operasi Keamanan* owed much, as previously, to the extensive support received from the traditional social and political networks of Timorese society. During the fence of legs, local people had used their knowledge of the terrain to steer troops away from Fretilin positions and they had concealed Fretilin members in the fence itself. Hamlets outside the resettlement villages had also provided refuge. In addition, the rebuilding of a national framework for the resistance movement before and after *Keamanan* had relied heavily on recreating ties between regional units which had survived because of their place in local kinship systems and political structures. This continued even when the population was concentrated in the strategic camps and resettlement villages. The social and political relations of the former hamlets and villages were reproduced in their new setting. Despite the military's attempts to impose new political frameworks, they survived and provided a basis for an organization of the resistance in resettlement areas, enabling it to maintain contacts with Fretilin groups outside. The Indonesians regarded this as a major threat to their system of control. The military manual captured at the end of 1982 was preoccupied with how to dismantle Fretilin networks and how to reduce contact between these and Fretilin groups outside the resettlement villages. The networks are described as composed of 'ordinary people, *Hansip* [Civil Guard]/ *Ratih* [people's unit] members and even community leaders; they are motivated by family ties, because they feel disgruntled towards ABRI [the Indonesian armed forces]'.[13]

Faced with these developments, several Indonesian commanders began to negotiate local ceasefires at the onset of the 1983 dry season. These culminated in discussions proposing a ceasefire for the whole country in March. Tapes and photographs of these discussions were carried abroad, reaching Lisbon in mid-June. From these it seems that the ceasefire was initiated by the Indonesian military, by the then commander of the armed forces, General Mohammed Jusuf, through his local commander in Timor, Colonel Purwanto. The first set of talks was held on 21 March in the village of Bubu Rate, when three Indonesian officials met a Fretilin delegation led by its president since 1979, Xanana Gusmao. The discussion focused on Fretilin's requests for the lifting of the naval blockade, contact with the outside world, the entry of foreign observers and an announcement by the Indonesian Government to the UN that it was engaged in ceasefire negotiations. The Indonesian stance, represented by one of the officials, Major Williem da Costa, was conciliatory. Xanana stated: 'We want good relations and peace. Seven years of war have passed and now we leaders . . . must join together to find a solution', to which da Costa replied: 'My soldiers and I have always sought this . . . I don't speak of politics, because I know nothing of them'. The talks concluded with an agreement to meet three days later, on 23 March, at the village of Lari Guto, near Ossu, in the central-eastern zone.

This second set of talks was attended on the Indonesian side by Colonel Purwanto, military commander of East Timor, Governor Carrascalao, a Tetum-speaking field commander from Eastern Lospalos, Major Iswanto, and on the Timorese side by the Fretilin delegation headed by Xanana Gusmao. During these talks, a ceasefire agreement was signed and Purwanto accepted a letter from Xanana to deliver to Suharto, outlining Fretilin's proposals for:

- the unconditional withdrawal of Indonesian occupying forces from East Timor;

- the entry of a UN peace-keeping force;
- the holding of free consultations with the people of East Timor; and
- the maintaining of Falantil troops in the mountains in order to keep people free from intimidation.[14]

Purwanto agreed that the Indonesian Government would inform the UN officially of the ceasefire.

The signing of this agreement was important for Fretilin forces. It enabled them to travel freely throughout the territory, to improve their networks in the resettlement villages and to receive medical treatment from doctors in Dili operating with equipment which was unavailable in Fretilin areas. It was important also because it was a clear recognition by sections of the Indonesian military in Timor of the war-weariness of their troops and the consequent need to find a solution which would reduce the level of fighting. The agreement was also crucial for the people of East Timor. After the ravages of *Operasi Keamanan* it provided a period in which much-needed crops could be grown for local consumption, as people were allowed to travel beyond the confines of the resettlement villages.

For the Indonesian military, the ceasefire agreement had more significance externally than internally. An Australian Labour Government had taken office in March with an anti-annexation policy, receiving widespread support in the party at large. Indonesia's aim was to reverse this policy and Australia's influence on other industrialized states at the UN. The military thus attempted to portray the agreement as a gesture of beneficence on its part, as a precursor to an amnesty offer which would herald the definitive ending of the conflict. Ignoring the terms of the agreement, Foreign Minister Mochtar declared: 'We have offered them a total amnesty'.[15] To assist their portrayal of the ceasefire as a conciliatory gesture, the Indonesian Government agreed to the proposed visit of the Australian fact-finding delegation, under conditions which appeared to provide the possibility of meeting both sides in the conflict. The delegation was thus given the first real opportunity since 1975 seriously to assess directly the validity of the differing perspectives whose contention had excused inaction by their government and its allies over a war which by 1983 had the second highest number of casualties of any in the world.[16]

The delegation's visit

Five members were selected for the delegation, two of whom had some knowledge of the Timor issue. The group was led by Bill Morrison, former defence minister during the Whitlam administration. Having agreed to the delegation, the Indonesian military immediately began to try and limit its scope for investigation: military interpreters should be used since they were most familiar with the local language; accommodation could not be provided for more than a handful of journalists; Indonesia should be visited as well as East Timor; the delegation would find it difficult to travel by road, etc. Above all, it should be less a commission of inquiry and more a goodwill mission, improving Indonesia's strained relations with Australia. Gaining some minor concessions on the interpreter and travel issues, the delegation nevertheless accepted the overall context suggested by the military. This is illustrated in the opening paragraphs of the report of its visit. Concerned that an overly-investigative approach might be counter-productive, it called for a 'realistic appraisal', since 'the Indonesians certainly regard the Timor question as a critical test of Australian–Indonesian relations, indicating that if differences persist the whole relationship will suffer'.[17]

East Timor was thus placed firmly in an Indonesian context at the outset. The delegation defined itself as more informative than investigative. It seemed prepared to accept much of the Indonesian version of events. It faithfully recorded that the military invaded to quell chaos, that Suharto was reluctant to intervene, that the vast majority of the people voted for the military in the elections, that food shortages were due to long dry seasons and even that malnutrition was due to a 'lack of variety in diet'.[18] During their ten-day visit, delegation members spent no more than four days in East Timor, three of which were spent travelling, mostly by helicopter. The military was informed in advance which villages the delegation wished to visit. Concessions granted to the Indonesian side were not accorded to the independence movement. Despite considerable difficulties, a letter from Xanana Gusmao was smuggled out of the territory and handed to the delegation by Fretilin's external representative. It suggested radio frequencies and places for contact. This offer was never taken up, despite the fact that it would have been relatively easy to arrange under ceasefire conditions. Fretilin was provided with no means for meeting delegation members. During its short trip, the delegation visited 12 villages. Its reports on these are instructive, particularly when compared with refugee and resistance accounts.

Requesting a visit to Lacluta, in the centre of the country, the delegation was taken to a resettlement village, Dilor. The following explanation for this was given and accepted: Dilor had been established in 1979 as a village resettling people from nearby Lacluta, since the latter 'has apparently been the site of some serious clashes in the war where the casualties have been high'.[19] In fact, Lacluta had been the site of the infamous massacre at St Antony Rock in September 1981, in which soldiers massacred at least 400 women and children.[20] During the delegation's visit, Dilor was 'uncannily empty'.

> The delegation's hosts explained that its residents were away working on their land . . . the few people to be found — mostly the old — appeared reserved, if not afraid. Only the schoolrooms were bustling with life and excitement at the visit, the children singing loyal Indonesian songs lustily.[21]

Refugee accounts painted a rather different picture of the Lacluta area, with families separated, work for long hours cultivating cash crops on alienated land, rigorous resocialization and control and regular food shortages.

In Quelicai, south of Bacau, the delegation reported:

The people were not so ready to smile and in a largish gathering of perhaps 500 at the school which formed to inspect the delegation, one estimate put the number of distended bellies among the children at one in eight.[22]

Again, like Dilor, Turiscai, south of Dili 'appeared relatively uninhabited and the delegation was told that most of the people were away picking coffee. They have to walk for a total of four to six hours every day to and from the coffee trees'. The town's police chief claimed: 'There has been no trouble since 1975'.[23] On the contrary, Turiscai was the site of some of the fiercest battles and Indonesian reprisals, up until the capture of Xavier do Amaral in late 1977. In June 1975, following an engagement, Indonesian troops executed all the civilian population remaining in the village, most of whom were women with their children.

Visiting Lospalos, in the east, the delegation was impressed by attempts to set up a sugar industry to 'stimulate the region's economy'[24] through exports. A few weeks earlier, Fretilin's Council of National Resistance had undertaken a detailed survey of social and economic conditions in many of the resettlement villages of Los Palos, concluding that:

> People have been forced out of their homes by armed troops and their huts then destroyed. When this happened they had to live under the trees for some time before new huts were built. People live almost entirely from wild roots and coconuts; the death rate from starvation is high.[25]

In all the villages visited by the delegation, the contrast between its commentary and evidence from refugee and resistance accounts was stark. In all cases, the delegation concurred with the military perspective, whether it be concerning reasons for resettlement, empty villages or malnutrition. No other view was presented or sought, even when the explanation seemed vacuous.

In addition to visiting villages, the delegation called in on Atauro island. Three months earlier, a Portuguese journalist had met with Atauro's inmates: 'The atmosphere is quite dreadful. People look bewildered. The children never smile'.[26] This was one of the very few occasions on which a visitor was able to disturb the rehearsed arrangements practised by inmates for weeks before each delegation's visit. As exiles from Atauro have detailed, all visits, even those of the ICRC, are rehearsed. The Australian delegation's visit was no exception. They concluded that: 'The physical conditions under which they [the detainees] live are moderately comfortable, and the people in Atauro looked as well-fed and dressed as the villagers in other areas visited in East and West Timor'.[27] The delegation noted, with some enthusiasm, 'that too rapid a return of the detainees to their home area could place too great a strain on the resources of these areas to support them, and it was much easier to ensure their physical well-being on Atauro'.[28] What one former detainee termed 'the practice of intimidation, surveillance and reprisals enacted on the population during and after each visit', had worked. (After the Portuguese visit, three of the detainees to whom the visitors had talked 'were cruelly tortured and sent to Dili', following which they were detained in the Comarca prison.[29]. The delegation even remained oblivious to the rather obvious contradictions encountered in their short visit. Their Indonesian guide informed them that only 2031 persons remained, whilst the figures they were given totalled 3237. Whilst the military claimed that people had been sent to Atauro after giving themselves up, not one person in that category was found by the delegation, even when delegates asked the entire population assembled before them at the end of their visit. Finally, and perhaps most depressing of all, they were handed a list of missing detainees by a terrified prisoner, but it similarly had little impact.[30]

Interception

The severest test of the delegation's ability to view the situation through the military perspective was presented by a direct encounter with a delegation from Fretilin itself. Showing considerable organizational ability and detailed inside knowledge of the Australians' itinerary, Fretilin representatives intercepted their convoy as it was travelling on one of the two overland trips during its visit. What transpired illustrated in microcosm the lengths to which the government of an industrialized state was prepared to go to view East Timor from within an Indonesian context.

On the second day of its visit, the delegation visited Lospalos, meeting the local *bupati* and officials. Three of its members, including Morrison, opted to travel to Baucau by car, the remaining two taking a return helicopter to Dili. West of the village of Laga, some 20km east of Baucau, was the resettlement village of Soba. Fretilin representatives had camped here, near the roadside, hoping to intercept the Australians. The delegation was travelling in five jeeps, the first three of which sped past the Fretilin group, reliably informed by Indonesian officials that they were local militia. The discrepancy between this commentary and the group's display of T-shirts embossed with the word 'Fretilin' was finally noted by Morrison, travelling in the fourth vehicle. He ordered a halt, and together with Timorese and Indonesian officials, embarked on a 30-minute meeting with the Fretilin group. Its leader was Cancio de Sousa Gama, a local commander. Since he only spoke Portuguese, his comments were translated into *Bahasa Indonesia* by a Timorese official, Thomas Ximenes, a member of the Provincial Assembly, and from *Bahasa* into English by an Indonesian official, Ruslan Suroso. This tortuous process was then reversed for Morrison's comments. The encounter was taped by a reporter from Radio Australia, John Lombard, who was accompanying Morrison.

The conversation centred on a number of issues, most importantly, the war, the conditions of the population, the ceasefire talks and areas of Fretilin control. Throughout, Morrison's tenor was dismissive, sceptical and condescending, reproducing faithfully the by now conventional military myths:

'What is the reason you want to stay in the jungle when there's [sic] only so few of you?'

'Fretilin does not occupy a strong position and your position is very weak. Why do you think you can win?'

'How old are you and your friends? You seem very young'.[31]

The aims of the Fretilin representatives, to present a document outlining the movement's position on negotiations and to arrange a meeting with a higher-level delegation which had taken over the nearby resettlement camp of Saelari, were largely ignored by Morrison. Not that the translation helped in this respect. Asking where Saelari was located, and before rapidly changing the subject to how and why Fretilin travelled there, Morrison was given the following reply, in translation: 'They have been there two months waiting for the delegation'. What de Sousa Gama actually said, according to Lombard's tape, was: 'The camp is a concentration camp built by the Javanese. We came here two months ago waiting for you, senhors'.

This same process was repeated throughout the conversation, particularly at critical junctures. For example, Morrison: 'If we wanted to get in contact with you again, how would we get in contact with you?'. Gama: 'The four people here present and four others in the village would like to take the delegation to *suco* do Saelari to get in touch with our leader who is at the present moment in Saelari, *suco* do Saelari'. His answer was translated as: 'They do not want to answer the question. But if you want to, really want to meet them . . . they are here four people and the other four is in Laga . . . and you come to Laga, they want to bring you to Saelari to discuss with their leader'.[32]

At the end of the meeting, Morrison promised: 'Somehow we will get a message to you. If we decide to come . . . I will talk to Governor Carrascalao'.[33] In fact, he did nothing of the sort, confining his actions to 'informing other members of the delegation' on his return to Baucau, and 'requesting' comments from Carrascalao. No attempt was made to contact the Fretilin representatives who remained in Saelari and were later surrounded and killed by Indonesian troops. 'Back in Baucau', notes the official report of the visit, 'the delegation leader informed other members of the delegation of the meeting before settling down to a night of bridge'.[34]

Some days later, speaking at a press conference on the delegation's visit, Morrison felt able to conclude that nothing they had seen contradicted the view that 'the administrative authority of the East Timor Government and the Indonesian Government is firmly in place', and that Indonesian development 'is for the people of East Timor, to overcome the scars that everybody admits are there'. Asked if he had any comment on external Fretilin reports of a forthcoming military offensive in August, Morrison replied: 'We have just been there and we have seen for our own eyes and we have discussed with the military commander . . . Certainly nothing we saw, nothing we were told there, gives any credence to that report'.[35]

The offensive was launched subsequently on 17 August, Indonesian independence day. Heartened by the delegation's supportive approach, Commander in Chief Murdani unilaterally broke the ceasefire, launching a new campaign called *Operasi Persatuan* (Operation Unity). He threatened: 'This time, no fooling around. We are going to hit them without mercy'.[36] It was a fitting epitaph to the Morrison mission. Charged with 'ascertaining the facts', it had fitted neatly into a military-generated mythical picture which it itself had helped to reproduce.

Massacre

As early as mid-June, Murdani had given notice of his intention to launch an offensive, but he had been restrained from breaking the ceasefire and banning the delegation's visit by politicians and generals, who supported the conciliatory approach of Purwanto. After the delegation's comments, however, Murdani was given free rein. The military build-up began no less than two days after the departure of the delegation.

The Indonesian press reported the campaign as a response to Fretilin attacks breaking the ceasefire agreement. In particular, it focused on an incident in the Viqueque area, on 8 August, in which 16 Indonesian soldiers were reportedly killed by former Fretilin members in a resettlement village. On 10 August it was further reported that 86 Timorese civil guards (*Hansip*) had deserted, with their weapons. Military action was thus justified. The reality of these events, however, was rather different, as accounts from refugee and official Timorese sources have since documented.[37] It seems that a village festival was raided by Indonesian soldiers, who abducted and raped several Timorese women; enraged, the villagers turned on the soldiers, among whom were a number of officers, and killed them; with their officers dead, the civil guards then defected.

Military reprisal was swift and thorough. Shortly after the incident, at least 80 people from a resettlement village nearby, Kraras, were killed as Indonesian soldiers set fire to their homes.[38] Following this, many people fled from the village to the slopes of Mount Bibileu, to the north of Kraras, west of the River Be Tuku. The military then conducted a 'clean-sweep' (*sapu bersih*) operation on the mountain with prolonged and intense bombing raids and encirclements. During this operation, according to several accounts, no less than 500 people were killed, many of them being executed *en masse* on the banks of the river. Those that remained were resettled in a new village, Klalerek Mutin, created specifically for this purpose.[39]

And so began a further onslaught: encirclement and annihilation, fence of legs and, now, 'unity', perhaps the most systematic, certainly the longest, campaign, particularly at its focal point, in the eastern sector. As with the massacre at Kraras village, the military claimed that there were no excesses: very few people were killed and no one was tortured; there was no need, since Fretilin was no longer a problem, reduced as it was to small, roving bands — 200 'remnants' according to Colonel Purwanto in discussion with Morrison.[40]

Such myths were soon to be shattered by the capture of a set of Indonesian military manuals, written by officers of the East Timor command for use by troops in the territory. Issued between July and September 1982, after *Operasi*

Keamanan, they were captured by a Fretilin group at the end of December and sent out to Europe in 1983. The manuals covered a range of strategic issues, such as security in towns and villages, military operations in resettlement areas, political propaganda and interrogation. They documented a widespread support amongst the population for resistance operations spread throughout the territory and outlined measures taken to contain this support. They substantiated the major features of military control as previously outlined in refugee accounts and testimonies. Villages were categorized according to the degree of Fretilin presence. Not one village mentioned is cited as free of 'support networks' for the resistance, and the preoccupation of four manuals was solely with isolating the population of the resettlement villages from contact with Fretilin. 'Family ties' were seen as the major means of support. The manuals described capture of family members, followed by interrogation, a transfer of subsequently discovered Fretilin sympathizers to the island of Atauro and operations to capture contacts living outside the resettlement villages. They outlined the difficulties of recruiting Timorese into the civil guard (*Hansip*), and people's units (*Ratih*), of ensuring that they remained loyal and did not pass information to Fretilin. One manual exhorted; 'Examine their background, their life history and their motivation for joining *Wanra* (*Hansip*) and *Ratih*. If there are any indications that any members are still sympathetic with the GPK (Fretilin), these persons must immediately be taken into custody'.[41]

A manual on 'Guiding the Village Comprehensively', went so far as to list the essential items, such as 'the genealogy of the chieftain', a 'list of catechists' and a 'sketch map of the old village (pre-upheaval)', in order that 'every level of the territorial apparatus will know for certain the inner workings of the villages'.[42] Perhaps most revealing of all, however, was the manual on 'Established Procedure for Interrogation of Prisoners'. Section 13 of this document stated:

> Hopefully, interrogation accompanied by the use of violence will not take place except in certain circumstances when the person being interrogated is having difficulty telling the truth . . . If it proves necessary to use violence, make sure that there are no people around (members of *Hansip*, *TBO*, *Ratih* or others to see what is happening, so as not to arouse people's antipathy'.

Cautioning, it suggested:

> Avoid taking photographs showing torture in progress (people being photographed at times when they are being subjected to electric current, when they have been stripped naked, etc). Remember not to have such photographic documentation developed outside East Timor which could then be made available to the public by irresponsible elements. It is better to make attractive photographs, such as shots taken while eating together with the prisoner, or shaking hands with those who have just come down from the bush, showing them in front of a home, and so on . . . If necessary, the interrogation should be repeated over and over again using a

variety of questions so that, eventually, the correct conclusion can be drawn from all these different replies.[43]

This notion, central to the manual's definition of interrogation, of drawing a 'correct conclusion' from replies which constantly denied this conclusion's inversion of reality, could also have been taken as a guide for the Indonesian military's relations with the governments of the industrialized states. The military tried their utmost to distort the reality of their brutal occupation by offering palatable images to these governments, who sifted through them in the hope of finding evidence to justify their inaction. The visit of the Australian delegation provided several such images. The delegation was careful in selecting them, avoiding all evidence which countered the Indonesian military perspective. In doing so, it refused the opportunity of reporting the situation directly and objectively. In this manner it reached its conclusions: that the resistance movement was a spent force and the occupying power a reluctant benefactor, despite some short-term difficulties in adjustment by the occupied population.

Further visits

Since the Australian delegation's visit, and particularly after the end of *Operasi Persuatan* in 1985, several foreign delegations have visited East Timor regularly each year. Almost all have been funded and selected by the Indonesian Government. In all cases, the military have gone to great lengths to ensure that their conclusions are supportive. Many refugees have reported on the rigour with which the military have prepared the ground for such visits. A former official in the Dili Information Office claimed that:

> Foreign visits to East Timor are organized by the Secret Service and by the Department of Information where I was working. The latter department is headed by a Timorese, but 95 per cent of the officials come from Indonesia. They choose which places are to be visited, as well as who may speak to the visitors.[44]

A former receptionist at the Hotel Tourismo, where many foreign visitors were placed, illustrates what this meant in practice:

> Protocol officials were always in contact with security by telephone. They received their orders from security — what they could say, what they couldn't say: 'You can't go to that place, choose another'. 'It is impossible to go to that spot by car, the road has been cut off by the rains, you will have to go by helicopter'. If they asked us what the chances were of visiting this or that area, we spoke of the rains and of the bad state of the roads. We always had to give a reply which followed what they had taught us. The government itself, the police, closed the roads. Visitors are always accompanied by

Indonesians. Everything they say is monitored. It is impossible to say anything.[45]

In 1983 [wrote a former student] my college was visited by a crew from Portuguese television. The crew was continually surrounded by secret agents who were taking note of our attempts to enter into contact with them. On my return to the seminary I was insulted and threatened by these agents.[46]

An official of the Indonesian administration who escaped to Darwin in December 1987 claimed that all visits by foreigners

are prepared down to the millimetre and to the second; itineraries are rigorously designed, and staged scenes having little to do with the reality of East Timor are enacted. Even the prisoners in the gaols visited are replaced by administration officials who have a good physical appearance. Several officials in my line of work had to take the place of prisoners. When acting as a guide for foreign delegations, I was instructed not to translate everything, and to not show a lot of things, in addition to not revealing that many of the civilians were Indonesian soldiers in civilian clothes.[47]

On several occasions, even the best laid plans have misfired. In an attempt to weaken support for a resolution put to the European Parliament in September 1988, the military invited four MEPs to visit East Timor in August. They duly visited Dili on 16 August, meeting Governor Carrascalao and attending an independence-day celebration the next day. Following this, they were taken out of the capital 'to see with their own eyes the real situation in East Timor'.[48] On board the helicopter one of the parliamentarians requested a map, to check their flight direction. After having claimed that there were no relevant maps, the pilot finally produced one. The group soon realized that, rather than being taken to Viqueque in the southeast, as promised, they were flying westwards. After two members threatened to pull out of the delegation if the helicopter did not change direction, the pilot made a sudden unscheduled landing, and returned to Dili. Here the delegation was told that the trip had to be abandoned because the blue skies were clouding over and that the helicopter needed to be repaired. After several phone calls to Viqueque and a two-hour delay, the helicopter took off. On arrival in Viqueque a delegation member noted: 'People did not come out to welcome the delegation, as happened elsewhere'.[49] In the town they saw many troops and military compounds, in an area in which the Indonesians claimed that there was no military activity. Back in Jakarta, the chair of the Indonesian parliament's Inter-Parliamentary Co-ordination Board, Theo Sambuaga, who had accompanied the delegation, concluded that: 'They might have seen many ABRI (armed forces) officers in East Timor and hastily reached the conclusion that the soldiers were there to fight. In fact, ABRI is also an agent of development. Such things cannot be seen through European spectacles'.

Sambuaga's view prevailed. The delegation's report proposed

> open and friendly discussions between provincial representatives and the
> Indonesian Government . . . to reach a maximum degree of autonomy
> within the flexible constitutional framework of the Indonesian Republic and
> in accordance with the principles of *Pancasila* to get the highest possible
> consensus to avoid future conflicts.[50]

And so the pattern evident in other delegations recurred. Events were
rigorously orchestrated to enable visitors to 'discover for themselves' the
validity of the military's view of the conflict. If events contradicted this, visitors
were persuaded that what they had seen was the 'exception to the rule', or that
they were not in East Timor long enough to fully appraise the situation, and so
on. Consequently, the status quo prevailed, unchallenged by any serious
investigative visits, enabling many governments to perpetuate their policy of
'having insufficient information to comment fully'. At the same time they also
tried to use Indonesian Government statements and information to justify their
acceptance of integration: 'Every news item, regardless of source', stated
President Suharto, 'should be censored carefully before being published'.[51]

Notes

1. Indonesia, Republic of, 1987, p. 9.
2. 'Suharto Justifies 1975 Invasion of East Timor', Hong Kong AFP (in English)
15.22 GMT, 16 August 1985, *BBC Summary of World Broadcasts*, Australasia, 20
August 1985.
3. *Sinar Harapan* (Jakarta), 5 May 1982.
4. Ibid.
5. Interview with refugee, Neobere, London, 11–13 May 1983.
6. East Timorese refugee, Anselmo Aparicio, testimony to the UN Sub-
Commission on Prevention of Discrimination and Protection of Minorities,
Geneva, August 1989.
7. *Suara Pembaruan* (Jakarta), 30 April 1987.
8. *Kompas* (Jakarta), 24 April 1987.
9. *Sydney Morning Herald*, 17 April 1987.
10. *Recent Developments in East Timor*, Hearing before the Sub-Committee on
Asian and Pacific Affairs of the Committee on Foreign Affairs, House of
Representatives, 97th Congress, second session, US Government Printing Office,
Washington, 14 September 1982, p. 76.
11. Letter received by a Timorese refugee in Lisbon, 22 November 1982,
translated by Jill Jolliffe.
12. Letter received by a Timorese refugee in Lisbon, 30 March 1983, translated by
Jill Jolliffe.
13. *Military Manual*, Section II: The Structure of GPK Support networks,
Military Resort Command, 164 Wira Dharma Intelligence Section 1982 (translated
by Carmel Budiardjo).

14. These proposals are set out in a publication by Fretilin's Lisbon office. *Fretilin Conquers the Right to Dialogue*. Lisbon, June 1983.

15. AFP. Jakarta, 30 June 1983.

16. See *A World at War*. Center for Defense Information, Washington DC, 1983, cited in *Canada Asia Currents*, Vol. V, No. 2, Summer 1983, p. 2.

17. Australian Government Printing Service, 1983, p. 3.

18. Ibid.

19. Ibid., p. 45.

20. See Chapter 9, n. 17.

21. Australian Government Printing Service, 1983, p. 46.

22. Ibid., p. 47.

23. Ibid., Appendix 24, pp. 175–6.

24. Ibid., p. 48.

25. Document on social and economic conditions in East Timor's resettlement camps and villages, compiled in the first six months of 1983 and signed by Xanana Gusmao on 25 July 1983. Each section of the report is hand-written in Portuguese (translated by C. Budiardjo).

26. Rui Araujo, 'Timor: Where Have These 116 Timorese Gone?' *ABC Monthly* (Lisbon), April/May 1983.

27. Australian Government Printing Service, 1983, p. 51.

28. Ibid., p. 52.

29. Testimony from an Indonesian visitor to Atauro camp, published in *Em Timor-Leste a Paz é Passivel* (Lisbon), February 1985, p. 32.

30. For details of these see ibid.

31. Australian Government Printing Service, 1983, Appendix 24B, pp. 157–60.

32. Ibid., Appendix 24C, pp. 161–4.

33. Ibid., p. 160.

34. Ibid., p. 50.

35. Ibid., Appendix 35, pp. 207–13.

36. *Sinar Harapan* 17 August 1983.

37. A report from a 'highly-placed Timorese official', in *East Timor Report*, No. 6, March 1984, Australian Council for Overseas Aid, concurs with the details of events recounted in letters to Timorese refugees in Lisbon in September. A Fretilin report of 1984 gives a different version — that ex-Fretilin members turned on the Indonesian guards in their villages in a more organized revolt, following a military killing of Fretilin troops during the ceasefire period in early August.

38. This account has been compiled from a number of sources but most notably from refugee accounts received by Amnesty International, and from Fretilin documents sent to Lisbon from East Timor early in 1984.

39. The Apostolic Administrator of East Timor during this period, Mgr Carlos Filipe Belo, later claimed in an interview on 12 March 1984, specifically of Kraras itself: 'I saw the graves. The places where these people were buried. In one place about 70 and in another place 14' (see 'Timor Bishop Accuses Military of Massacring 84 Villagers', Peter Millership, *Reuters* (Dili), 1 March 1984).

40. Australian Government Printing Service, 1982, Appendix 29, p. 188.

41. *Instruction Manual* No.JUKNIS/06–IV/1982, 'Babinsa/TPD Activity in Developing and Phasing out Trained People's Resistance Forces', Military Region Command (Korem), 164 Wira Dharma Intelligence Section, translated by C. Budiardjo (p. 26 in translated document).

42. *Instruction Manual* No. JUKNIS/01-A/IV/1982, 'The Village as a Focal

Point of Attention and How to "Guide" it Comprehensively'. Military Region Command (Korem). 164 Wira Dharma Intelligence Section, translated by C. Budiardjo (p. 14 in translated document).

43. *Instruction Manual* No. PROTAP/01-B/VII/1982, 'Established Procedure for Interrogation of Prisoners', Military Region Command XVI Udayana, Military Resort Command, 164 Wira Dharma, 8 July 1982 (p. 34 in translated document).

44. Joao Maria dos Reis, testimony to UN Sub-Commission on Prevention of Discrimination and Protection of Minorities, Geneva, August 1989.

45. Carlos Barbossa, interviewed by Jean-Pierre Catry, Lisbon, 1988 (transcription available from author).

46. Anselmo Aparicio, testimony to UN Sub-Commission on Prevention of Discrimination and Protection of Minorities, Geneva, August 1989.

47. These quotes are selected from interviews with Inacio de Moura, contained in *Diario de Noticias* and *Expresso* (Lisbon), 20 February 1988, translated by Wesley Edward Kerney, Catholic Relief Services Language Service, April 1988.

48. This quote is from Indonesian Foreign Minister, Ali Alatas, in *De Gelderlander* (Amsterdam), 5 August 1988.

49. Beate Weber, Member of European Parliament, Comments on the Delegation's Visit to East Timor, contained in *Tapol Bulletin* (London), No. 89, October 1988.

50. *Report of European Parliamentary Delegation to East Timor*, Strasbourg, September 1988.

51. *Jakarta Post*, 11 December 1987.

11. The Development of Opposition and Indonesian Plans for the Resocialization of East Timor

With *Operasi Persatuan* well underway, Commander in Chief of the Armed Forces Benny Murdani visited military posts in East Timor on Christmas Day 1983. Describing how Christ's birth 'presented a picture of nobility and glory in the midst of suffering and hardship, a picture that was relevant for every soldier', he announced 'that everyone who surrendered would be treated humanely'.[1] In January 1984, students from the Dare Seminary, near Dili, presented a document to the Indonesian Bishops' Conference detailing massacres of children in Lospalos, Viqueque, Ainaro and Sumalai. Earlier in November, letters received by refugees in Lisbon and Darwin had described the systematic burning of villages, notably in the eastern sector. Most people who had been captured or surrendered between August and December had been either executed, imprisoned on Atauro or sent to prisons in Bali.[2]

The military build-up leading to these events had begun in earnest during September. Refugees leaving Dili reported that Hercules transport planes were arriving every two or three days with paratroops and heavy equipment. Bronco OV-10s were seen flying off on regular missions to the eastern sector. They were assisted by Skyhawks flying from Baucau and specializing in incendiary, cluster and anti-personnel bombs. Exasperated by the increasing rates of defection of Timorese *Hansip* and *Ratih* troops,[3] the military relied on their élite commando *Kopassandha* Red Beret units, who were dropped by helicopter to mop up after bombing raids. It was they who were responsible for most of the village burnings.

With scant concern for international reaction, Murdani restricted ICRC contacts to such an extent that the organization found itself unable to distribute food.[4] Similarly he declared Governor Carrascalao 'inactive', and ordered Purwanto's replacement by Colonel Rudito, an experienced field officer who, in line with the 'no fooling around' policy, 'resolved to fight to the end'.[5] Armed with the evidence of its fact-finding delegation, the Australian Government dutifully conveyed its concern, and urged 'restraint'.[6]

As the campaign developed, it became clear that once again Fretilin was mounting a fierce resistance. Before December, attacks had been made on Indonesian troops in Dili and Fretilin units had mounted surprise assaults in the eastern sector, where the Indonesians had concentrated 12,000 troops along a line from Baucau to Viqueque prior to their eastward advance. By the middle of the dry season, in December and January, Fretilin had also begun to mount co-ordinated attacks in the central and northwestern border areas. A Fretilin communiqué, released in Lisbon in April 1984 and reporting two central command meetings between 16–18 March, claimed that: 'The Indonesians are growing more and more demoralized by the fact that our activities cover almost the whole territory'.[7]

As with earlier campaigns, the most serious effect was on cultivation. Crops were burnt and food stocks destroyed and, following the relatively more relaxed atmosphere of the ceasefire period, people were once again prevented from leaving their resettlement villages to tend their crops. Food shortages were most acute in the areas of Viqueque and Lospalos, both targets of Indonesian attacks. Refugees displaced from villages by red berets were herded into centres in towns such as Lospalos, where 3000 were reported to have been moved into its environs by the end of December.[8] As the recently appointed Apostolic administrator, Carlos Filipe Ximenes Belo put it, in a letter to his predecessor, Mgr Costa Lopes: 'In the Kabupatens of Lospalos, Viqueque, Baucau and Ainaro, there is war and the population is corralled. They suffer illness, hunger, lack of liberty and persecution'.[9]

This suffering referred to by Belo was documented in many refugee accounts. A letter dated 6 January 1984 claimed that in the mountain areas around Viqueque, Indonesian soldiers were 'doing what they like' with 14-year-old girls, and that it is the same in Lospalos. Couples who are suspected are dying in each other's embrace in common graves, riddled with bullets. The least suspicion leads to liquidation'.[10] On a more personal note, a letter from Bobonaro in March described how

> a pupil of the mission school who attended the SMP [Indonesian lower middle school] lost his father and two uncles. All these were murdered by the military. Then, this schoolboy, whose name is Pedro, being full of anguish and sorrow, went to complain to the red berets. Their response was to tie a rope round his neck and hang him on a tree. This is how the young Pedro, pupil of the SMP at Bobonaro, died for having wept for the death of his father.[11]

Such actions by Indonesian troops evinced an increasing frustration with yet another seemingly floundering operation. The Indonesian daily *Merdeka* went as far as it possibly could under military censorship: 'Although General Murdani did not provide a detailed account of the security situation in East Timor in his speech [Christmas Day 1983] the impression could be gained that the armed gangs have yet to be crushed'.[12] An American military attaché, cited in a Canadian paper, put it rather more directly, after a visit in early 1984:

> It's a running sore. They have tried the hearts and minds approach and it didn't wash. Now they have gone back to the big-stick policy and it doesn't seem to be working much better. This thing is going to go on and on until we all get old.

In the same article, the ageing architect of *Operasi Komodo*, Ali Murtopo, was openly pessimistic, concluding that most regular soldiers were incapable of dealing with Fretilin, and that 'our army is shooting at shadows'. It was to be his final comment, before his death in 1984, on the East Timor situation which he had done so much to create.[13]

In February 1984, a new offensive was begun, increasing the number of troops first to 14,000 and then to 20,000, with the ultimate aim of a final obliteration of Fretilin, 'to the fourth generation', as one Indonesian commander put it.[14] A letter written in March told of the country swarming with troops, preparing for 'a grand campaign of extermination'. Unlike its wet-season predecessors this campaign was not confined to the east but extended into the central and northwestern regions to cover villages which had supported earlier Fretilin attacks. As in previous operations like *Keamanan* the population was recruited into fence of legs groups. All males between the ages of 15 and 50 were involved in the central, northwestern and eastern sectors. A priest wrote that:

> During the months of March, April and May in various regions (Baucau Laga, Quelicai, Fatumaca, Venilale, Ossu, Viqueque, Bobonaro, Ainaro and Same), the men and youths were forced to go with the Indonesian military to the mountains to search for the armed resistance. The military only gave a little bit of corn to these people. The operations lasted from one week to fifteen days. They came back full of hunger, tired and sick. The result of the military operation was zero.[16]

Faced with the possibility of such recruitment and the restrictions on travelling to grow or collect food, many Timorese appear to have broken out of their resettlement villages while Indonesian troops were away on their search missions. A 'movement to the hills', similar to that of 1976–7, appears to have occurred after March.[17] A new feature, introduced in this campaign, was referred to by refugees as 'popular judgements': 'In Lospalos and Iliomar [as they reported] 'those implicated in contacts with people in the bush were murdered in front of the assembled people — with knives, swords and sticks'.[18]

And so it continued throughout 1984–5 — a 'generalized warfare' of encirclements, bombing, uprooting of the population, malnutrition and generalized brutalities:

> During the month of May about one hundred people from Alas, mostly men and youths, were imprisoned and taken to Same. They were terribly tortured in an effort to confess that they had contacts with Fretilin. A witness affirmed that he heard the piercing screams of the victims and that he could not sleep.[19]

'Pray for these people', wrote a priest, 'nothing has changed for the better. We feel that everything is worse than in 1975–7'.[20]

Fighting spread to the southern sector, with naval bombardments and four to eight jet raids daily. Less confident than he had been the previous Christmas, Murdani confided that 'The East Timor conflict will take some time to resolve'.[21] The cost of such an attempt was illustrated in a statement by the Catholic Church in early 1985, reiterating that at least 200,000 people had died in the nine years since the December 1975 invasion.[22]

The role of the church and the growing opposition to Indonesian rule

Charting the course of the fighting in East Timor during the post-ceasefire campaign had been easier than in previous operations because of the wealth of material sent out, not only from letters, refugee accounts and the independence movement which briefly re-established a radio link with northern Australia during 1985, but also by material from church sources. This reflected an increasing opposition to the Indonesian presence, not only from parish priests but also from the more highly placed prelates. It thus seemed that the church was beginning to play a qualitatively new role, one of opposing a colonial power controlling East Timor.

The post-Pacific War developments narrowing the gap between colonial (urban) and rural élites had largely passed the Catholic Church by. The division between the parish priests working in the villages and the hierarchy in Dili remained marked. Furthermore, with some exceptions, priests located in regional centres often remained aloof from the population and disdainful of 'traditional' Timorese society. Church was identified clearly with state in East Timor, particularly during the Salazar period (1933–71), when the missions were charged with implementing government policies. In 1940, for example following the signing of the *Concordat* with the Vatican, Catholic missions became the official agency for the education of 'indigenous peoples'. Institutionally, the church was viewed by Timorese as the place where they went to become 'civilized', necessarily since one had to be educated, yet also reluctantly since education entailed a gradual loss of traditional culture through the acquisition of Portuguese mores. Although each town or village had its church, priest and Catholic rituals, generally these remained distinct from local culture. As late as 1975 no more than one-third of East Timor's population had been baptized, and of these a preponderant number were from *suco* chief and *liurai* families, consolidating their status by acquiring a Portuguese education. Certainly, in the years leading up to the Indonesian invasion, church leaders, particularly the bishop and his Portuguese and Goan priests, distanced themselves from the independence movement, even though several members of Fretilin had been training for the Catholic priesthood in the Jesuit seminary at Dare, near Dili. 'Dialogue is alright at the European level of culture but not here where the people are not as sophisticated', claimed the Bishop of East Timor, Dom José Joaquim Ribeiro, in March 1975, referring to the growth of the independence movement.[23] In a subsequent sermon, he cautioned against adopting Angolan practices, such as the clenched-fist salute in greeting: 'Far better to wave and say hello',[24] he advised. An earlier pastoral letter had reminded Timorese that the church forbade Catholics to vote for either socialists or communists.[25]

In the years following the invasion, and particularly after the 1978-9 campaign of encirclement and annihilation, this began to change. Many priests had retreated into the interior with their villagers during 1976, and had lived subsequently in Fretilin areas. Those who were captured and deported to Lisbon spoke enthusiastically of Fretilin's organization and popularity, at the same time as condemning Indonesian brutalities. Refugee reports also described how priests were supporting and defending the local population. The most crucial change occurred when Ribeiro, totally distraught by the killings in Dili, requested retirement in 1977. He was replaced in May by his assistant, Martinho da Costa Lopes, formerly a member of the National Assembly in Lisbon. Unlike the Portuguese-born Ribeiro, Costa Lopes was a Timorese with an excellent knowledge both of the parishes and their priests, amongst whom he was widely respected. Receiving reports from the countryside regularly in the post-invasion years, he was able to build up a detailed picture of the course of the war. News from his priests confirmed his worst fears from his experiences in Dili.

Initially he tried dialogue, culminating in discussions with Jusuf, Dading and Murtopo in Baucau in the early months of *Operasi Keamanan*. Since this proved fruitless, he turned to more public statements, allowing letters to friends in Australia to be published. Decisive here was his communication to the head of the Australian Catholic Relief Organization, describing the Lacluta massacre and the famine produced by the 1981-2 fence of legs operations. The Indonesian military retaliated by using 'visitors' reports' to discredit Costa Lopes, most notable of which was that by former Australian Prime Minister Gough Whitlam who, in May 1982, denounced him for failing to divulge his sources. Despite these efforts, the protests of Costa Lopes and other priests became increasingly influential, even having some impact on the Catholic Church in Indonesia itself. From 1982 onwards the Indonesian Bishops' Conference began to take up the issue, culminating in a document released in November 1983 which belatedly and hesitantly called for support to combat 'the misery of the masses who are involved in or who are victims of cruel oppression'.[26] This was no great step forward, particularly since the document was not circulated in Indonesia, but it had some impact in Indonesian political circles, and stood in marked contrast to the Protestant Church which regarded the Indonesian occupation as an opportunity for gaining more converts, and stressed the need for army battalions from Protestant areas to develop community programmes funded by the Indonesian Council of Churches, focusing on building links with Indonesian Timor through evangelical motivators.

Although the military achieved a minor success with the early retirement of Costa Lopes in May 1983, under pressure from the Pro Nuncio in Jakarta, Bishop Puente, and his replacement by Carlos Belo, a young Timorese who had just returned after 13 years' study in Portugal and Rome, the opposition of many of the clergy continued, marked by their refusal to attend Belo's inauguration. Despite his youth and inexperience, however, and his willingness to allow Indonesian clergy into East Timor, Belo did not prove to be as sympathetic as the military had wished. Indeed, only five months after his inauguration, in a sermon in Dili cathedral, he protested vehemently against the 'arrests and violence' characterizing *Operasi Persatuan*. Despite strong protests from the military, Belo visited the Oecusse enclave in January 1984 and dispatched a detailed critique of military oppression during *Operasi Persatuan* to Lisbon in February. Disseminated widely it had some impact on the Portuguese Catholic hierarchy. Speaking of the 'popular judgements' in Lospalos, Belo wrote: 'The Indonesians laugh contentedly, rubbing their hands, saying they are not to blame . . . It is a macabre situation in which we live'.[27]

Belo's account, combined with pressure from the European and American Catholic churches, appeared to produce some results: a Papal tour to Indonesia was cancelled. Greeting the new Indonesian ambassador to the Vatican in July, the Pope expressed the hope that in East Timor 'particular consideration will be given in every circumstance to the ethnic, political and cultural identity of the people', and 'earnestly recommended respect for human rights'.[28] Spurred by these statements, the Council of Priests in Dili, representing the East Timorese clergy, produced its most trenchant criticism yet of the Indonesian occupation. In an official statement released by the Council on New Year's Day 1985, the following conclusion was presented:

> Having experienced with the people all the events which, since 1975, have deeply affected the social and political life of this same people, the Church bears anxious witness to facts that are slowly leading to the ethnic, cultural and religious extinction of the people of East Timor.[29]

During the next few months the church kept up the momentum. In March, Belo dispatched from Dili a list of people killed in the Kraras massacre of August 1983. He also published a pastoral letter criticizing the methods used in Indonesia's birth-control programmes, implying that many East Timorese were being forcibly sterilized.

In response, the Indonesian military went onto the offensive. Belo was placed under constant surveillance.

> The Bishop of Dili is being intimidated [wrote a Dili resident]. He is under surveillance day and night . . . Everyone in Dili knows it, that is why the people are afraid to visit the bishop or to go and confide in him. Doors and windows are monitored and so are conversations. And if a visitor should visit him, a sophisticated listening device is employed.[30]

Priests subsequently were beaten, churches entered and their congregations arrested. Belo responded by withdrawing his priests from the regular *Pancasila* indoctrination sessions organized by the military.

As the conflict between church and the military intensified, the Indonesian

Catholic hierarchy gradually retreated from its earlier tentatively supportive position, and distanced itself from Belo's statements, thus restricting the effectiveness of his actions. Most significantly, it began to agree to the military's continual requests for the removal from East Timor of Portuguese priests who were critical of the Indonesian occupation. By 1987, the Vatican's diplomatic representative in Jakarta went so far as to claim that, 'compared with the past, of course, the human rights situation is better', and that the only reason for not integrating the East Timorese diocese into the Indonesian Bishop's Conference was a legal one, in that it would pre-empt the eventual international settlement of the issue.[31] At the same time, Frans Seda, a leading Indonesian Catholic politican and a member of the Vatican's Pontifical Commission for Justice and Peace, called for the church to recognize officially the integration of the East Timorese into the Indonesian Catholic church.

The Indonesian church's shift in position began to have an impact at a higher level. In April 1986 the Vatican requested Belo to hold a secret meeting with Xanana Gusmao, proposing that Fretilin leaders should surrender in exchange for a safe conduct out of East Timor. They duly met, with Xanana replying that it was not simply a matter of personal interest or choice. 'Are they going to remove all the Timorese from Timor?' he asked.[32]

At the end of 1987, the Pope greeted yet another incoming Indonesian ambassador to the Vatican, as he had done in 1984. He again called for 'particular consideration' to be given to East Timor, but this time it was only for its people's ethnic, religious and cultural character'. Gone was any reference to the country's 'political identity'.[33] It was a significant change, indicating that East Timor could no longer rely on a sympathetic hearing from the external Catholic hierarchy to criticisms of the Indonesian occupation. This was illustrated most clearly in the Vatican's response to a letter sent by Bishop Belo to the UN secretary-general and the Portuguese president, in February 1989, in which he described continuing human rights abuses and called for a referendum: 'Indonesia says that the people of East Timor have already chosen integration, but the people of East Timor themselves have never said this'.[34]

In March the Vatican announced that the Pope would visit Indonesia, including East Timor, in October. A Portuguese newspaper commented that his visit 'goes against all the rules of diplomacy; the Pope would enter the territory under the auspices of the occupying power, whilst for the Vatican and the UN, Portugal continues to be the legitimate administering power'.[35] The Indonesian military was delighted. The armed forces newspaper, *Angkaten Bersenjata* concluded that 'the visit is very positive for Indonesia because it promotes international recognition of East Timor.'[36] The clergy of East Timor were rather less enthusiastic, writing to the Pope to protest against his proposed visit which, in their view, 'would constitute a formal act of recognition', and against the holding of an open air mass in *Bahasa Indonesia* at Taci-Tolu, near Dili, which had been a site for the massacre of thousands of East Timorese after 1975.[37] Urging the clergy and laity to welcome the Pope, Belo wrote in a pastoral letter: 'The Pope does not come to defend integration, nor does he come to defend independence, nor to indicate political solutions to the problem of East Timor . . . An attitude of authentic faith behoves us to accept the Pope, whether or not he is to our taste'.[38]

In response to these criticisms, the Vatican envoy preparing the Pope's visit, Father Tucci, concluded that the mass could be held in Latin, and perhaps in Tetum, and arranged for a short meeting between a group of East Timorese priests and the Pope during his visit, the latter being scheduled by Tucci for three hours. He cautioned the East Timorese clergy to limit their demands: 'We are not going to sacrifice all Christendom on account of 400,000 Catholics', he said.[39]

In the months leading up to the Pope's visit, some 1500 people were detained and levels of intimidation intensified.[40] The Indonesian military headquarters in Ermera threatened that: 'If the people of Ermera should do anything, or in any way come out in favour of, or publicly support, Bishop Carlos Belo, all the churches and objects of worship in the area will be destroyed'.[41] Just before the Pope's arrival Belo claimed that, because of the impact of his February 1989 letter, the military 'are threatening me physically and psychologically. They send me anonymous letters. They want to kill me'.[42]

On 12 October the Pope consecrated the cathedral in Dili and celebrated mass to 100,000 people at Taci-Tolu. Many others were prevented from attending because they were held at military check-points set up at 20km intervals on all the roads leading to Taci-Tolu. During the mass, the Pope spoke from a platform fashioned to represent *Pancasila* values, beneath a gigantic portrait of himself and President Suharto. Acknowledging the brutality of Indonesia's occupation, he nevertheless hoped that 'those who have responsibility for life in East Timor will act with wisdom and goodwill towards all'.[43] As he ended the mass with '*Ite missa est*', dozens of people started shouting independence slogans in Tetum and Portuguese, and called out, 'Long Live the Pope'. The site of the mass then became a battlefield, with demonstrators beaten and journalists having their cameras snatched and films exposed.[44] Forty demonstrators were arrested and beaten into making confessions claiming that the event had been organized by priests and students. A letter written by the leader of the Salesian priests in East Timor, and by the directors of the Fatumaca Technical College claimed later that:

> the boys who were arrested told us that they were invited to raise banners like those of the demonstrators, while a photo-camera waited to catch them in front of a background of a video-screen with the scenes of the demonstrators at Taci-Tolu.[45]

In the following weeks, intimidation continued. On 4 November, a group of around 20 people were arrested outside Bishop Belo's house, after gathering there following rumours that the army was planning to enter his residence. At the end of the month, this finally happened, with the security forces removing students who had taken refuge after being shot at by the army in their college.

Following his visit to Dili, the Pope 'had not been disturbed by the protests', according to a Vatican spokesman.[46] He subsequently made no comment, apart from a telegram sent to Belo expressing his gratitude for the way in which he had been received by the Catholics of East Timor.[47] The closest the Pope ever came to making any criticism of the Indonesian occupation came in the most general of references on the first day of his trip, in Jakarta, when he stated that: 'At times, nations are tempted to disregard fundamental human rights in a misguided search for political unity based on military and economic power alone. But such unity can easily be dissolved'.[48]

Despite Vatican *realpolitik* and the attempt by the Indonesian Catholic Church to avoid the issue, the church in East Timor has become a major focus for opposition to the Indonesian occupation during the 1980s. Through their repeated documentation of human rights abuses, calls for a referendum, and the protection they have given to critics of the occupation, East Timorese clergy have played a crucial role in defending people's rights and publicizing the plight of East Timor internationally. 'The church, the priests and the religious are the three factors which threaten East Timor's integration with Indonesia', claimed Suharto's son-in-law, Major Prabowo, adding that 'the people must turn against them'.[49]

The importance of the changing attitude of the church in the late 1970s and 1980s should not be underestimated. Its opposition to the forcible Indonesian annexation marked the culmination of a process of growing institutional rejection. Almost all social groups, economic classes and political élites from pre-invasion East Timorese society now defined themselves primarily through their alienation from the military project. The differentiated social structure of the pre-invasion period, with its divisions between colonial, rural and nationalist groups, reflecting religious, cultural, educational and economic cleavages, converged ideologically and politically as a result of the military occupation. Furthermore, just as the opposition united previously disparate groups, so too did it include a growing number of students and young people, the so-called second generation, which the Indonesians had hoped to 'resocialize'. Consequently, there were increasingly fewer social groups and institutions on which the military could rely to achieve its objectives.

This explains why the military had to introduce such drastic changes as re-education, resettlement and restructuring of the agricultural mode of production. A total resocialization was required in order to construct a new social and economic framework for its military rule. Forced through after the encirclement and annihilation campaigns of the late 1970s this process had only been partially successful by the onset of *Operasi Persuatan* in mid-1983, but was intensified in the years that followed, aiming for a total change in the social structure, eradicating all traces of indigenous society and culture.

The ultimate transformation: Indonesian strategies for birth control

Resettlement has profoundly affected the East Timorese way of life. Villages have been relocated and divided, agriculture undermined and movement curtailed. Following *Operasi Persuatan*, resettlement areas (*daerah pemukiman*) have been superseded by what are termed '*desa binaan pangkal perlawanan*' ('guided villages as bases for resistance'). A 'gigantic project' was announced by the military in July 1984, to establish 200 such villages, 'to reinforce stability and security, and facilitate all aspects of development activity', according to the secretary-general of the Department of the Interior.[50] Four months later this figure of 200 was extended to 400, to be located 'in areas which can be easily supervized and patrolled'.[51]

Existing settlements were fortified, with groups placed in specific areas within the perimeter and new villages created with populations moved from resettlement areas. The new villages were located in 'safer' areas, away from Fretilin zones, and their links with military plans for economic development were strengthened by each village specializing in a particular type of export crop. According to the Department of Agriculture, the aim was to change the agricultural sector into a neatly organized 'cottage garden', with large plots growing export crops.[52] Resettlement was thus made permanent, an integral part of East Timor's new colonial development.

Since Indonesian colonialism had also eliminated most of the relatively small pre-existing professional group of administrators, it needed to create a basis for its political control by building up a new administrative élite. As one might expect, most administrators had been recruited from the civil service in Java. Attracted by higher salaries, with hardship bonuses of anything up to 99 per cent, they were rewarded with more rapid promotions after their Dili postings. All the major programmes in East Timor are run by regional offices headed by Indonesians responsible directly to their relevant departments in Jakarta. With the exception of Governor Carrascalao, most Timorese are located in the lower echelons. According to the governor, many of them are salaried although they do no specific job and are there primarily for propaganda purposes.[53] As a Javanese administrator put it: 'These people are so simple that they have to be taught even the most basic procedures of administration'; another immigrant spoke even more plainly: 'you have to overcome their hill-tribe mentality before you can get any use out of them'.[54]

Beyond these additional restructuring measures, however, the most insidious form of control was yet to come. In the aftermath of the invasion and particularly after the campaigns of encirclement and annihilation, refugees described incidents of women being sterilized without their knowledge and the widespread use of contraceptive drugs, such as *Depo Provera*. The sterilization occurred during surgical operations, such as caesarian sections, in provincial-centre hospitals. These practices were institutionalized in a 'Family Planning Programme' introduced in 1980, aiming to control population growth by disseminating advice on contraception via provincial and local clinics. This provoked widespread opposition, stemming largely from the intense pressure placed on women to participate in the programme, the fact that the population had already been devastated and, last but not least, the tremendous love which Timorese have for children. As one commentator remarked: 'To understand the present brutality, one must understand the past gentleness, the rhythms, the magic place of Timor-Leste, where children are valuable people'.[55]

The work of Indonesian 'dynamizers', moving from one centre to another, encouraging sterilization and contraception, thus achieved little success in the post-1980 period. Consequently, the programme was extended dramatically in 1985. In April of that year a large two-storey family planning centre was built in Dili, financed to 95 per cent of its cost by the World Bank. A further 67 local centres were planned in addition to the 183 already in existence. The aim was simple: 'to prevent an increase in the population of the province'. Governor Carrascalao's speech-writer spelt this out on the occasion of the opening of the Dili centre. He concluded that there was an 'imbalance' between numbers of children requiring education and provision of schooling, between labour supply and jobs available, between health facilities and housing and the numbers needing them. Thus, the quality of life could only be improved by limiting population size.[56]

Such statements should be read together with military pronouncements on transmigration. In addition to the overall plan to move families from Java to Indonesia's Outer Islands, including East Timor, in recent years birth control has been imposed by the military on people living in areas designated for transmigration. The link between the two was emphasized by the military governor of South Kalimantan, who stated that since transmigration was to occur, 'there is therefore no alternative — it (South Kalimantan) must reduce its rate of population growth'.[57] The World Bank agreed:

> There is no inherent contradiction between the government's population and transmigration programme. We believe that family planning and health projects are a suitable form of assistance in the area (East Timor), as they are capable of providing important economic and social benefits to all concerned.[58]

Refugees gave rather different accounts: 'Timorese women don't accept it . . . they defend their right to give birth to children to compensate for the many people who have died since the invasion'.[59] A letter from East Timor described how:

> officials of the state family planning programme are present in every little village and hamlet to make people limit their number of children, and each family is only allowed to have three children. In the interior the military force our women to receive injections, and pills are being distributed to them for the same effect. All the women are forced to take part in this. It is one way the enemy has to make our ethnic identity disappear.[60]

Thus transmigration and birth control appeared to go hand-in-hand, inextricably linked in the military plan. Timorese women have lost the right to control their own bodies, to choose freely whether or not they wish to give birth. Whilst the Timorese population is reduced, the Indonesian population is increased through job creation and transmigration. The logic is inescapable;

whether it be in areas such as agriculture, health or education, the argument remains the same: the excess of need over supply is met by reducing the need, which is itself reduced by limiting those who create that need, namely the East Timorese people. The problem of 'Timur–Timur' as the military choose to call it, can thus be resolved by dealing with its root cause, the Timorese themselves and their wish to live and exist as Timorese. 'The success or failure of this programme', claimed an Indonesian newspaper, 'will determine the success or otherwise of efforts to create social prosperity.'[61]

According to the head of the Dili centre, almost 32 per cent of women involved in the birth control programme were being injected with *Depo Provera* in 1985. From what we know from refugee accounts, it is likely that many of this 32 per cent had inadequate knowledge of what was being done to them, and that many agreed to the treatment only under considerable pressure. As one of Indonesia's leading feminist writers put it:

> In pursuit of political and economic objectives, the status of women has been so degraded that they are treated like cattle who can be told when to produce children and 'castrated' when they are no longer required to do so.[62]

In recognition of his government's support for population control, President Suharto received the UN Fund for Population Activities Prize in 1989. Presenting him with a medallion and a cheque for US$12,500, UN Secretary-General Perez de Cuellar praised Suharto's strong support for 'family planning'.

Military stalemate

Alongside the attempts to resocialize East Timorese society, the war continued. The aim of Operation Unity had been to close off the country east of a line from Baucau to Viqueque and divide this zone into smaller areas which could then be surrounded. These operations were intensive: of the 20 battalions present in the 18 months after the 1983 Kraras massacre, no less than 15 were located in the east. All attacks were accompanied by heavy aerial and naval bombardment yet no significant successes were achieved by the military, and by the end of 1984 they pulled back their troops, withdrawing them to the towns, resettlement villages and major routes.

From this time onward, the war settled into a pattern similar to that of 1977, before 'encirclement and annihilation'. The military held on to their strategic locations, whilst Fretilin troops organized base areas and mobile units in areas away from routes and resettlements. The base units, located in the central, border and eastern sectors, each contained about 50 families, and provided support for the mobile companies and detachments which linked up with networks inside villages. The detachments, which were unarmed, were involved mostly in reconnaissance and co-ordinating with the population in the resettlement villages. The mobile companies ambushed Indonesian troops, attacking supply lines and bases. Their aim was to capture weapons and disrupt military operations with minimal losses. In the population units, according to a member of Fretilin captured by the army, 'Fretilin were still highly disciplined, lived in semi-permanent forest settlements complete with schools and were well-armed with weapons captured from Indonesian soldiers'.[63]

The Indonesians continued to organize local fence of legs operations, particularly during two intensive campaigns, from June 1986 to May 1987 (codenamed *Operasi Kikis*) and during the summer and autumn of 1987, under a new commander, Colonel Soenarto. In both these campaigns the focus was on the eastern sector, with the over-riding objective of capturing Xanana Gusmao and leading Fretilin commanders.

In the late 1980s, and particularly after President Suharto's visit to Dili in October 1988, Indonesian strategy underwent a major change, to what was described by one refugee as a 'fortress system' (*benteng stelsel*) strategy.[64] In this, the army set up military posts and sealed off large tracts of land in areas where Fretilin forces were thought to be located. Troops then recruited men from the local population and organized them into groups to search for Fretilin guerrillas. The aim was either to capture them or keep them constantly on the move. When they were spotted, aircraft and helicopters were called in to wipe them out. At the same time, the army also stepped up its counter-insurgency operations in the towns, locating and breaking up clandestine organizations.

During the period before the Pope's visit in October 1989, Indonesian military campaigns were increased dramatically, with an estimated 32 battalions, or 21,000 troops, operating between May and August. Many of these units were highly mobile, constantly at the ready to be dispatched to the latest reported sighting of Fretilin forces. A visitor to Dili in May 1989 related how, on the Sunday when he arrived, the town looked calm. On Monday, however, it was transformed with army helicopters bringing in reinforcements and truckloads of troops speeding out of the city. According to a bystander, the troops were bound for Maubisse, 'where some people are not too happy about things'.[65]

Journalists who have been allowed to visit the territory since 1985, and have asked about troop deployments, have found that the level of fighting is greater than the military is prepared to admit. When a group of foreign correspondents visited in July 1985, their trip to Baucau was cancelled 'because of recent incidents in the area between Fretilin and the army'.[66] Despite a rebuke from Carrascalao they visited the cemetery in Dili where they discovered 22 soldiers dead in March in that area alone. As one correspondent concluded: 'the casualties seem high for a conflict as dormant as the East Timorese civil war is said to be'.[67] Visiting Dili around the same time, a Catholic relief worker was told that one soldier was buried daily.[68]

Maps captured and produced by the independence movement in July 1985 gave a clearer picture of areas of control. They indicated that Indonesian troops were concentrated in Dili and along a line from Baucau to Viqueque. Everywhere east of this line was dotted with tank and artillery units.

Furthermore, most of the regular Indonesian units tended to have fairly high-ranking field commanders, particularly in the more isolated areas. Other areas of concentration were in the south, from the west of the Baucau–Viqueque line to Ainaro and Same. By contrast, the border areas (west of a line from Dili to Suai) and the regions south and southeast of Dili seemed to be pacified, with little or no Fretilin presence. On the basis of this information, taken together with subsequent journalists' and refugee reports, it would seem that in the late 1980s we had a situation in which, across about one-third of the territory, mostly in the east and southeast, an average of 10–12,000 Indonesian troops faced 1200–1500 Fretilin troops in a pattern of foray and ambush, with occasional but decreasing numbers of direct confrontations.

In contrast to the situation on the ground, the picture accepted by most foreign governments was one which stressed stability and evidence of a return to 'normality'. They tended to focus selectively on incidents which could substantiate the Indonesian perspective. Such were the trials of political prisoners begun during 1984 in Dili. The military claimed that their occurrence proved that the emerging political system was *en route* to both stability and democracy. By the end of the year, 195 prisoners had been tried in Dili's District Court, most of them under Articles 106, 108 and 110 of the Indonesian Criminal Code. This involved both them and the much smaller numbers who have been tried in subsequent years being accused of offences such as 'being involved in armed rebellion' or 'conspiring to bring about the secession of a part of state territory'. Sentences have varied from 2 to 17 years. Whilst much has been made of these prisoners being tried after as many as ten years' detention, little has been said of the conditions under which they have been tried. These were highlighted in the Indonesian daily, *Sinar Harapan*. A representative of the Third Parliamentary Commission of the Indonesian Parliament, which deals with issues of law and justice, was told by the head of the Dili District Court that:

> If all trials could be like those in East Timor, the task of the legal profession would be easy. Those who came before the green baize [those who are tried] are all honest. When they are asked if the accusation of the prosecutor is correct, they always say yes.[69]

No one denied the charges against them because, supposedly, all the evidence was complete, and most of the accused 'had been caught in the act', anyway. Furthermore, all defendants had been represented by a government-appointed defence team. One defendant tried to claim that the court was not competent to try him, since it was an Indonesian court. 'When he persisted in this, he was reportedly threatened with death, and desisted'.[70] Like many others, he was imprisoned subsequently in Cipinang and Tangerang prisons, some 2500 km away in the alien society of Java. One-fifth of those imprisoned suffered this fate, the remainder being re-imprisoned in Dili or a regional prison. Little justice was apparent in this system. After three years of such 'trials', in 1988 Amnesty International concluded that many of the prisoners appear to have been tried on the basis of false or coerced testimony after long periods of incommunicado detention during which some were reportedly told that signing a 'confession' and being brought before a court would enable them to receive visits from their families. Many apparently did not understand that they had the right to appeal against their sentences, and in some cases were told that if they did not accept their sentence without appeal, it would be increased.[71]

Such procedures did not prevent an Indonesian defence lawyer commenting: 'It adds up to months and months that we spend in Dili on these hearings, and all at state expense. What more proof could you ask of the government's seriousness about wanting to provide these defendants with a fair trial?'[72]

The validity of such proof is hardly borne out in many cases. One documented case is that of Aleixo Guterres, sentenced in 1986 to seven years imprisonment for 'collaborating' with Fretilin. Interviewed by a British parliamentary delegation in March 1989 he described how, like other prisoners, his testimony had been extracted under duress and how he was unable to choose his own lawyer.[73] Further details of the trial process have been provided in other refugee accounts:

> Before being brought to court we were all interrogated, this time by the police, though everything had been fixed beforehand by the military. During these interrogations they tried to force us to make false statements which would then be used for a trial. These interrogations went on for three to four months. They had something written down which we were asked to sign. We were asked whether we wanted to be brought to trial. They kept saying that if we refused to go on trial we would never be released . . . They asked us over and over again, with the result that many agreed in the end to be tried. Before this we weren't allowed any family visits. After this our families were allowed to come to the prison to bring food, but they were not allowed to meet us . . . Some of the prioners who agreed to sign false statements were illiterate people who knew nothing about politics. They had no idea what it meant to be tried, and they were people who never had any contact with Fretilin. The Indonesians used their ignorance to stage the trials.[74]

Playing down the continuing war, much of the international press focused on the trials as evidence of an improving process of normalization. Following a 24-hour visit in the company of Australia's Northern Territory Minister, a journalist concluded that: 'The agony of East Timor following its incorporation by Indonesia could be approaching an end as human rights and living standards improve'.[75] Leading politicians were similarly optimistic. According to former US Secretary of State, George Shultz, during President Reagan's meeting with Suharto in May 1986 human rights issues, including the question of torture and murder in East Timor, were discussed: 'There has been a considerable amount of progress over the years', Shultz said.[76] The

Australian Government, meanwhile, used the atmosphere of a more favourable climate to achieve its major objective, an agreement in principle with the Indonesian military on exploration on the vast oil resources in the Timor Gap. In March 1988, a zone of co-operation was agreed for the area.

Just as they had focused on the trials, so too did foreign governments stress the release of prisoners during the late 1980s. During 1987–8 some 150 detainees were released from Dili's prisons. However, these were prisoners with relatively light sentences averaging two years, most of which had been completed; no information was provided on prisoners detained in areas outside Dili. At the same time, people were constantly being arrested and re-arrested. Refugees have recently provided the names of 200 people arrested in the period around President Suharto's visit to Dili in November 1988, although the actual number was probably far greater.[77] These arrests were then followed by another wave of detentions before, during and after the Pope's visit in 1989.

Meanwhile, it had been reported that the Chinese population of 20,000 in 1974 had been reduced to 'a few thousand' by July 1985, and that there were no less than 21,833 orphans and 11,231 homeless children in areas under Indonesian control. A relief worker on a visit to the eastern sector in 1986 was informed by a dispenser in Fatumaca that, since 1980, the mortality rate for children under five had been between 50–60 per cent, with most deaths occurring after the first year of life, mainly from malnutrition. In 1988, it was reported in the Indonesian press that 38,000 children under five were suffering from malnutrition in the Dili region.[78] 'We Indonesian soldiers do not need Timorese', stated the commander of the Dili military garrison. 'We deal with the Timorese as we deal with pigs — we slaughter them whenever possible.'[79]

Notes

1. 'Christmas in East Timor: Commander in Chief Again Appeals, Those Who Report Will Be Well-Treated', *Sinar Harapan*, 27 December 1983.

2. 'Indonesian Soldiers Burning Villages', *Canberra Times*, 2 November 1983. The information on Atauro and Bali is contained in letters to refugees cited in *Canberra Times*, 28 January 1984. The report of the Dare seminarians is contained in *Asian Bureau Australia*, May 1984.

3. Reports from different sources estimate the number of defections varying from 130 (*Australian*, 6 January 1984) to 500 (*Canberra Times*, 19 November 1983).

4. ICRC, *East Timor Situation Report No. 10*, Geneva, September 1983.

5. The text of this statement is contained in *East Timor Report*, No. 5, ACFOA, Canberra, November 1983; the quote is from the *Australian*, 6 September 1984.

6. 'Affrontements, Meurtriers à Timor-Est', *Agence France Presse*, Jakarta, 19 February 1984.

7. The most extensive reproduction of this communiqué is contained in the *Canberra Times*, 17 April 1984.

8. 'Timorese Face Starvation as Military Operations Disrupt Food Production', *Australian*, 6 January 1984.

9. Letter from Carlos Filipe Ximenes Belo, Apostolic Administrator, to Mgr Costa Lopes, dated Dili, 16 February, translated from the original Portuguese. In Mgr Lopes' possession. Copy available from author.

10. This letter is cited in the *Canberra Times*, 28 January 1984.

11. Letter received in Lisbon, dated March 1984. Correspondent's name withheld. Letter in author's collection.

12. 'Security in East Timor', editorial, *Merdeka*, 29 December 1983 (translated from *Bahasa Indonesia*).

13. 'Shadow Battle Hobbles Army in Indonesia', *Toronto Globe and Mail*, 10 February 1984.

14. *South China Morning Post*. 11 March. The 14,000 figure was that given by the Indonesian military, and the 20,000 figure by refugees arriving in Lisbon at the end of April.

15. 'Bishop Tells of Mass Arrests, Executions', *Canberra Times*, 3 May 1984.

16. Letter from a priest in East Timor, dated 2 July, received in Lisbon in August. Correspondent's name withheld. Letter in author's collection.

17. 'Timor, Leading Toward Generalized Warfare', *Canberra Times*, 29 June 1984.

18. Letter from the Bishop of Dili, Mgr Carlos Belo to Mgr Costa Lopes, dated 18 February 1984. Letter in possession of Mgr Lopes.

19. Letter from a priest in East Timor, dated 2 July, received in Lisbon in August. Correspondent's name withheld. Letter in author's collection.

20. Ibid.

21. *Reuters* (Jakarta), 17 December 1984.

22. 'The Harassment of the Church in East Timor', *Catholic Leader* (Brisbane), 5 August 1984.

23. Bishop Ribeiro, in an interview with an Australian Parliamentary Delegation visiting East Timor in March 1975 cited in Jolliffe, 1978, pp. 93–4.

24. This statement was reported to me by several refugees interviewed in Lisbon in June 1982. It occurred in May 1975, although the exact date is not known.

25. Bishop de Dili e o Sell Concelho Diocesano de Presbiteros, *Perante una Nova Situacao: Costa Pastoral*, Dili, 25 January 1975.

26. Majelis Agung Waligereja Indonesia, 'Letter from the Bishops' Conference of Indonesia to the Apostolic Administrator of the Diocese of Dili, Mgr Carlos Filipe Belo, and to the Priests, Brothers and Sisters of the Diocese of Dili, Jakarta, 17 November 1983.

27. Letter from Carlos Belo to Costa Lopes, dated 18 February 1984 (translation). Letter in possession of Mgr Lopes.

28. *Le Monde*, 3 May 1984.

29. *Statement of the Apostolic Administrator and the Presbyterian Council of the Dili Diocese*, 1 January 1985, p. 2.

30. *Em Timor Leste Paz e Possivel*, Lisbon, January 1986 (translated from Portuguese) (the letter was dated June 1986).

31. *Indonesian News Service* (Maryland, USA), No. 37, 7 October 1987.

32. *East Timor News* (Lisbon), Subject Memo No. 8/88, 8 August 1988.

33. The Pope's 14 December 1987 statement is printed in full in 'Church News', *Timor Link* (London), Nos. 12/13, April 1988.

34. *East Timor News* (Lisbon), Subject Memo No. 1/89, 5 May 1989.

35. *O Jornal* (Lisbon), 7 April 1989 (translated from Portuguese).

36. *Angkatan Bersenjata* (Jakarta), cited in *Tapol Bulletin* (London), No. 93, June 1989.

37. Letter printed in ibid.

38. Belo's pastoral letter is published in full in *East Timor News* (Lisbon), Subject Memo No. 1/89, 5 May 1989.

39. Quoted in documents received in Lisbon from Dili and Jakarta, cited in *East Timor News* (Lisbon), Monthly Memo 5/89, 21 June 1989.

40. See *East Timor News* (Lisbon), Monthly Memo No. 28, 7 December 1989, for details.

41. Document from East Timor, 15 July 1989, published in *East Timor News* (Lisbon), Monthly Memo No. 28, 7 December 1989.

42. Telephone interview with Bishop Belo, published in *Independente* (Lisbon), 9 October 1989.

43. The text of the Pope's speech is printed in *Timor Link* (London), Nos. 20/21, February 1990.

44. This description is compiled from reports appearing in *El Pais* (Madrid) and *La Stampa* (Italy), 13 October 1989.

45. This letter is printed in *Timor Link* (London), Nos. 20/21 February 1990.

46. The quote comes from an article on the Pope's visit in *Tapol Bulletin* (London), No. 96, p. 14.

47. Reprinted in *Sabado* (Lisbon), 23 December 1989.

48. See *Timor Link* (London), February 1990, Nos. 20/21.

49. Quote given in *Le Paix est Possible au Timor Oriental*, No. 38, August 1989, Lisbon (no author cited).

50. Statement by the Secretary-General of the Department of the Interior, *Topik* (Jakarta), 18 July 1984.

51. *Sinar Harapan* (Jakarta), editorial, 28 November 1984.

52. See 'Indonesian Colonialism in East Timor', *Tapol Bulletin* (London), No. 72, November 1985, p. 11.

53. See *Asiaweek*, 2 August 1985; also Lincoln Kaye, 'East Timor Depends on Jakarta's Largesse', *Far Eastern Economic Review*, 8 August 1985.

54. Kaye, ibid., p. 20.

55. Jill Jolliffe, 'Scenes from East Timor', *Alternative News Service*, Melbourne, Australia, May 1976.

56. See 'East Timor Governor: Birth Control Programme Still Faces Delays', *Berita Yudha*, 26 August 1985 (translated from *Bahasa Indonesia*).

57. *Sinar Harapan* (Jakarta), 30 August 1985.

58. Letter from the head of the Indonesia Division Country Programme Department, East Asia and Pacific Regional Office, World Bank, to Ms C. Budiardjo, *Tapol Bulletin* (London), 12 September 1985.

59. Interview with East Timorese refugee, Lydia Mota, by Mariet Peeters, of the Women's Group of the Dutch *Komite Indonesia*, August 1984.

60. Personal letter to Mgr Costa Lopes, dated 20/2/86, in Mgr Lopes' possession.

61. 'East Timor Governor: Birth Control Programme Still Faces Delays', *Berita Yudha*, 28 August 1985 (translated from *Bahasa Indoensia*).

62. Fanny Carmilla, in *Sinar Harapan* (Jakarta), 29 June 1985.

63. See Danny Gittings, 'Army Still Strikes Fear in Villages', *South China Morning Post*, 12 August 1989.

64. East Timorese refugee, José Guterres, interviewed in *Ampo*, a Japanese–Asia quarterly journal, published in Tokyo, Vol. 20, No. 3, 1988.

65. Report on a visit to East Timor by Pat Walsh of the Australian Council for Overseas Aid, August 1989 (available from the author at the ACFOA Human Rights Office, 124 Napier St, Fitzroy, Australia 3065).

66. Jacques Guillon, *Agence France Presse*, Report from Dili, 7 July 1985.

67. Lincoln Kaye, 'East Timor Depends on Jakarta's Largesse', *Far Eastern Economic Review*, 8 September 1985.

68. Personal communication to the author. Catholic Relief Worker's name withheld on request.

69. *Sinar Harapan* (Jakarta), 3 September 1985.

70. This case is cited in Amnesty International, 1985.

71. *Unfair Trials and Further Releases of Political Prisoners*, Amnesty International, London, April 1988.

72. Lincoln Kaye, 'Political Prisoners Get Fast Justice in Court', *Far Eastern Economic Review*, 8 September 1985.

73. Amnesty International, 'Statement to the United Nations Decolonization Committee', New York, August 1989, p. 3.

74. Interview with East Timorese refugee, Christiano Costa, Geneva, published in *Tapol Bulletin* (London), No. 86, April 1988.

75. *Niugini Nius* (Papua New Guinea), 'Focus' section, 7 March 1986.

76. Susan Page, 'Friction Marks Reagan–Laurel Meeting in Bali', *Newsday* (USA), 2 May 1986.

77. Amnesty International, 'Statement to the United Nations Decolonization Committee', New York, August 1989.

78. These items are from, in order: Lincoln Kaye, 'East Timor Depends on Jakarta's Largesse', *Far Eastern Economic Review*, 8 September 1985, *Suara Karya* (Jakarta), 27 March 1986 from a personal communication to the author.

79. Quote cited in a paper presented to the *Fourth Christian Consultation on East Timor*, 22–4 January 1990, Lisbon.

12. In Their Best Interests: Strategies for East Timor in the International Community

In addition to their claiming that they have inadequate information, the governments of the industrialized states have always insisted that, whilst they were concerned about the war, there was very little they could do about it. Behind this lay an assumption, at times made explicit, that the country was small and insignificant and that, tragically, the politics of pragmatism in the international arena dictated that principles such as self-determination be relegated to a minor role in the Southeast Asian regional context. As the Australian ambassador to Indonesia put it in a cable to his government just after the invasion:

> On the Timor issue . . . we face one of those broad foreign-policy decisions which face most countries at one time or another. The government is confronted by a choice between a moral stance, based on condemnation of Indonesia for the invasion of East Timor and on the assertion of the inalienable right of the people of East Timor to self-determination on the one hand, and a pragmatic and realistic acceptance of the longer-term inevitabilities of the situation on the other. It is a choice between what might be described as Wilsonian idealism or Kissingerian realism. The former is more proper and principled but the longer-term national interest may well be served by the latter.[1]

It was within such a framework that the governments of the industrialized states supported Indonesian annexation, reluctantly yet necessarily, with the *caveat* that the East Timorese would benefit in the long run when the excesses of the initial invasion years had abated. Behind these arguments, however, lay a rather different reality. For each of the nation-states there were crucial reasons why annexation had to be supported.

Strategy, economics and politics

For the United States the most important aspect was strategic. The Ombai–Wetar straits had to be retained at all costs. With the southward movement of the Soviet fleet enhanced by its ability to obtain bases in Indochina after the defeat of the US in 1975, it was vital that the American navy had maximum undetected mobility for its nuclear submarines between the Indian and Pacific Oceans. This urgency was reinforced by the impending introduction of new Law of the Sea agreements, which although likely to establish Indonesian control over the waters of its archipelago, were quite unlikely to include agreed rights for underwater passage by a foreign power. Their retention would depend, rather, on the good-will of the Indonesian military. Thus, whilst all the general benefits of the prize of Indoensia, as Nixon had so aptly put it, came into play, it was undoubtedly the strategic concern that was uppermost in the American administration's planning in the invasion period. Both the Ford (1974-6) and Carter (1976-80) administrations went out of their way to re-affirm their support for the Indonesian military, in ways which went beyond accepted conventions for dealing with friendly states committing acts of aggression against neighbouring countries. For example, whilst claiming that it had temporarily stopped processing new arms sales to Indonesia in the six months following the invasion, in line with congressional rulings that arms should not be supplied for external aggression, the Ford administration doubled its military aid, from US$83 million in 1975 to US$146 million in 1982.[2] Ninety per cent of the weapons used in the invasion were supplied by American companies. Justifying military aid on the grounds of *de facto* recognition at a very early stage (1976), the United States increased its arms supplies to Indonesia dramatically after the invasion, with peaks coinciding with the offensives in 1978-9 and 1981-2. In the period 1982-4, military sales exceeded US$1,000 million, including weapons particularly useful for the 1983-4 offensive. This pattern continued throughout the 1980s, with the most significant purchase being twelve F-16 fighter aircraft, costing US$337 million in 1986. All these arms sales to the Indonesian military have, of course, contravened the 1958 United States-Indonesian Mutual Defense Agreement which states that, 'Any weapon or other military equipment or service purchased by the Government of Indonesia from the Government of the United States shall be used by the Government of Indonesia solely for legitimate national self-defense'. It is accepted as self-evident that the Government of Indonesia as a member of the United Nations Organization (UN), interprets the term 'legitimate national self-defense' within the scope of the UN Charter as excluding an act of aggression against any other territory.

In a similar manner, successive US administrations have pressed other governments not to let the East Timor issue influence their relations with the Indonesian military, despite East Timor's presumed 'insignificance'. Thus, shortly after his election as prime minister, Malcolm Fraser was cautioned by high-ranking American officials in the Ford administration not to let opposition to the invasion upset his relations with Jakarta.[3] In much the same way, the American delegation at the UN worked hard to lessen the impact of resolutions condemning the Indonesian invasion. A cablegram published in the *New York Times* on 28 January 1976 had the then ambassador to the UN, Daniel Moynihan, applauding the 'considerable progress' made by US strategy at the UN 'toward a basic foreign-policy goal, that of breaking up the massive blocs of nations, mostly new nations, which for so long have been arrayed against us in international forums'. The cablegram dealt specifically with the General Assembly vote on East Timor the previous December. Many other cases of influence followed in the next nine years with the repetition of a common theme. 'No nation has pursued the goal of independence in a more responsible manner than Indonesia', claimed President Reagan, some seven years into the military campaign.[4] Visiting Suharto in April 1986, Reagan praised the Indonesian president for being, 'a most responsible influence in world affairs',[5] whilst Secretary of State Shultz, answering questions on East Timor, concluded that: 'There has been a considerable amount of progress over the years'.[6]

During the last years of the Reagan administration and into the Bush presidency, American officials tried to influence international opinion to consider East Timor as a bilateral issue between Indonesia and Portugal rather than as a case of decolonization: 'East Timor is an issue which should be solved between Portugal and Indonesia, without outside interference', concluded the US Ambassador on a visit to Lisbon in February 1987.[7] During a visit to Dili on 17 January 1990, US Ambassador to Indonesia, John Monjo, was met by demonstrators calling for independence and Indonesian withdrawal. According to eye-witnesses he spent an hour in discussion with the student demonstrators, promising to pass on their views to his government and to the UN. Immediately after his departure from the scene of the demonstration, the students were beaten by Indonesian troops and police, and at least one was killed. Although the ambassador's aides witnessed this attack on a peaceful demonstration, the US embassy subsequently commented that Monjo had had a 'one-hour grievance session' with the demonstrators, and that there had been no arrests prior to the ambassador's departure. No further action was taken by the ambassador or by his government.

Whilst strategic interests dominated American policy, Australian concerns were primarily economic. The objective of jointly exploring one of the most productive oil fields in the world influenced all areas of Australia's East Timor policy. Certainly, there were other factors: trade and investment in the region, the state's increasing political involvement in Southeast Asia in the aftermath of the Indochina war, and its leading politicians' aversion to small states in the western Pacific; but the over-riding concern was to 'close the Timor Gap', to generate energy and revenue for the Australian economy. So essential was this to Australian policy that it was raised in all the discussions on annexation and incorporation which were held with the military government. When, in early January 1978, the Fraser Government gave *de facto* recognition, it began to drill more extensively for oil in the Challis and Jabiru fields adjacent to the Timor Gap in an area claimed by Indonesia. Again, when *de jure* recognition was given later in the year, discussions on the Timor Gap area ensued immediately. When integration was recognized by the Labour Government in April 1985, discussions moved to a new stage — a joint development zone with the Indonesian military. This was pursued further in an agreement establishing a 'zone of co-operation' between the two governments in September 1988. Just over a year later, on 11 December 1989, in a ceremony held on a plane flying over the Timor Gap, Australian and Indonesian foreign ministers Ali Alatas and Gareth Evans signed a treaty formally dividing the area into zones with exploration rights for each country.

Since 1986, the Australian Treasury has received $Aus31 million from sales of permits to oil companies. Foreign Minister Bill Hayden put the position most succinctly, in a speech to the Joint Services Staff College, in April 1984:

> There is as you know a large gap off East Timor in the sea-bed boundary. In that gap are positioned natural gas fields and probably oil fields. We would not be regarded with great public celebration if we were to make a mess of those negotiations, and yet the implication of the negotiations is that as the area open or undefined at this point is off East Timor, a certain recognition must be established to East Timor. For some people in my party who have expressed concern about the pressure of Indonesia on East Timor, this is a cold, hard, sobering reality that must also be addressed in respect of those other interests we must attend to.[8]

It could hardly have been put more bluntly.

As distinct from both the United States and Australia, the interests of the third major power involved in East Timor, (Portugal) were primarily political. The post-Caetano government preferred integration because it provided a relatively quick and easy solution, or so it thought. As in the colonies of Angola, Mozambique and Guinea-Bissau, the essence of the matter lay in its timing. Faced with the enormity of the task of dragging the Portuguese economy into the twentieth century, and threatened constantly by political opposition from left, right and centre, most of the leaders of the Armed Forces Movement (AFM) wanted to shed the colonial burden as rapidly as possible and focus on the twin objectives of modernization and democratization of their home country. For most, the notion of East Timor as 'non-viable' and its subsequent need to be incorporated in a neighbouring state which could oversee its development in a regional context were accepted as the most satisfactory solution to the problem of ditching the distant Southeast Asian colony. If this incorporation could be brought about peacefully and with an aura of legitimacy, so much the better. If not, then force might have to be condoned, however reluctantly.

For the leaders of the Portuguese revolution, independence was never a serious alternative, despite the views of those AFM officers who had served in the colony and were committed to decolonization. Acquiescence characterized their approach at each stage: in their 1974–5 discussions with the Indonesian military in Lisbon, London and Rome; in their rejection of proposals coming from their officers in Dili; in their failure to return and complete the decolonization process after the UDT coup attempt; and in their disregard of the many proposals made by the Fretilin administration in the period between coup attempt and invasion. As governor Lemos Pires, stranded on the island of Atauro with no policy forthcoming from Lisbon, later put it: 'The position of Lisbon was one of almost complete abandonment'.[9] This continued after the invasion. Apart from a formal condemnation at the UN, the main activities of the Lisbon Government in 1976 centred on a meeting held just three weeks before East Timor's Provisional Government adapted its 'petition for integration'. AFM General José Morais da Silva travelled to Jakarta for the first discussions to be held with the Indonesian Government since the invasion. He discussed neither the invasion nor the reports of atrocities, nor even the legality of Indonesia's actions, but rather Portuguese recognition of Indonesia's takeover, the payment of provisions for ex-Portuguese soldiers, the payment of reparations to the Provisional Government and the repatriation of Portuguese citizens. With the July elections in Portugal in mind, da Silva's main objective was to secure the release from Indonesian detention of 23 Portuguese soldiers captured by UDT in August and taken across the border into Indonesian Timor as hostages.

And so it continued, through the late 1970s and into the 1980s — a neglectful Lisbon Government tried to extricate itself from a situation it had helped to create, whilst at the same time arguing that it was ultimately neither responsible nor influential. With the exception of a brief period of social-democratic rule in 1979–80, when they made some criticisms of Indonesia's occupation, Portuguese governments were, in the words of Fretilin's UN representative José Ramos-Horta, 'pathetic bystanders' in the diplomatic arena, where 'there was no consultation or support, let alone a joint strategy'.[10] This 'do nothing' policy, as one newspaper described it, gave other governments the excuse they needed for inaction, following the lead of the nation which, in formal terms, still retained legal responsibility for East Timor in international law.

In contrast to government policy, however, support for East Timor's right to self-determination remained a live issue in Portuguese public opinion. Many Portuguese were appalled by the events of the invasion, and felt a deep sense of sorrow and guilt that Portugal had failed to do anything to prevent the atrocities in its former colony. This was reinforced by the way in which the Indonesian military constantly blamed Portugal for the economic and social failures of Indonesian policies: health, education and welfare conditions were poor because of Portuguese-promoted underdevelopment; the economy was unable to meet subsistence needs due to centuries of colonial neglect; and so on. These popular sentiments were harnessed by Portuguese politicians, and particularly by critics of the AFM, who were constantly searching for evidence that, even in its most successful area, that of decolonization, the movement had not upheld national honour.

In 1982, an erstwhile leader of the AFM, General Ramalho Eanes was elected to the presidency. Angered by accusations from the right that the AFM bore the main responsibility for the debacle of 1975, he adopted East Timor as one of his personal concerns. This, together with a strengthening of public support for the issue, led to some improvements in government policy on East Timor. Eanes called for a 'common front of all Portuguese-speaking nations'[11] on the Timor issue, and persuaded the then Prime Minister, Pinto Balsamao, to present East Timor as 'the main priority of foreign policy' in a speech to the UN General Assembly.'[12] Following his re-election to the presidency in 1984, Eanes again called for more decisive action, although his Foreign Minister, Jaime Gama, remained lukewarm, arranging talks with the Indonesian military, putting forward general proposals, but then not following them up. At every available opportunity he stressed that Fretilin could have no role to play in the negotiating process. Shortly after Eanes' re-election, however, Mario Soares, the newly elected leader of the Socialist Party, became prime minister. Previously relatively unconcerned with the East Timor issue, he now sided firmly with Eanes, issuing a joint statement to the government calling on all its members to help achieve 'East Timor's inalienable right to self-determination'.[13]

During the next two years, from 1984–6, some progress was made in formally re-opening diplomatic contacts with Indonesia and in making public the Portuguese Government's opposition to the occupation by, for example, withdrawing its ambassador from Canberra when, in 1985, the Australian Labour Government agreed to the annexation recognized by previous governments. This continued when Soares succeeded Eanes as president in May 1986. The Portuguese Government's interventions in UN Forums such as the Human Rights Commission, the Decolonization Committee and the General Assembly were much more vigorous, focusing on the necessity for self-determination. Similarly, after entering the EC in 1987, the Portuguese regularly raised the East Timor issue, refusing to attend meetings of foreign ministers from the EC and the Association of Southeast Asian Nations (ASEAN), boycotting moves to upgrade the EC's Jakarta office to embassy level and, perhaps most seriously, proposing that the Indonesian and Australian governments be taken to the International Court of Justice at the Hague over the issue of their October 1989 agreement on the Timor Gap.

Yet, alongside these moves, there were others in which Portuguese policy seemed to be much more conciliatory. Whilst presidents and prime ministers spoke of 'inalienable rights', other ministers referred to East Timor as primarily a 'humanitarian, cultural and religious issue'.[14] Similarly, ministers criticized the conduct of the 1987 elections in East Timor, whilst Portuguese negotiators, in discussion with their Indonesian counterparts, advanced the idea of elections as providing means for measuring support for integration. Again, in the late 1980s, the Social Democratic Government referred repeatedly to self-determination as a 'fundamental and unquestionable tenet',[15] yet refused to include such a statement in its government's foreign-policy programme, even though East Timor's right to independence remains as Article 297 of the Portuguese Constitution.

Such actions and statements made Portuguese policy on East Timor appear contradictory in the eyes of the international community. Added to this was an evident trend for Indonesia to brush aside any conciliatory gestures made by the Portuguese. Floating ideas of elections as a measure of integration and removing electoral statements on self-determination from government programmes were treated by the Indonesian military as expressions of appeasement and were represented as such by their diplomats. At no stage has any Portuguese Government accorded any meaningful role to Fretilin, either in its discussions with the Indonesians or in its statements on negotiations. Not surprisingly, Xanana Gusmao concluded in one of his dispatches during 1987 that, ultimately, little was to be expected from Portugal.

Overall, Portuguese foreign policy has offered too little, too late. International actions taken by the government to publicize the plight of East Timor have generally been either statements of principle or minor thorns in the side of Indonesian diplomacy. At times, Portuguese policies have also been both contradictory and defensive. In the years immediately following the invasion, the Portuguese Government tried to abdicate responsibility in the interests of political expediency by attempting to bury the East Timor issue. When this failed, it offered to seek an 'honourable solution'. In pursuing this, however, its past actions, its contradictory approach and its 'flexibility' in such key areas as self-determination and elections have all placed severe limits on the efficacy of its policy of defending national 'honour'.

Monitoring and commitment

Because the integration of East Timor into the Indonesian Republic was important, strategically, economically and politically, to the states most deeply concerned, each one followed events very closely. Through monitoring by their respective intelligence services, Australia and the United States received daily reports on developments on the ground. They probably knew what was happening in greater detail than the Indonesian military itself during the months leading up to the invasion. Similarly, even after the withdrawal of the Portuguese colonial administration to the island of Atauro in the wake of the UDT coup attempt, the Lisbon Government followed events in the minutest detail through its own monitoring system. Surveillance by the Australian and American governments continued after the invasion. They retained the capacity to follow in detail the campaigns through which the military tried to incorporate its newly acquired colony, from the exchanges between commanders in the field to the instructions transmitted from Jakarta. Just as Australian intelligence monitored reports of the journalists' deaths in October 1975, so too were they able to monitor the ground instructions to jets bombing the Matebian mountain in 1978 and the co-ordination between Indonesian commanders during the fence of legs operation in 1981. For each year of the occupation, the US State Department Annual Report on Indonesia has outlined in detail the course of events in East Timor, documenting cases of torture, disappearance, imprisonment, forced entry and resettlement.

By following events in this way it soon became apparent to governments such as those of Australia and the US that the Indonesian military had neither the ability nor the capacity to achieve their objectives quickly and that the process of incorporation might not proceed as smoothly as they had hoped. Consequently, they enhanced Indonesian military capacity by supplying the very weapons which would fill crucial military gaps in the Timor campaign, and in several cases by improving the military's ability to use this hardware through training. In so doing, these governments, and particularly that of the

United States under the Carter (1976–80) and Reagan (1980–88) administrations, created a climate in which Indonesian requests for arms supplies were treated favourably. That these supplies were crucial to the annexation campaign rather than for general defence purposes is obvious. Whether they were F1-11 jets, A-4 bombers or Bronco OV-10 from the United States, or Hawk ground-attack planes from Britain, they all met particular military needs at specific moments in the campaign. The encirclement and annihilation operation required saturation bombing, hence the A-4 and the Hawk, both supplied in 1978. The fence of legs strategy with its chasing of Fretilin units required rapid troop movements across moutains, hence the 'Puma' helicopter, produced under French licence in Jakarta in 1979, and the supply of the more sophisticated Alouette in 1982, in preparation for the 1983 offensive. Similarly, the isolation of East Timor since the invasion has depended on a rigorous naval blockade which could not have succeeded without the supplying of high-speed, rapid-firing patrol boats from the Netherlands and South Korea, submarines from West Germany and frigates and submarine communications systems from Britain.[16] Tracking population and troop movements in the territory has been eased by the supply of command and control information systems, giving the military the latest information on the positioning of land, air and sea forces,[17] whilst the responses of armoured personnel carriers have been greatly improved by supplies of newly fitted guns,[18] and the movement of military vehicles has been speeded by the supply of prefabricated bridges.[19]

Condoning the annexation of East Timor did not only entail military support, however. Just as crucially, it involved a commitment by friendly governments to minimize the adverse publicity generated by accounts of the horrific results of annexation for the people of East Timor. Generally this involved counterbalancing refugee reports and visitors' accounts with contradicting statements, and then claiming, quite falsely, that there was no independent means available for governments to assess the validity of these competing claims. A recipe for inertia was thus concocted, although the Indonesian ingredient at times made its presentation seem less than credible. This was readily apparent when, for example, at the height of the encirclement and annihilation campaign of 1978 the US State Department claimed that 'most of the human losses in East Timor appeared to have occurred prior to Indonesia's intervention'[20], or, in March 1977, when the State Department's Country Officer for Indonesia testified that the people were 'happy' with integration: 'They have decided their best interest lies, at this time, in incorporation with Indonesia'.[21]

In other statements, the results of Indonesian military campaigns were presented as reasons for the military to incoporate East Timor to ease the country's emergence from its 'primitive' state. Replying to questions from members of parliament on the subject at the height of the 1978 bombing campaign in which the only recourse for the Timorese was to hide in mountain caves, the British Minister for Overseas Development wrote:

I had a talk with the Foreign Minister of Indonesia two weeks ago. Amongst other points which arose was one which startled me. He said that GNP per head was only sixty dollars, and that the living conditions were appalling: he said that many people still actually live in cave dwellings.[22]

Other erroneous statements were made in relation to a whole series of events: the elections of 1982 as an act of self-determination, the starvation of 1978–80 as a result of traditional seasonal food-shortages, and so on. In each case, the determination of representatives of friendly governments to provide a counterbalance to reports from refugees or perceptive foreign visitors and journalists produced results which exposed the transparency of military claims and suggested complicity on the part of these governments.

Doubtless they would have preferred to express openly the sentiments of a member of the US House Subcommittee on Asian and Pacific Affairs, when he wrote in 1976, that 'it is in all our interests to bury the Timor issue quickly and completely',[23] but given the reality of the conflict this proved impossible — which did not prevent these governments continually trying to close the issue by underwriting Indonesian positions, such was their commitment to integration. Each year, they coupled their support for Indonesian positions with claims that the situation was gradually improving, no matter what the reality. In desperation, when faced with a barrage of questions on human rights and self-determination at a Lisbon press conference in 1988, a US State Department spokesman finally admitted that 'the United States accepts the incorporation of East Timor into Indonesia, recognizing that there was no valid act of self-determination'.[24]

Through their support for Indonesia, governments such as those of the United States and Australia created an international climate in which Indonesian actions could be condoned without too much diplomatic risk or guilt. Moynihan's statement, for example, sent a clear signal at an early stage that the US government would turn a deaf ear to the question of self-determination. UN delegations rapidly fell into line, aggressively supporting Indonesian annexation as in the case of Japan, or quietly abstaining as in the case of most European delegations. In the crucial Security Council debate in April 1976, for example, which concluded by calling on Indonesia to 'withdraw its forces from East Timor without delay', the Japanese delegate claimed that this withdrawal was already underway because it had been ordered by the Provisional Government in Dili, and that the resolution was redundant. Rather more weakly, the British delegate was 'pleased to hear from the representative of Indonesia and from some representatives of the people of the territory that the situation in East Timor is returning to normal'.[25] One of the representatives was none other than Guilherme Gonçalves, former Apodeti leader and supplier of Timorese for guerrilla training in Indonesian Timor. US intelligence had followed his career closely through its monitoring in the previous twelve months.

As far as friendly governments and their allies in the industrialized states of Western Europe and the Far East were concerned, forums for debating the war in East Timor after 1978 soon became a means for deflecting the central issue of self-determination by raising or supporting objections which were weakened versions of Indonesian arguments. Most abstained or voted against resolutions calling for Indonesian withdrawal in international forums. This trend influenced the votes of other states. Some, of course, did not require persuasion. They supported Indonesian actions for reasons other than that of the conflict itself — as Islamic brothers or as newly colonizing Third World states. For many governments, however, the reluctance of the former colonial power to muster support in the early post-invasion years, the unwillingness of a major regional power, Australia, to take up the issue and the determined stand taken by US delegations in favour of integration meant that it was not worth supporting the issue of self-determination and, indeed, that such support might be given at a cost to one's relations with other UN member states. Take, for example, the case of the Pacific State of Vanuatu whose representative was quietly informed by the Australian delegate during the UN Fourth Committee debate on East Timor in 1982 that his government might curtail its aid to Vanuatu unless its prime minister took a less supportive stance on independence for East Timor.[26]

In the years following the invasion, the UN General Assembly each year passed a motion reaffirming East Timor's right to self-determination and calling for negotiations between Fretilin and the Indonesian and Portuguese governments. As a general rule, the governments of the industrialized states abstained. Many African, Asian and Latin American states voted with Indonesia, against the motion, with the Islamic bloc being particularly influential. The Soviet Union voted against but, in the early years of the 1980s, several Eastern European governments broke ranks and moved to an abstentionist vote. Early Chinese support for East Timor faded rapidly in the late 1970s. As one would expect, many smaller states, ranging from Costa Rica to Iceland, tended to support independence. The strongest advocates of self-determination were the former Portuguese colonies of Angola, Mozambique, Guinea-Bissau, Cape Verde, Sao Tome and Principé, together with Zimbabwe, Algeria, Benin and Vanuatu. In the 1980s, these states were joined by Portugal and Brazil. The voting breakdown for the East Timor resolution averaged around 60 votes in favour, 30 against, with approximately 40 abstentions. In 1982, however, several states moved from abstention to rejection and the motion was passed only narrowly, by 50 votes to 46, and this after the wording 'interested parties' had been substituted for the previous reference to Fretilin, in order to persuade delegations to vote for the motion. Since 1982, the motion has not been resubmitted for debate, not only because of fears that it could be defeated but also because in that year it charged the UN secretary-general with 'exploring avenues for achieving a comprehensive settlement of the problem'.[27] From then on, any return to the General Assembly was dependent upon progress being made in negotiations between 'all parties directly concerned', under the auspices of the Secretary-General's Office.[28]

The Secretary-General Perez de Cuellar interpreted the General Assembly resolution's brief in a narrow sense, arguing that there were really only two important parties to the East Timor conflict, Portugal and Indonesia.

According to Fretilin's representative at the UN, José Ramos-Horta, the under-secretary appointed by de Cuellar to deal with the negotiations, 'argued that Fretilin was not recognized by the UN; and that furthermore, Res. 37/30 (the 1982 resolution on East Timor) makes reference only to Portugal and Indonesia'.[29] Consequently, the objective of de Cuellar's task became to achieve some agreement, however limited, between these two governments. Until 1984, Portugal made little serious effort and, of course, at all stages Indonesia blocked any progress. The reports issued annually by the Secretary-General's Office to the General Assembly have, therefore, been schematic, bland, ill-informed, and have contributed little to the development of any meaningful negotiations. Discussions between the Portuguese and Indonesian foreign ministers have got no further than meetings to discuss 'humanitarian issues', and the secretary-general has been able to offer little more than the hope of a solution 'acceptable to the international community', in the words of his 1988 report. Consequently, fundamental issues have never been addressed, even though the Indonesian occupation violates almost every human rights provision in the UN Charter, the Universal Declaration of Human Rights and the International Bill of Rights.

In addition to the General Assembly, within the UN there are two institutions whose specific purpose is to protect human rights by assessing cases of violation. These are the Human Rights Commission and the committee which prepares its agenda, the Sub-Commission on Prevention of Discrimination and Protection of Minorities. The latter is composed of government officials from 43 member states. After adopting annually resolutions condemning human rights abuses in East Timor, the Human Rights Commission, in private session, voted to remove the issue from its agenda in 1985 for reasons which have never been made public, and this despite extensive and detailed documentation being presented on specific violations in the years following the 1983 ceasefire. Both in that year and those that followed, Indonesian pressure on sub-commission members has been intense, to prevent the East Timor issue being placed on the Human Rights Commission agenda. When the subject has been debated, the Indonesian Government has had, on average, ten diplomats lobbying sub-commission members. As the member from Norway, Asbjorn Eide, described it during the debate on East Timor in 1989, without naming any country, 'pressure from governments last year came close to being contempt of court'.[30] Thanks largely to a prolonged campaign mounted by non-governmental organizations (NGOs) in the late 1980s, the sub-commission re-adopted a resolution in 1989, recommending the Human Rights Commission to 'consider the human rights situation and fundamental freedoms in East Timor'.[31] The extent to which the commission's members heed this advice will depend not only on specific UN features such as the political composition of the commission and the views of the secretary-general but also on developments in two other bodies, the Non-Aligned Movement (NAM) and the European Community (EC).

As a founder member of the NAM Indonesia still retains some prestige within it, although its image was tarnished by the brutal way in which its present rulers came to power in 1965–6. It thus came as something of a shock to the military when, after the 1975 invasion, at a meeting of the NAM heads of state and government, members called on Indonesia to withdraw from East Timor in line with UN Security Council resolutions. This was repeated in subsequent NAM meetings in the late 1970s, which all reaffirmed the UN General Assembly resolutions. Pressure from the Indonesian Government at the ministerial and heads of state meetings in 1981 and 1983, however, led to East Timor being removed as an issue from the NAM agenda. Through saturation lobbying, Indonesia has subsequently kept East Timor on the sidelines. At the 1985 ministerial meeting in Luanda, when the Angolan Government, as the host of the meeting, inserted a paragraph on East Timor into the draft political declaration, the Indonesians arrived with a 40-member delegation to brief ministers on the issue. Foreign Minister Mochtar commented that 'the main task of the Indonesian delegation this time is to eliminate the East Timor question from the draft declaration'.[32] The subsequent five-hour debate in the NAM's Political Commission did much to deprive President Suharto of one of his main political ambitions, the presidency of the NAM. Similarly, at the 1986 summit in Zimbabwe the Indonesians went so far as to open a new embassy in Harare in the months preceding the meeting and to dispatch a roving ambassador to non-aligned governments, with the task of winning support for Indonesia on the East Timor issue. This trend was followed during subsequent NAM meetings in the 1980s. At considerable political, diplomatic and financial expense, Indonesia has succeeded in keeping the discussion of the conflict peripheral, but it has not removed it completely from the non-aligned agenda. Suharto's political ambition remains unrealized, and this failure was one of the reasons for Mochtar's replacement as foreign minister in March 1988 by Indonesia's representative to the UN, Ali Alatas.

Just as the East Timor issue has remained a diplomatic thorn in Indonesia's side in the NAM, so too have the actions of the European Parliament, particularly in the 1980s. Resolutions urging the Council of Ministers of the parliament 'to take measures enabling a referendum to be held, with the people being allowed freedom of choice on the future of East Timor',[33] have been combined with critical reports from the parliament's Human Rights Commission and, most significantly, in May 1988, the adoption of a common stand on East Timor by all the foreign ministers of the EC in favour of 'a comprehensive and internationally acceptable settlement'.[34] Subsequent to this decision, the EC states have acted more collectively on East Timor, following the lead of the Portuguese Government. Such policy decisions led Ali Alatas to comment that: 'East Timor is still a nuisance internationally, leading to many misunderstandings, even among our allies, and creating difficulties in our diplomatic work'.[35]

Other options

One of the greatest tragedies of the East Timor conflict is that, contrary to the thrust of their policies in the mid-1970s, governments such as Portugal, Australia and the United States could have influenced the outcome in a very different direction without jeopardizing their long-term relations with the Indonesian military. As an official of the US CIA put it, at the end of 1980: 'It [East Timor] would have been a viable entity if we and some other governments had made it clear to the Indonesians that there would be a price to pay if they went ahead and invaded'.[36] In the case of Portugal, for example, the newly installed AFM Government could have built on the widespread international support for an administration that had just overthrown a fascist regime. At the very least, it could have afforded some protection to East Timor by acceding to long-established UN requests from the Caetano period that it become a UN protectorate. This would have internationalized the issue at an early stage and made it much more difficult for the Indonesian military to interfere in the country's internal affairs in 1974 and 1975. In the case of the Australian Government, rather than doing its utmost to accommodate the Indonesian military, it could have played a more constructive brokerage role. As the regional power most concerned with the resolution of the conflict, it could have offered to mediate between Portugal, Indonesia and Fretilin, without damaging its long-term regional economic and defence interests. This might not have resulted in independence but undoubtedly it would have reduced significantly the chances of an armed invasion. In the case of the US Government, it too could have exercised a restraining role given its crucial levels of military supplies and economic aid, particularly at a time when the Indonesians were modernizing their armed forces and rebuilding their petroleum industry in the aftermath of the Pertamina debacle.

Despite such options, the need for each of these governments (Portugal, the United States and Australia) to appease the Indonesian military became paramount, eclipsing other possibilities. The stakes, it seemed, were too high in the mid-1970s. The risks of failure were viewed as too great strategically, economically and politically. And once support had been given to the Indonesian line it had to be followed through to the end no matter what the consequences, since the reasons for accepting integration were now reinforced by the need to prove the correctness of the policy. As the American ambassador to Jakarta put it in 1975, US policy was 'to take at face value Indonesia's professed desire for orderly self-determination'.[37]

With support for East Timor limited internationally, much of the work of keeping the issue alive has been carried out by NGOs, church institutions, support groups and individuals trying to co-ordinate actions undertaken in their respective countries. In the United States, for example, in contrast to the official government position, an increasingly influential campaign has been organized in both the House and Senate, condemning human rights violations, criticizing resettlement and calling for the entry of international aid agencies into East Timor. From the organizing of senate hearings in the 1970s to the tabling of motions in both houses and the signing of protest letters to successive secretaries of state in the 1980s, the campaign has been supported across the political spectrum. On each occasion President Suharto has visited the United States, or when the American president has travelled to Indonesia, the occupation of East Timor has been given widespread publicity in the media. Prior to President Bush's meeting with Suharto in June 1989, 118 members of Congress urged him to raise the issue of East Timor. Some nine months previously, almost half the Senate (47 members) and 182 members of Congress had written to Secretary of State Schultz, highlighting food shortages, lack of medical supplies, imprisonment, torture and 'the virtually non-existent freedom of expression for the citizens of East Timor'.[38] Similar campaigns have been organized in Australia, Japan, Canada, the EC countries and Britain in particular to publicize the East Timor conflict and organize support for self-determination.

Assisting these groups, and organizing international lobbying, was a group of Fretilin members who had either left Dili just before the Indonesian invasion, or who had already been representing Fretilin in Lisbon. Charged with raising diplomatic and material support, their task was extremely difficult. Initially, with the exception of two members, José Ramos-Horta and Mari Alkatiri, they had little experience of diplomatic work. Thrown into the arena of international diplomacy and lobbying, they received advice and support from the representatives of only four governments — Mozambique, Angola, Guinea-Bissau and Cape Verde. They had to learn all the diplomatic tricks and skills in a very short time, in a situation in which they were either politely dismissed or treated with benign tolerance by most governments. Their links with the movement inside East Timor, always precarious, were severed in 1978 and not restored until 1985, only to be broken again shortly afterwards. As a result, actions outside and inside could not be co-ordinated, information from inside was received several months after the event and proposals made to the external delegation by UN, Indonesian or other representatives could never be discussed in any detail with those leading the movement in East Timor. Furthermore, having to rely on a wide range of groups in different countries to disseminate information, members of Fretilin's External Delegation became subjected to differing and often contradictory influences. Tutored by academic and political experts of varying persuasions, receiving advice from a plethora of groups, individuals and political parties, their pre-existing differences of opinion (manifest in events such as the dispute over the Macau Conference in 1975) at times were exacerbated, to the detriment of their work. Shades of opinion became differences of position and political division. This reached a low point in November 1978 when the most diplomatically exposed member of the delegation, Ramos-Horta, was detained by its other leading members in Maputo on the grounds that he was negotiating unofficially both with the Indonesian military and Alarico Fernandes, who had recently surrendered to Indonesian troops in East Timor. In the 1980s the members of the delegation seemed to overcome most of their differences and presented a united diplomatic front. Recently, however, splits have re-emerged, with Ramos-

Horta leaving Fretilin and forming a new group in Australia, vying with the official delegation based in Lisbon under the leadership of Abilio Araujo.

Contrast these limitations and difficulties with the position of the Indonesian Government and the resources on which it can draw, economically, politically and socially. Throughout the entire 15-year period since the invasion, Indonesia has made East Timor a priority in the diplomatic work of all its embassies and delegations. Offers of trade, investments and markets, together with offers of political support and financial inducements, have been made whenever the issue of East Timor has been raised. Once again, vast resources have been deployed to ensure that this highly significant war is portrayed as insignificant.

Notes

1. Bruce Juddery, 'Envoy Puts Jakarta's View', *Canberra Times*, 10 January 1976.
2. In a 1978 hearing before the US House of Representatives International Relations Committee (Sub-Committee on International Organizations) it was stated by a government spokesman that the policy of curtailing arms supplies had, in fact, never been implemented in 1975–6. See, *US Policy on Human Rights and Military Assistance: Overview on Indonesia, 15 February 1970*.
3. M. Richardson, 'Fraser Given Blunt Warning at Washington Talks: Don't Anger Jakarta', Melbourne *Age*, 3 August 1976.
4. Visit of President Suharto of Indonesia to the United States; remarks by President Reagan at the Arrival Ceremony, 12 October 1982, *Weekly Compilation of Presidential Documents*, 18 October 1982.
5. *Washington Post* (USA), 27 April 1986.
6. *Newsday* (USA), 2 May 1986.
7. *Timor Link* (London), No. 9, March 1987.
8. *Canberra Times*, 18 April 1984.
9. Interview with Lemos Pires, *Expresso* (Lisbon), 3 July 1976 and *O Tempo* (Lisbon), 8 July 1976.
10. José Ramos-Horta, 1987, p. 129.
11. *Diario de Noticias* (Lisbon), 10 June 1982.
12. *Age* (Melbourne), 1 October 1982.
13. *Age* (Melbourne), 21 July 1984.
14. See, for example, Jaimé Gama, in a speech to the UN General Assembly, *Diario de Noticias* (Lisbon), 23 September 1985, or Cavaco da Silva in *Expresso* (Lisbon), 30 April 1987.
15. See Joao de Deus Pinheiro, in a speech to the UN General Assembly, UN General Assembly *Record*, 23 September 1987.
16. Frigates from the United Kingdom were supplied by the Vosper Thornycroft Company (*Kompas*, Jakarta, 7 March 1986), whilst Communication Systems for submarines were supplied by Marconi UK (*Military Technology*, London, No. 12, 1985).
17. *Jakarta Post*, 24 May 1988.
18. Information supplied by GKN, a London-based comapny, in July 1988.
19. *Jakarta Post*, 8 April 1987.

20. US State Department, *Human Rights Report on Indonesia, 1978*.

21. *Human Rights in East Timor and the Question of the Use of US Equipment by the Indonesian Armed Forces*, hearing before the sub-committees on International Organizations and Asian and Pacific Affairs of the Committee on International Relations of the House of Representatives, 23 March 1977.

22. Judith Hart, Minister for Overseas Development, letter to Geoffrey Edge, MP, 27 December 1978.

23. Congressman J. Herbert Burke, minority member of the committee, cited by Noam Chomsky, *Statement delivered to the Fourth Committee of the United Nations General Assembly, November 1978*, republished in Retbøll (ed.), 1980.

24. *Diario de Noticias* (Lisbon), 2 November 1988.

25. UN Security Council, *Provisional Verbatim Record of the Nineteen Hundred and Fourteenth Meeting*, 22 April 1976, New York, S/PV 1914/15 Japanese delegate, p. 12, UK p. 17, resolution p. 33.

26. This incident, which occurred during the 1982 debate on East Timor in the Fourth Committee of the United Nations, was reported to me by two sources, both of whom attended, and both of whom did so independently of the other.

27. See UN General Assembly Resolution number 37/30, 1982.

28. Ibid.

29. Ramos-Horta, 1987, p. 169.

30. *Tapol Bulletin* (London), No. 95, October 1989, p. 1.

31. The resolution is printed in full in ibid, p. 2.

32. *Kompas* (Jakarta), 30 August 1985.

33. For a detailed analysis of the 1989 European Parliament Resolution on East Timor, see *Tapol Bulletin* (London), No. 95, October 1989, from which this quotation from the resolution is taken.

34. Hans-Dietrich Genscher, German Federal Republic Foreign Minister, press conference statement issued after EC Ministers Meeting in Dusseldorf, May 1988. The quote is taken from the press statement.

35. *Tempo* (Jakarta), 16 May 1988.

36. *Christian Science Monitor*, 17 December 1980.

37. Van Atta and Toohey, 30 May–12 June 1982.

38. Letter to George Shultz from Senate members, sponsored by Senator David Durenberger, 28 October 1988.

13. What of the Future? Scenarios for East Timor

What, then, of the future? How is the conflict in East Timor likely to develop over the coming decade? A number of scenarios is possible, each of which can be assessed in the light of recent trends:

- *There is the possibility of an Indonesian military victory over Fretilin*. The Indonesian armed forces concentrate their military might in a final onslaught on Fretilin strongholds in the eastern and southeastern zones. Combining fence of legs operations with intensive aerial and naval bombardment, they capture or eliminate the Fretilin leadership, destroy the movement's base areas and run to ground surviving groups. Publicizing this defeat internationally, Indonesian diplomats insist that the East Timor issue be brought back to the UN General Assembly, in which an even weaker resolution than the one carried narrowly in 1982 is defeated. Despite attempts by NGOs, supported by Portuguese diplomacy, criticisms of Indonesia's annexation in international human rights forums begin to fade away. The issue can no longer be raised in any meaningful sense within the NAM, and governments previously critical of the Indonesian stance are forced to accept grudgingly that resistance finally has been quelled. Reluctantly, Portugal is persuaded to accept a negotiated settlement with Indonesia, in which integration is recognized, with guarantees for a respecting of human rights and Timorese cultural identity. Meanwhile, in East Timor, the military presses ahead with a token Timorization of the administration, with Javanese effectively holding power. Support for this administration is bolstered by the creation of pro-Indonesian political groups, possibly based on the former Apodeti, which provide a counter to any potential criticism, however limited, from members of the Provincial Parliament in Dili, notably Governor Carrascalao and his former UDT allies. Church opposition is neutralized by the Vatican agreeing to the transfer of Bishop Belo and the removal of priests who have acted as mediators between the Indonesian army and Fretilin groups. With the most minimal of changes in its policies and system of military control, the Indonesian Government is thus able to undermine potential bases for opposition to its continuing occupation, and to remove the issue of East Timor from the international agenda.

What are the chances of this occurring?

Under present circumstances it would seem fairly unlikely. The Indonesian military have undertaken many concerted campaigns with the stated aim of eliminating Fretilin but none of them have succeeded, even if the 1978 campaign came close to it. The difficulties for the Indonesian army of fighting in East Timor's terrain, the ease with which Fretilin groups can conceal themselves in their mobile base areas and the strength of their support amongst the population will continue to make an outright military victory unlikely. Furthermore, it has become clear during the course of the occupation, and particularly during the 1980s, that entrenched interests in the Indonesian armed forces are quite happy for the conflict to continue at its present low-intensity level. It provides troops with combat practice and enables commanders to gain promotion through their military achievements in engaging and capturing Fretilin units and controlling dissent. Indeed, many of Indonesia's current military leaders earned their stripes as a result of their successes in East Timor. In addition, many members of the armed forces have benefited financially from the activities of companies like P. T. Denok, in addition to their profits from daily corruption and bribery. For such people, the adverse diplomatic results of Indonesia's rapacious colonialism are of secondary concern. This, together with the ability of Fretilin to continue fighting, means that an outright victory by the Indonesian armed forces is unlikely in the foreseeable future.

- *It is unlikely that Fretilin forces will be able to defeat Indonesia militarily.* Estimates of Fretilin's current strength vary considerably but a reasonable figure seems to be around 2000 active troops, located mostly in the eastern and southern zones and armed with weapons captured from the Indonesians. Although Fretilin has strong support from networks in the towns and villages, it is clearly impossible for it to mount an offensive which could seriously challenge Indonesian military control. Indeed, the number of engagements with Indonesian troops dropped significantly in the late 1980s, and it seems that much of Fretilin's energies are now being devoted to maintaining their base areas — cultivating crops, hunting for food and providing adequate shelter. The only developments which might enable Fretilin to make a breakthrough militarily would be either a significant upsurge by separatist movements in areas of eastern Indonesia, such as West Irian, or a prolonged conflict between military factions in Java itself, related to a succession crisis to Suharto's presidency. Neither of these seems likely in the immediate future. Consequently, it appears that, militarily, the stalemate will continue, with Indonesia maintaining its campaign of attrition against Fretilin groups who sporadically harass Indonesian units as they move around the territory.

- *The Indonesian Government organizes a referendum in East Timor, whose carefully orchestrated outcome would be a vote for integration.* Indonesia has previously stage-managed such an event in West Irian in 1969 when, under UN auspices but using Indonesian personnel, the military orchestrated an Act of Free Choice in which 'local representatives' organized in regional councils 'consulted' their populations and then, following discussions among themselves and with Indonesian government representatives, decided to remain within the Indonesian Republic.[1] Such an outcome in East Timor could be used to legitimize integration internationally, particularly if the military could secure limited UN involvement or, even better, a Portuguese presence during the referendum. To a certain extent, Indonesia has already floated this suggestion, both in 1982 and 1987, when it was argued by government officials that the results of the elections for East Timor's Provincial Assembly gave some guide to the level of support for integration.

What is the likelihood of this taking place?

Several factors currently mediate against it. Most seriously, perhaps, is the point that Suharto and his immediate entourage seem to be opposed to it, arguing that it would entail a greater opening up of East Timor and enable opposition, and particularly the Catholic Church, to give full vent to its criticisms of the occupation. They cite events surrounding the Pope's visit in October 1989 as a small-scale example of what could happen. Furthermore, since the international community is by now well aware of the methods used by the military to secure the West Irian result, many governments would be unhappy accepting the outcome of a referendum, whilst others would re-open the West Irian case as a means of criticizing Indonesia. Consequently, from the present regime's viewpoint, a referendum might bring unwelcome intrusions into East Timor and provoke unwanted international criticism. Since in addition no foreign government or international agency is likely to put forward such a suggestion, its chances of emerging as a serious or viable way out of the present situation are remote.

● *A variation of what the Indonesian officers involved in negotiating the 1983 ceasefire, termed the 'Sulawesi Solution'* would begin with a negotiated ceasefire, followed by a more prolonged agreement, demarcating Indonesian- and Fretilin-held zones. As in 1983, Fretilin troops and their families would be allowed to enter Indonesian-held areas, primarily to get access to medical facilities. The Indonesians would take the opportunity offered by the ceasefire period to discuss with Fretilin and church leaders a series of measures whose enactment would result in an East Timorese province integrated into the Indonesian Republic, but with a limited degree of political autonomy. These proposals would include a Timorization of the administration, with some powers devolved to Dili's Regional Assembly to direct areas of the economy, to oversee the implementation of regional plans, to suggest policies for maintaining East Timorese culture and so on. They would also entail a substantial increase in educational provision for East Timorese, in order to build up a corps of trained workers for both the local economy and bureaucracy. Fretilin members would be offered an amnesty, with the longer-term possibility of participation in the Dili Government. The introduction of these policies would be accompanied by a limited military withdrawal, campaigns to deter human rights abuse and a general 'winning of hearts and minds' approach adopted by the armed forces.

Under present circumstances, such developments seem rather remote. There is little sign of any lessening of Indonesian brutality or of any serious intention to involve East Timorese in the running of the political system or the organization of the economy. The 1983 ceasefire agreement was revoked by a military hierarchy whose members remain in predominant positions in Indonesian politics, and subsequent attempts at local ceasefires — arranged through church intermediaries — have collapsed before they have even begun to be implemented. Whilst Fretilin would probably welcome a ceasefire, as they did in 1983 when they were able to re-group their forces, their leaders have made it clear on several occasions that they have little interest in any proposals for a federal solution which are put forward by the present regime in power in Jakarta.

The scenarios suggested above have focused on potential developments within Indonesia and East Timor. It is conceivable, of course, that changes could also be brought about by influence or pressure from foreign governments and the international community. These would probably involve the former colonial power, which brings us to a further possibility.

- With the exception of a small number of governments, there have been few sustained criticisms of Indonesia's occupation since the invasion. Due largely to the work of committed diplomats, and to Fretilin's representatives in New York, the issue has been kept alive in the UN, but only just. Much the same has occurred in other forums, such as the NAM. Within the international human rights network, various NGOs have succeeded in keeping East Timor on the agenda of bodies such as the UN Human Rights Commission. In terms of pressure on the Indonesian regime, this has produced regular diplomatic embarrassment, and much time and money have been spent by Indonesia in containing criticisms internationally. Indonesia's status as a co-founder of the NAM has been damaged by its actions in East Timor. Yet international pressure of this kind, although successful in its own terms, is limited in scope. It can never constitute a serious threat nor provide any basis for sanctioning Indonesia in any serious way. As we have seen, this could only have been achieved by the governments of countries such as the United States, Australia and Japan, and only then in the months leading up to and after the invasion. It is unlikely that these governments will apply any pressure on Indonesia to reverse the process of integration or to lessen the brutalities of its impact unless there is a major political change within Indonesia itself.

Many governments, and notably those of the EC, might well have responded to Indonesia's diplomatic overtures in the early 1980s had it not been for their relations with Portugal, whose actions have tempered Europe's support for Indonesia resulting, for example, in the development of a common abstentionist policy on the East Timor issue at the UN. In the coming years, Portugal undoubtedly will remain an important influence on the East Timor issue in the international arena. If it continues with its present policies, its diplomatic pressure on Indonesia, particularly through the EC, will help keep the issue alive internationally. It is conceivable, of course, that Portuguese policy might return to its earlier acquiescence and lethargy, with the result that Indonesia would be able to secure concessions from the former colonial power. *In such a scenario, Portugal, reluctantly accepting* de facto *integration, would conclude an agreement with Indonesia which accepts the* fait accompli *but secures guarantees from the military to respect human rights, permit religious freedom and preserve East Timor's cultural identity. Portugal would then claim that it had done the best it could under difficult circumstances and had withdrawn in as 'principled' manner as possible.* This would then be supported by other EC governments, who would join with the majority of governments in removing East Timor from the UN agenda. This would make it extremely difficult for NGOs to raise the issue in any serious way in UN human rights organizations. In East Timor the military would simply carry on as normal, exercising control with even less concern for international reaction than previously.

Currently, this outcome seems far less likely than it did in the early 1980s since the Portuguese Government has repeatedly stated the necessity for an act of self-determination. On the other hand, it should not be forgotten that this stand taken by Portugal has depended primarily upon the commitment of a number of leading politicians, notably presidents Eanes and Soares, and that, throughout the 1980s, one can find counter-statements by other political leaders. Consequently, there is always the possibility that Portugal will exit by taking the 'honourable' route. *For the moment, however, Portuguese policy probably constitutes the most effective thorn in the side of Indonesian diplomacy, through raising the issue in international forums and embarrassing Indonesia in its dealings with the EC through such bodies as ASEAN.*

Changes in Indonesia

In drawing up these scenarios we have assumed that the present regime remains in place in Jakarta. Clearly, if this were to change, it could have a profound effect on the conflict. Scenarios which we have assessed as unlikely, notably the referendum and the Sulawesi Solution, might well become possible. If this happened, then obviously the international picture would also change. But what are the chances of a change of regime in Indonesia? Can a government emerge which might be less oppressive towards East Timor, allowing its people a greater say in the running of their affairs, and perhaps even granting some degree of political autonomy?

The issue dominating politics in Indonesia in the early 1990s will be the succession to the Suharto presidency. In other Southeast Asian states a change of presidency might not be that fundamental an issue, but in Indonesia's case its impact could be profound. Suharto and his entourage have exercised a rigorous and tight system of control over Indonesian politics for 25 years. They have overseen the destruction of political parties and the creation and maintenance of an authoritarian state whose influence has extended to the remotest village level. Militarily, Suharto has skilfully played off one armed forces faction against another in maintaining his rule. Politically, his cadres have remoulded political parties in the military image whilst at the same time restructuring the apparatus of government to ensure an in-built majority for the military. Economically, the president has similarly built up a system of centralized control in which his family plays a predominant role, with assets greater than those of the late President Marcos of the Philippines. Major strategic industries in areas such as oil, gas, communications and plantations are run by state companies controlled by Suharto loyalists. Alongside these companies, and linked with them, are private companies owned by the Suharto family or its close associates. As the *Asian Wall Street Journal* put it, referring to his more immediate family:

> In recent years the Suharto sons (of which there are three) have put together a maze of businesses giving them a stake in almost every important commodity or service in the country. In most cases these businesses originate from and thrive on state contracts, government decrees or licences giving concerns tied to the Suharto sons and their associates special rights to handle the import, manufacture or distribution of such goods or services.[2]

Current estimates of Suharto's family and business associates' wealth in the 1980s vary from US$2–3 billion.[3]

For a growing number of influential military and political groupings in Indonesia Suharto's rule is increasingly becoming counterproductive. His entourage's handling of the economy and its involvement in extensive corruption, together with the failure of his government to modernize resource-rich Indonesia at a rate similar to neighbouring countries such as Thailand and Malaysia in the 1980s, have led to demands from within the military both for changes in the political system and, by implication, for the president's retirement at the end of his current term, in 1993. It has become more and more apparent to such groups that Indonesia faces urgent problems in its development which the present government seems unwilling to address. Despite its tremendous potential, the Indonesian economy is burdened with high levels of debt-servicing, and its attempt to modernize through restructuring its industrial base, established largely in the 1950s, has made limited progress in the 1980s. Furthermore, many of the present government's economic policies are having highly adverse cultural and social effects on the population in a growing number of regions in the archipelago. Such factors have meant that in the 1980s Indonesia was viewed less favourably as an area for trade and investment. This was brought home most forcibly when, in 1986, the *Economist* in its annual analysis of the prospects for developing countries placed Indonesia in the 'high-risk' category, three points behind South Africa and six behind El Salvador and Zaire, citing the 'authoritarianism' and 'staleness' of its government.[4] If Indonesia is to change such perceptions, then a number of crucial issues need to be dealt with in the 1990s, and in many of these it would seem that the Suharto Government may form part of the problem rather than the solution. The scale of the problems facing the Indonesian economy can best be illustrated by taking two examples, in the areas of debt and economic growth.

Indonesia's official debt stands at just over US$35 billion, and almost 40 per cent of foreign-exchange earnings have to be used to service this debt annually. The debt-service ratio has increased to this level from 19.75 per cent in 1985 and 32.7 per cent in 1986. Consequently, indebtedness is increasing fairly rapidly, and this is evidenced, for example, in 36.6 per cent of state receipts being allocated to buy foreign currency to repay the country's overseas obligations. The main reason for this lies in the sharp decline in earnings from oil exports due to severe price falls since the end of 1985. However, it also reflects a longer-term trend, namely that if Indonesia is to increase its growth rate it will have to boost its non-petroleum exports, since the latter currently provide around 70 per cent of export revenue. This means that the country's manufacturing base will have to be diversified; in order to achieve this, more domestic and overseas investment is required fairly rapidly. Most commentators, and notably such bodies as the World Bank and the International Monetary Fund, have stressed this point repeatedly in recent years and have underlined the urgency of diversification if Indonesia is not to fall behind neighbouring ASEAN economies in the 1990s.

Thus far, however, policies to attract increased investment and to promote industrial diversification have had only partial success. Measures such as devaluing the rupiah, providing incentives for export companies and doubling the number of economic sectors open to foreign investment have resulted in limited increases in investment and diversification. For many potential investors there still seems to be a failure to tackle fundamental problems, centring on the nature of control over leading economic sectors, and more particularly on what economic commentators have aptly described as 'restrictive licensing and other valuable concessions which favour certain individuals but disadvantage the economy as a whole'.[5] This is a rather thinly veiled reference both to the widespread corruption resulting from the corporate power exercised by the Suharto group in the commodity-export sector and to the restrictions the group has placed on companies trying to enter manufacturing and importing sectors where it has immensely profitable monopolies.

For the future development of the economy, it is crucial that these restrictions be weakened and that deregulation involve a reduction in the economic power of the Suharto monopolies. Investors are deterred both by the corruption at every level of business and by the limited success of the government in shifting resources from Suharto-dominated sectors to new manufacturing industries and export-oriented production. Such delays have a negative impact on growth potential and contribute little to increasing foreign-exchange earnings to alleviate the debt problem. Hence the need for austerity measures and substantial cuts in public expenditure budgets in the late 1980s.

These trends seem to indicate a conflict between the increasing demands of the Indonesian economy for modernization, based upon deregulation and diversification, and the entrenched interests of monopolies supported and sponsored by companies aligned with the Suharto family. This conflict needs to be resolved in favour of economic diversification if the Indonesian economy is to attain the levels of development currently reached by less well-placed economies in the Southeast Asian region. The present regime is promoting this diversification, but one of the conditions of its long-term success is a weakening of the economic interests of the Suharto group and, by implication, a weakening of the economic basis for its exercising of political power.

Indonesia similarly faces serious environmental problems, whose impact will intensify during the next ten years. In addition to petroleum and its related products, Indonesia has for many years exported other primary commodities: a wide range of raw materials, coffee, rubber and, increasingly since the 1960s, timber which now provides 14.4 per cent of the country's non-oil exports, earning US$1.6 billion per year. Ten per cent of the world's tropical forests are located in Indonesia, comprising some 90 million hectares of land. On average during the 1980s, one million hectares have been felled each year. Most of this has not been replaced, which is indicative of the government's cavalier attitude to forestry management. Most logging operations leave behind huge quantities of organic waste which are highly combustible. A fire in East Kalimantan in 1982–3 burnt down 3.6 million hectares of tropical forest, an area slightly larger than the Netherlands. Cutting has resulted in the destruction of the forest canopy and the exposure of the forest soils to the tropical sun. This leeches the soil of its nutrients and, together with erosion, makes any natural regeneration impossible. The micro-climate of areas such as Kalimantan and Eastern Indonesia is beginning to be affected by the current rapacious rates of timber exploitation.[6] Furthermore, forestry exploitation in several areas has robbed indigenous peoples of their homelands — the Kubu in Sumatra, the Penan in Kalimantan, and perhaps most importantly the Korowai in West Irian. These societies, who have lived for centuries by shifting cultivation and hunting and gathering, are increasingly threatened.

The Indonesian Government's treatment of its forested environment cannot be discussed without also mentioning the related issue of transmigration. Policies in this area aim to move millions of landless poor from the central islands of Java, Madura, Bali and Lombok to the less densely populated islands, mostly in the east. Despite the stated aim of this movement, to reduce population pressure, much of it seems to be occurring largely for security reasons. As General Murdani stated: 'The population of sites and the removal of obstacles to land availability need to be given special focus because the choice of locations is related to the concept of territorial management'.[7] Transmigration has involved widespread human rights abuses, including forced resettlement, as have been rigorously documented by many commentators.[8] The government has made it clear that an additional aim is to undermine non-Javanese societies and cultures. Hosting a meeting on transmigration in Jakarta, Minister of Transmigration Martono promised that:

by way of transmigration, we will try to realize what has been pledged, to integrate all ethnic groups into one nation, the Indonesian nation. The different ethnic groups will in the long run disappear because of integration, and there will be one kind of man.[9]

Current estimates for the period covering the present Five-Year Plan put the loss of tropical rain-forest resulting from the clearing of transmigration sites at 3.3 million hectares. In addition, many transmigration sites have proved totally unsuitable for farming and their settlers have abandoned them for surrounding areas, causing further deforestation.

The Indonesian Government's handling of the environment, its transmigration policies and its treatment of its minority peoples have all led in recent years to growing opposition, both domestically and internationally. In Indonesia itself, many NGOs campaigned on these issues throughout the 1980s, and a whole range of international bodies has raised them as urgent priorities, claiming that unless Indonesia alters its policies it will face regional unrest and, in the longer term, ecological disaster.

The government has countered these criticisms aggressively. An advertisement costing US$46,000 placed in the *New York Times* attacked environmental groups 'who want Indonesia managed as one big protected park', whilst the blame for deforestation has been placed firmly on shifting cultivators or on transmigrants, who the Minister of Transmigration was reported to have described as 'mentally unprepared (*tidak siap mental*)' for life in their new settlements.[10] Conservationists have been described as belonging to 'a movement supported and financed by our competitors, because they feel threatened by our expanding exports', according to the chairman of Indonesia's timber cartel.[11]

Much of the tone of this response has been influenced strongly by the views of Suharto himself who, through family members such as his eldest son, Sigit Harjoyudanto, and his long-time business associate, Bob Hasan, exercises extensive control over the timber industry. Hasan, a lifelong friend, is one of Suharto's small group of financial and economic advisers. He chairs all the organizations involved in forestry, notably the Plywood/Woodpanel Association which sets prices and quotas and is the only organization which can issue export licences. As with Suharto in recent years: 'Hasan accepts no consultation. He thinks he is doing the right thing'.[12] With a mandate from the president, he exercises decisive control over the future of Indonesia's tropical forests. Like Suharto, he seems determined to press ahead with forestry exploitation, with scant concern for environmental consequences.

As was the case with economic policy, we have a government in power which, due to its centralizing and monopolizing role, seems unwilling to address crucial environmental issues facing Indonesia's development. Other economic and social areas, equally as serious, could have been analysed, and similar trends would have been observed. Overall, it seems that the Suharto regime remains largely an authoritarian system, impervious to demands for greater responsibility and openness (*keterbukaan*). Consequently, as Indonesian society shows some signs of an emerging potential for a limited form of political pluralism, the government appears to be responding with a reassertion of its traditional paternalistic notions of 'guided democracy' in which political consensus is reached through government direction, which, in reality, is imposed from above through the direct use of state power. Recent years have seen, for example, a tremendous increase in the activities of NGOs. Since both parliament and political parties have been emasculated by the military, political activities have shifted to these organizations, many of which have become local bases for voicing criticisms of the government. Similarly, there has been some discussion amongst academics and even in parliament itself on the opening up of the political system. Suharto's model of consensus has been confronted with an alternative model of decision-making through majority voting, with the existence of an opposition. Suharto and his military entourage have tried to silence these criticisms and, of course, the NGOs' movement has been strongly attacked, its activities castigated as 'reprehensible for the development of the nation'.[13] Despite such criticisms, the extensive NGO network will not go away, nor will the criticisms from academic, intellectual and dissident political groups. Indeed, the grounds for dissent will recur, as the government's reluctance to give up some of its powers in the interests of economic and political development results in policies disadvantaging significant sections of the population.

In this context, it is possible that Suharto may not be elected to his sixth presidency. Indeed, he himself has indicated in his autobiography that he might step down in 1993. If this occurs Indonesian politics will face a succession problem, particularly since Suharto has failed to groom an acceptable successor to his rule from within his entourage. What, then, might be possible alternatives to Suharto?

In the late 1970s, a number of dissenting factions within the armed forces argued that the army's role in civilian affairs had become far too great, that it had extended itself economically, politically and socially, becoming bureaucratized, unprofessional and corrupt. Before the removal of its leading exponents, the leading faction, known as the *Hankam* group of generals (so-called because its base was in the Department of Defence and Security), put forward the notion that the army should be the 'guarantor' of the political system rather than running it directly. Its role should be to oversee political decision-making, whilst itself remaining in the barracks, only intervening to 'restore order' if the political system was threatened, operating the 'Turkish Model', as one commentator termed it.[14]

Recently such views have again been expressed, but this time by a newer, younger generation of generals most of whom graduated from military academies in the early 1960s. Overall, they seem to be more concerned with their status as professional soldiers and would prefer a greater involvement by civilians in government, and notably in local government. For this generation, although they will not yet state it publicly, the policies of Suharto and his managers are becoming problematic, when faced with the issues Indonesia must address in the 1990s: the president should either retire or step down to be replaced by a more civilian-influenced regime, if Indonesia is to modernize in line with other ASEAN states.

Such a scenario may seem rather far-fetched under current circumstances, when Suharto is still able to command overwhelming support in controlling any opposition,[15] but given his delays in restructuring the economy and his unwillingness to ameliorate the exploitative effects of his policies on the environment and in areas such as transmigration there seems little doubt that opposition will recur.

In such a situation it is possible that the present form of government in Indonesia could be replaced by one with limited but genuine civilian representation, whose economic policies might involve a thorough deregulation of the economy and a weakening of the power of state corporations. Combined with such changes, and facilitating the development of a more export-oriented economic structure, there would probably be attempts to reduce expenditure on high-cost military ventures and to develop a more professional army — less corrupt, less wasteful of resources. Such a regime might also attempt to improve Indonesia's tarnished international image by alleviating some of the more rapacious aspects of its policies towards areas outside Java. What policies might such a government follow towards East Timor?

With the aims of improving Indonesia's image, weakening the control of Suharto-sponsored monopolies and limiting excessive expenditure, it might well favour a 'Sulawesi Solution' in which the military would retreat, the army and administration would be Timorized and a limited degree of autonomy be given to East Timor as a province. However, against this should be set the rather obvious point that most of the generals of the early 1960s generation who would implement the Turkish Model have gained promotion through their 'battlefield experience' in East Timor. Consequently, there would be great reluctance on their part to admit in any way that the occupation and annexation had been a misadventure. The most that could be conceded would be that the army had been too rapacious, due to its involvement in the economic exploitation of the territory. This could then be attributed to the power of the Suharto and Murdani monopolies, which would provide the rationale both for a reduction in their powers and for a civilianization of the Dili administration.

By such means, a post-Suharto Government of this type might implement changes in East Timor. The most it could grant, however, would be a very limited degree of autonomy, with a provincial administration having a degree of control over social, cultural and, perhaps, economic affairs. All this, of course, assumes that such a regime can emerge in Indonesia. At present this seems rather unlikely but, in the 1990s, it is possible to envisage the conditions for its emergence developing.

Whichever scenario develops, it seems certain that events in the international arena, or within the Southeast Asian region itself, are unlikely to influence signficantly the outcome of the conflict in East Timor during the next decade. International pressure will succeed in keeping the issue alive, whilst Fretilin forces will maintain their areas under fairly adverse conditions, and will occasionally be capable of ambushing Indonesian troops and harassing Indonesian positions, in a continuing military stalemate. Opposition from the church and from within the administration will also continue, as will regular outbreaks of spontaneous protest in the main towns and villages. Major changes, however, will only come as a result of political changes in Indonesia itself, where a post-Suharto regime may adopt a less brutal and exploitative policy towards East Timor. The limited degree of autonomy allowed by such a regime might then enable the independence movement to pursue its aims in a situation which is no longer dominated by a continual recourse to the requirements of armed conflict.

Whatever the outcome, there is little doubt that East Timor will continue to resist Indonesia's occupation. The capacity of East Timorese society to maintain itself in the face of determined attempts at incorporation emerges clearly from our analysis of its history. Just as the Portuguese were never able to pacify their colony, so too were the Japanese unable to quell resistance to their occupation. During the Indonesian invasion and subsequent occupation, the independence movement has shown incredible resilience in its fight against annexation. In all areas of East Timorese society there is a continuing opposition to attempts at Indonesianization, whether it be in education, the economy, culture or, indeed, in the political system introduced by the Indonesian military. Most recently, some of the most effective and vociferous opposition has come from the generation of East Timorese raised during the years of Indonesian rule.

This ability to resist incorporation owes much to the nature of East Timorese society, which we described briefly in our account of the Portuguese period, and returned to in our analyses of such areas as resettlement, Indonesian military campaigns, the development of opposition and, most notably, the organization of Fretilin during and after the Indonesian invasion. The most important feature of East Timorese society has been its kinship system and the social and political alliances which this has engendered both within and between its constituent communities. This system has influenced profoundly all areas of life, from economic organization to culture and religion. The maintenance of kinship has enabled communities to remain cohesive, integrated and highly resistant to outside incursion.

In the final years of their colonial rule, the Portuguese began to realize the importance of the kinship system in the organization of opposition to their control, and many of their policies in the twentieth century were devoted to its undermining. The Fretilin administration was successful because many of its policies were based upon ideas derived from cultural values emanating from indigenous society. Fretilin's political reorganization introduced novel ideas of democracy, whilst at the same time combining these with pre-existing notions and respecting the existing pattern of political alliances. Fretilin was able to mount its campaigns of resistance to the Indonesian occupation and reorganize itself under the most unfavourable conditions in the late 1970s because it was still able to rely on support from local communities, despite the destruction of its national organization.

The Indonesians had little awareness of these aspects of East Timorese society when they invaded, and were clearly taken aback at the strength of opposition to their annexation attempt. Only by pouring in arms and troops in large quantities were they able to control Fretilin. They were equally surprised by the extent to which the population resisted Indonesianization. Gradually they realized that, in the face of such strong resistance, their only hope of successful integration lay in a destruction of much of the existing social structure and its replacement by one more amenable to control. Consequently, from the end of the 1970s they began their intensive resocialization and restructuring campaigns of economic reorganization, control of family life, resettlement, undermining of Timorese culture and systematic inculcation of Javanese values.

These campaigns were carried out brutally and were accompanied by widespread military intimidation. The Indonesian government needed changes to be carried out as rapidly as possible to support its diplomatic arguments that East Timor was becoming increasingly Indonesian and that opposition was weakening.

Many writers and commentators have seen in the Indonesian occupation an example of the methods used by the military against opposition in Indonesia itself. This is a valid point, but it doesn't present us with a complete picture. From our analysis it would seem that the only way to colonize East Timor successfully and subdue opposition to colonial rule is by undermining the reproduction of the basic structures of its society and, in particular, its kinship system. Hence the overwhelming focus of the Indonesian military on the need for resettlement of communities throughout the territory as a precondition for the success of Indonesianization. Given the particular structure of East Timorese society, it can only be colonized fully by a fundamental reorganization, in which the lives of its members are profoundly transformed. The Portuguese tried this and failed, perhaps because they concluded that both for themselves and the Timorese the costs ultimately were too high. The Indonesian military has had no such reservations. Despite the strength of opposition to its invasion and occupation, the military has pushed ahead with its attempts to impose as thorough and determined a colonial control as is possible. The results have been disastrous for the people of East Timor, as detailed in the evidence presented in our account.

Yet, despite its determination, the Indonesian military has not yet succeeded either in successfully controlling all the territory or in establishing any firm support for its annexation amongst the East Timorese population. In spite of its policies, the social relations and values of the pre-invasion period persist, providing a framework for continuing opposition. In addition to this, the brutalities accompanying the implementation of these policies have reinforced opposition, notably amongst the younger generation. This latter development has particularly annoyed the military, many of whose members had pinned their hopes on their successful socialization of the second generation.

Following the demonstrations organized during the visits of the Pope, in

October 1989, and the American ambassador, in January 1990, General Murdani addressed a meeting of civilian, military and religious leaders in Dili on 3 February. In a speech aimed at humiliating and intimidating his audience, he proclaimed angrily:

> Don't dream about having a state of Timtim (the Indonesian phrase for East Timor). There is no such thing! In the past, there were some small states that wanted to stand on their own, and without hesitation the Indonesian Government took steps to stop that. All the forces at our disposal were used to prevent the creation of small states. And this also applies to Timtim . . . ABRI (the Indonesian armed forces) may fail the first time, so it will try for a second time and for a third time. There have been bigger rebellions, there have been greater differences of opinion with the government than the small number calling themselves Fretilin, or whoever their sympathizers are here. We will crush them all! I repeat, we will crush them all![16]

As General Murdani was addressing this Dili meeting a group of Indonesian anthropologists from Gajah Mada University in Jogjakarta was carrying out a one-month study in sub-districts in Ainaro and Ermera, as a follow-up to earlier research in 1981 and 1989, funded by the Bank of Indonesia. The group's findings were to have been presented to a seminar in Dili on 19 April but this was subsequently postponed, and the report of the group presented to a closed session of senior army officers who demanded successfully that most of the findings be censored. Criticizing the 'monopolistic practices' of East Timor's 'war economy' and describing the ineffectiveness of education and local government, the report concluded that the whole process of resettlement had been so traumatic for the East Timorese population that it should be abandoned altogether:

> Considering the close bond between villagers in East Timor and their land and customs, it is recommended that the resettlement programme should be halted. The people in the resettlements should be allowed to return to their original villages so that they can till their own land and live in accordance with their own customs.[17]

The contrast between the findings of this report and the statements of General Murdani, whose career has been tied closely to the subjugation of East Timor, could not be greater. On the one hand we have a determination to intensify the military policies followed since the invasion of 1975, and on the other a study by Indonesians, concluding that, in almost every sphere of social life, these policies have been counterproductive. Most telling of all was the recommendation that resettlement, the foundation of military strategy, be abandoned since it had not achieved its objectives and, of all policies, it had caused the greatest resentment amongst the population.

The findings of the anthropologists' report were a testimony to the remarkable capacity of the East Timorese both to resist the implementation of military policies and to counter military propaganda by describing in detail the horrendous impact of the Indonesian occupation on their daily lives. The report similarly showed the futility of gaining any meaningful support for the occupation within the framework of the strategies pursued since the invasion, particularly those followed in the 1980s. Juxtaposed to this, we have a determination by the military to continue with these policies, which undoubtedly will fuel opposition during the coming years.

Indonesia has neither been able to control East Timor successfully nor legitimize its occupation by generating any real basis for support within East Timorese society. There is no reason to suppose that this situation will change soon unless there is a significant shift in existing political parameters, particularly in Indonesia. Yet there is an urgent need for alternative strategies in East Timor if its people are to overcome the terrible trauma of the years of Indonesian occupation and return to the task begun in 1974, of charting a path to development based on an assessment of their needs decided through a genuine act of self-determination.

Notes

1. For a description of the events surrounding the 'Act of Free Choice' in West Irian, see May, 1978, Chapter 5, 'The United Nations Fiasco'; also, *West Papua: the Obliteration of A People*, Tapol Books, London, 1983.

2. *Asian Wall Street Journal*, 24 November 1986.

3. See *Far Eastern Economic Review* (Hong Kong), 7 April 1983, *Sydney Morning Herald*, 10 April 1986, and *Asian Wall Street Journal*, ibid.

4. For details of this, see the league table of countries published in the *Economist* (London), 20 December 1986.

5. *Far Eastern Economic Review*, 16 June 1986.

6. Herwasono dan Kuswata Kartawinata, 'Dampak Sosial dan Ekologis dari Pembangunan Kehutanan di Indonesia', *Diskusi INGI*, Jakarta, February 1988.

7. *Sinar Harapan* (Jakarta), 8 March 1985.

8. See, most notably, 'Banking on Disaster: Indonesia's Transmigration Problem', London, the *Ecologist*, April 1984.

9. *Proceedings* of the meeting between the Indonesian Government's Department of Transmigration and representatives from the Inter-Governmental Group on Indonesia (unpublished), Section 4:41, Jakarta, 20 March 1985.

10. Quotation cited in *Tapol Bulletin* (London), No. 76, July 1986.

11. *Berita Hutan* (Jakarta), No. 16, January/February 1989.

12. *Far Eastern Economic Review*, 6 April 1989.

13. This phrase was reportedly used by a minister in Suharto's cabinet during one of its sessions, on 5 July 1989.

14. This phrase was first used in reference to the Indonesian military government under Suharto by David Jenkins, in *Suharto and His Generals*, Cornell University Press, Ithaca, 1984.

15. For example, in July 1989 Suharto was able to replace a number of generals who had spoken in favour of *keterbukaan*.

16. Speech by General Murdani, Dili, 3 February 1990, transcribed from tapes by Liem Soei Liong, and translated by Carmel Budiardjo. The speech is available as a *Tapol* document.

17. The anthropologists' report was sent to the author, with some 70 of its pages missing. The quotes (translated by Carmel Budiardjo) are from this copy. Selections from the report have appeared in *Kompas* (Jakarta), 17 April 1990.

Chronology of the Main Events in East Timor since 1974

1974

April 25   The AFM coup in Lisbon leads to the overthrow of the Caetano regime.

May 5   The governor of East Timor issues a proclamation for the establishing of political parties.

May 11   The *Uniao Democratica Timorense* (Timorese Democratic Union, UDT) is founded.

May 12   The *Associacao Social Democratica Timor* (Timorese Social Democratic Association, ASDT) is formed.

May 27   The *Associacao Popular Democratica Timorense* (Timorese Popular Democratic Association, Apodeti) is formed.

June 17   Following a meeting in Jakarta between Indonesia's Foreign Minister, Adam Malik, and ASDT's representative, José Ramos-Horta, Malik writes to Horta assuring him that Indonesia supports independence for East Timor.

Sept 6   Australian Prime Minister Gough Whitlam meets President Suharto in Wonosobo, a village in Central Java, and agrees that the eventual integration of East Timor into the Indonesian Republic is inevitable.

Sept 12   ASDT becomes the *Frente Revolucionara do Timor Leste Independente* (Fretilin).

Oct 14   General Ali Murtopo, head of the Indonesian Government's Special Operations Unit (OPSUS, Military Intelligence), visits Lisbon and has secret talks with leaders of the AFM. *Operasi Komodo*, the Indonesian Government's plan to annexe East Timor, is launched the same day.

Nov 25   Colonel Lemos Pires is appointed as the new governor of East Timor.

December   Fretilin begins its anti-illiteracy programmes and starts to set up co-operatives.

1975

Jan 20   A coalition is formed between the UDT and Fretilin parties.

Jan 31   The Portuguese Government's National Council for Decolonization rejects the idea of internationalizing the East Timor issue.

Feb 18	The Indonesian military carries out a simulated invasion of East Timor in Lampung, South Sumatra.
March	Elections begin in East Timor, supervised by the Decolonization Committee of the Portuguese parliament.
May 26	The UST withdraws from its coalition arrangement with Fretilin.
June 26	Two days of talks begin in Macau between the Portuguese Government and East Timor's political parties. The Indonesian Government is allowed to send observers to the talks. For this reason, Fretilin refuses to attend.
July 17	Constitutional Law 7/75 is passed in Lisbon, setting October 1976 as the date for popular elections for a General Assembly to determine East Timor's future. Colonial control is set to end in October 1978.
July 29	The results of the elections for local councils are announced: Fretilin candidates gain 55 per cent of the popular vote.
Aug 11	After a meeting in Jakarta with Indonesia's leading generals, the UDT leadership launches a coup in Dili to wrest power from the Portuguese and halt the growing popularity of Fretilin.
Aug 27	The Portuguese governor and administration withdraw from Dili to the island of Atauro in Dili harbour.
Sept 24	UDT forces retreat into West (Indonesian) Timor, leaving Fretilin in control of East Timor.
Oct 6	Indonesian troops attack Batugadé, a border town in East Timor.
Oct 16	Two Australian, one New Zealand and two British journalists are killed by Indonesian troops in the East Timorese village of Balibo.
Nov 28	Fretilin declares East Timor an independent state.
Nov 29	In the presence of leaders of the UDT and Apodeti in Kupang, West (Indonesian) Timor, Adam Malik signs a declaration formally integrating East Timor into Indonesia.
Dec 7	Indonesian forces invade East Timor.
Dec 22	The UN Security Council calls on Indonesia to withdraw its armed forces from East Timor.
Dec 25	Indonesia is estimated by Australian intelligence to be deploying 15–20,000 troops in East Timor.

1976

Jan 13	Following its occupation of Dili, Baucau and the border region, the Indonesian military establishes a 'Provisional Government' formed from Apodeti and UDT members. This body invites Indonesia to proclaim its sovereignty over East Timor.
Feb 14	Lopez da Cruz, President of the Provisional Government and former UDT leader, claims that 60,000 East Timorese have been killed since the Indonesian invasion.
Apr 3	A revolt by UDT members in Dili is suppressed by the Indonesian military.
Apr 22	The UN Security Council again calls on Indonesia to withdraw. It receives a report from a special envoy of the UN Secretary-General, who visited Indonesian-held areas in February. The envoy,

Winspeare Guicciardi, states that he is unable to produce a full report of the situation inside East Timor because the Indonesian military prevented him from contacting or travelling to Fretilin-held areas.

May 15   Fretilin holds a two-week national conference in the central region, to co-ordinate the campaign of resistance to the invasion.

May 31   An East Timorese 'Popular Assembly' is convened by the Indonesian military. It approves a petition, addressed to President Suharto, calling for full integration into Indonesia.

Jul 12   First reports are received of resettlement camps being set up in East Timor.

Jul 17   President Suharto signs a bill integrating East Timor into Indonesia.

Sept 29   The Australian Government confiscates a transmitter used to receive messages from East Timor.

Nov 19   Indonesian relief workers visit East Timor and report that 100,000 people have been killed since the invasion.

Nov 19   The UN General Assembly rejects Indonesia's annexation of East Timor, and calls for an act of self-determination to be held in the territory. (The voting is recorded as 75 in favour, 20 against, with 52 abstentions.)

1977

Feb 2   First reports are received of American Bronco OV-10 jets being used in East Timor.

Mar 13   US congressional hearings on East Timor commence in Washington. Former Australian Consul to East Timor, James Dunn, provides details of Indonesian atrocities in East Timor in the months following the invasion, on the basis of interviews he conducted with East Timorese refugees in Lisbon.

Mar 17   Lt General Howard Fisk of the US air force testifies to the congressional hearings that US military equipment was used in the invasion of East Timor.

May 7   Fretilin forces report that they control just over 80 per cent of the territory. Radio broadcasts from Fretilin areas describe food production and distribution, the use of traditional medicines and the conduct of anti-illiteracy campaigns.

Sep 5   Fretilin forces report heavy bombing raids on Bobonaro and a long military engagement with the Indonesian army in Quelicai. The bombing raids mark the beginning of the Indonesian encirclement and annihilation campaign of 1977–8.

Sep 7   The President of Fretilin, Xavier do Amaral, is arrested by the Central Committee of Fretilin, allegedly for opening negotiations with the Indonesian military. Nicolau Lobato subsequently is elected president in early November.

Sep 23   First reports are received of East Timorese being imprisoned without trial on the island of Atauro, north of Dili.

Nov 28   The UN General Assembly rejects integration and calls for an act of self-determination to be held in East Timor. (The voting record is 67 in favour, 26 against, with 47 abstentions.)

1978

Jan 20	The Australian Government gives *de facto* recognition to Indonesia's occupation of East Timor.
Apr 4	The British Aerospace Company signs a contract with the Indonesian Government to supply eight Hawk ground-attack aircraft to the Indonesian air force. These planes are ideally suited for use against ground forces in difficult terrain.
Apr 6	Lt General Mohammed Jusuf is appointed Commander in Chief of the Indonesian army. He states that a resolution of the war in East Timor is one of his priorities.
May 12	Letters received by East Timorese refugees in Lisbon provide evidence of the first campaigns of enforced sterilization organized by the Indonesian military.
May	A special co-ordinating group for East Timor is established by the Ministry of Defence. It is chaired by Brigadier-General Benny Murdani.
Jul 18	President Suharto pays a brief visit to the towns of Dili and Maliana.
Aug 4	The US Government sells 16 A-4 counter insurgency bombers to the Indonesian air force.
Aug 30	Former Indonesian president Xavier do Amaral is captured by Indonesian troops.
Sep 7	Ambassadors from several countries visit Dili, Baucau, Remexio, and Maliana, to assess food shortages and medical supplies. They are shocked by the extent of malnutrition.
Nov 20	The UN General Assembly calls for the withdrawal of Indonesian troops and for the right of self-determination to be exercised in East Timor (voting record: 59 in favour, 30 against, with 46 abstentions).
Dec 12	Fretilin's Radio Maubere ceases transmitting.
Dec 31	Fretilin's President, Nicolau Lobato, is shot and killed by Indonesian troops.

1979

Apr 2	The ICRC concludes that 'tens of thousands of people displaced by military operations are facing starvation unless aid is brought to them rapidly' (cited in *East Timor News*, Sydney, No. 6/12, November 1979).
Oct 19	The ICRC begins a relief programme in East Timor.
Nov 2	Peter Rodgers, Jakarta correspondent of the *Sydney Morning Herald* publishes photographs taken in East Timor. They reveal that malnutrition is widespread throughout the territory.
Nov 12	In London, Indonesian Foreign Minister Mochtar Kusumaatmadja admits that only half of the pre-1975 population of East Timor is under Indonesian control, and that 120,000 people have died since the 'civil war' began in East Timor in 1975.
Dec 13	The UN General Assembly passes a resolution condemning the Indonesian occupation and calling for an act of self-determination

	to be held in East Timor (voting record: 62 in favour, 31 against, with 45 abstentions).
Dec 25	A report in the *Times* of London claims that the Indonesian military are using napalm in East Timor.

1980

Jan 16	East Timor is designated an official resettlement area for Indonesian transmigrants from Java and Bali.
May 13	It is reported by Associated Press from Dili that there are 150 resettlement camps in East Timor.
June 10–11	A six-hour attack on Dili is mounted by Fretilin forces.
Nov 11	The UN General Assembly again calls for Indonesian withdrawal and self-determination for East Timor (voting record: 58 in favour, 35 against, with 46 abstentions).
Dec 4	A set of secret documents on Australian foreign policy on East Timor during the 1970s is published in the Melbourne *Age*. The documents show that the government had an extensive knowledge of, and acquiesced in, events prior to the invasion.
Dec 17	A US CIA official states that the US Government could have prevented the invasion of East Timor, without any adverse effects on its long-term policy aims towards Indonesia.

1981

Jun 3	A report written by the members of the Indonesian-appointed East Timor Regional People's Assembly (the parliament set up by the Indonesian military in 1976) is sent to President Suharto. It is highly critical of the Indonesian presence, citing cases of torture, maltreatment and disappearances. It complains bitterly of the actions of P. T. Denok, a trading company controlled by the Indonesian military.
July	Reports are sent from East Timorese students in Baucau, Laclo and Manatuto to Jakarta and thence to Australia, describing preparations for a new Indonesian offensive, referred to as *Operasi Keamanan*.
Aug 19	The forced recruitment of the East Timorese population into 'fence of legs' (*pagar betis*) operations begins, as part of *Operasi Keamanan*.
Oct 24	The UN General Assembly repeats its call for self-determination for East Timor (voting record: 54 in favour, 42 against, with 46 abstentions).
Dec 20	The ICRC is given permission by the Indonesian Government to re-enter East Timor.

1982

Jan 11	Mgr Costa Lopes, Catholic Apostolic Administrator of East Timor,

	alleges that at least 500 East Timorese were massacred by Indonesian troops at the Shrine of St Anthony, near Lacluta in September.

Feb   Catholic Church sources in East Timor report that approximately half the population is facing serious food shortages.

May 4   Elections are held in East Timor, in which the Indonesian military party, *Golkar*, obtains 98.8 per cent of the votes cast. The London *Economist* (8 May) describes the election results as 'hard to swallow'.

May 16   The Pope states that the Vatican will not accept East Timor as part of Indonesia.

May 18–28 A small group of journalists visits East Timor and produces reports highly critical of the actions of the Indonesian military. Their reports are published in the *Philadelphia Inquirer*, 28 May, and the *Asian Wall Street Journal*, 14 June.

Jun 10   The newly elected President of Portugal, Antonio Ramalho Eanes, initiates a new policy on East Timor, calling for a 'common front' of Portuguese-speaking nations to oppose the Indonesian occupation.

Aug 4   Figures for detention on the island of Atauro indicate that 6800 people are imprisoned there.

Oct 13–14 During President Suharto's visit to Washington, many of the major American newspapers are highly critical of Indonesia's occupation of East Timor.

Nov 3   The UN General Assembly again condemns the annexation of East Timor and calls for an act of self-determination. The motion, which is passed by 50 votes to 46 with 50 abstentions, also instructs the UN Secretary-General to initiate consultations with all concerned parties in order to 'achieve a comprehensive settlement of the East Timor issue' (UN General Assembly Report, 4 November).

Dec 30   Indonesian military manuals, captured by Fretilin troops, are released in Lisbon. They deal with such issues as the destruction of Fretilin networks, the interrogation of prisoners and the control of resettlement villages.

1983

Feb 7–12 Portuguese television journalist Rui Araujo visits East Timor for two days with the permission of the Indonesian Government. His report, which is deeply critical, describes conditions on the island of Atauro, the daily oppression experienced by East Timorese and the use of the contraceptive drug Depo Provera.

Feb 16   The UN Human Rights Commission condemns human rights abuses in East Timor, and calls for self-determination (voting record: 16 in favour, 14 against, with 10 abstentions).

May 13   A document signed by a group of priests in Dili states, 'We foresee the implacable extermination of the people'.

May 16   Mgr Costa Lopes resigns as Apostolic Administrator of East Timor. He is replaced by a young East Timorese priest, Mgr Carlos Felipe

	Ximenes Belo, who has not lived in East Timor since the Indonesian invasion.
Jun 25	A ceasefire is reported to have been signed by the Indonesian Commander of East Timor, Colonel Purwanto, and Fretilin President Kay Rala Xanana.
July 28–31	An Australian Parliamentary Delegation visits East Timor.
July (late)	The ICRC halts its operations as Indonesia withdraws facilities in preparation for a new offensive.
Aug 8	The Indonesian military launches a new campaign against Fretilin forces, thereby breaking the ceasefire.
Aug 16	Fretilin forces attack the military section of Dili airport.
Aug 21–2	200–300 people are executed by Indonesian troops in the village of Kraras, near Viqueque.
Sep 9	A state of emergency is declared in East Timor by the Indonesian Government.
Sep 14	President Suharto orders a 'clean sweep' of East Timor.
Sep 23	The UN General Assembly discusses East Timor and votes to defer consideration of the issue for a year, giving the secretary-general time to complete his report requested in 1982's resolution.

1984

Jan 6	Reports in both the Indonesian and international press describe how the offensive begun in September (codenamed *Operasi Persuatan*) has severely disrupted food production.
Feb 24	First reports are received of trials of political prisoners in Dili.
Mar 16	The ICRC is allowed to visit prisoners in Dili, but is still prevented from resuming its food aid programme in mainland East Timor.
Mar 31	The Portuguese Government announces that talks are planned with the Indonesian Government on the East Timor issue.
Apr 1	22 US senators write to Secretary of State George Schultz, asking him to raise East Timor as an issue on his forthcoming trip to Jakarta.
May 2	A letter written by Mgr Belo, received in Lisbon, refers to disappearances, trials and 'popular judgements' carried out 'on the spot' by the military. He refers to settlement villages as 'corrals', and criticizes mass conscription for 'fence of legs' operations by the military. He claims that the Indonesian army is not winning the war despite the presence of ten battalions (10,000 troops).
Jul 12	When the new Indonesian Ambassador to the Vatican presents his credentials, the Pope hopes of East Timor that 'every consideraiton will be given in every circumstance to the ethnic, religious and cultural identity of the people' (*Washington Post*, *Le Monde*, *Vatican Daily*).
Jul 21	Portuguese President Eanes and Prime Minister Mario Soares make a joint statement on East Timor, calling upon the Portuguese Government to assist in 'bringing about the inalienable right of the people of East Timor to self-determination' (Melbourne *Age*).

Jul 25   The UN Secretary-General publishes his 'progress report' on negotiations between Indonesia and Portugal. He concludes that little progress has occurred. The General Assembly agrees subsequently to defer discussion of East Timor to its 1985–6 session.

Dec 17   General Murdani, Indonesian Armed Forces Commander in Chief, states that the East Timor conflict 'will take some time to resolve' (*Reuter*, Jakarta).

1985

Jan 1   A statement written by the Council of Catholic Priests in East Timor refers to the military organizing regular 'clearing up' operations, using children in 'fence of legs' operations, arresting people *en masse*, promoting resettlement and demanding that the inhabitants of resettlement villages undertake 'night watch' duties. It describes the 'Indonesianization' of the administration and the suppression of Christianity and Animism.

Jan 5   The Indonesian Government publishes a Five-Year Plan for 1984–9. For East Timor it plans birth control for 95,000 women and the resettlement of 6800 transmigrants from Indonesia. The Birth Control Campaign is to be supported by the World Bank.

Mar 15   The UN Human Rights Commission removes the charges against Indonesia on East Timor from its agenda.

May 8   131 members of the US Congress send a letter to President Reagan before his visit to Lisbon, expressing concern at the situation in East Timor.

Jul 3   A US government State Department report estimates that there are approximately 12,000 Indonesian troops in East Timor.

Jul 7, 10 Reporting from East Timor, a correspondent of *Agence France Presse* states that he was not allowed to visit Baucau because it was considered unsafe by the military.

Aug 8   Reporting on a trip to East Timor a journalist states that the Chinese population has been reduced from 20,000 in 1975 to a 'few thousand'. He reports fighting five miles from Dili and describes recent transmigration and political trials in Dili (*Far Eastern Economic Review*, Hong Kong).

Aug 16   In a speech marking the fortieth anniversary of Indonesia's independence, President Suharto justifies the invasion of East Timor as 'a positive response to the people's movement in East Timor to set themselves free from the shackles of foreign colonialism' (*Agence France Presse*, Hong Kong).

Aug 18   Australian Prime Minister Bob Hawke recognizes Indonesian sovereignty over East Timor on behalf of his Labour Government.

Aug 22   The UN General Assembly again votes to defer action on East Timor pending reports from the secretary-general on the talks initiated under UN auspices between the Portuguese and Indonesian governments in the 1983 General Assembly resolution.

Sep 14   Reports from East Timor describe intense bombardment by the Indonesian air force between August 1983 and June 1984.

Sept 24	The first formal diplomatic contacts are established between the Portuguese and Indonesian governments since the 1975 invasion.
Oct 27	The Indonesian and Australian governments begin discussions for a joint exploration programme in the disputed Timor Gap area, south of East Timor.
Nov 28	The Indonesian Government states that it intends to set up 400 strategic villages in East Timor.
Dec 9	The Indonesian and Australian governments announce that they will jointly develop the petroleum resources of the Timor Gap.
Dec 12	An upsurge in fighting in East Timor is reported, with ambushes of Indonesian troops by Fretilin forces across the territory.
Dec 20	A massacre by Indonesian soldiers of 60 inhabitants of a village is reported (*Guardian*, London).

1986

Mar 4	Bids from oil companies for drilling sites in the Timor Gap area have already produced $Aus31.5 million for the Australian Government, according to the *Sydney Morning Herald* (4 March).
Mar 7	Reporting from Dili, a journalist is told by Governor Carrascalao that 100,000 East Timorese have died since the 'civil war' of 1975.
Mar 31	In Lisbon, Fretilin's External Delegation and representatives of the Timorese Democratic Union (UDT) announce the formation of a coalition.
Apr 17	70 Japanese parliamentarians from both houses of the *Diet* call for self-determination in East Timor in a letter to UN Secretary-General Perez de Cuellar.
Apr 18	A set of maps, some captured from the Indonesian military and some drawn by Fretilin units in East Timor, is released in Lisbon. They indicate that most military activity is occurring east of a line from Baucau to Viqueque. The Indonesian army appears to have built a military gate across the island, with the aim of moving eastwards from the Baucau–Viqueque line to encircle Fretilin areas.
Jul 11	The European Parliament passes a motion criticizing the Indonesian annexation of East Timor, and calling for the exercise of self-determination.
Jul 11–15	Portuguese parliamentarian Miguel Anacoreta Correia, of the Christian Democratic Party, visits East Timor. His report concludes that although there have been some economic gains from integration, 'rejection and mistrust towards Indonesia are generalized feelings throughout East Timor' (*Christian Science Monitor*).
Jul 17	Governor Carrascalao is reported to be critical of Indonesian control over East Timor's administration (*International Herald Tribune*, Paris).
Sep 16	The UN General Assembly agrees a motion, sponsored by Malaysia, that postpones further discussion of East Timor until the UN Secretary-General delivers his final report on negotiations between the Portuguese and Indonesian governments.

Sep 19   Letters received by refugees in Lisbon and Darwin, Australia, describe a wave of arrests in eastern areas, with those arrested being taken to Baucau.

Nov 16   Fretilin's external delegation describes a new offensive in East Timor, involving 50 Indonesian battalions, 12 of which are searching exclusively for Xanana Gusmao.

Dec 21   Fretilin military successes are reported during the previous month's fighting in the western, central and eastern sectors, notably in the Viqueque area.

1987

Jan 2   A new military commander of security operations, Brigadier General Mantiri, is appointed in East Timor.

Jan 3   Governor Carrascalao calls on Fretilin members 'to come home and build the province' (*Jakarta Post*).

Feb 10   The UN Human Rights Commission reinstates hearings on East Timor.

Mar 6   It is reported from Dili that 38,000 East Timorese children under the age of five are suffering from malnutrition (*Jakarta Post*).

Mar 20   A new offensive is launched by the Indonesian military, deploying 30,000 troops.

Apr 13   The US Catholic Bishops' Conference officially criticizes the Indonesian occupation. Its statement focuses particularly on the enforced birth control campaign.

Apr 15   The Indonesian Ambassador to Australia states that there are 15,000 Indonesian troops in East Timor.

Apr 25   Elections are held in East Timor resulting in an overwhelming majority for the Indonesian military party, *Golkar*.

Jun 5   40 members of the US Senate criticize the Indonesian occupation of East Timor in a letter released to the press.

Jul 14   Another offensive is launched by the Indonesians, to coincide with the appointment of a new military commander, Colonel Soenato.

Sep 2   The UN Sub-Commission on Prevention of Discrimination and Protection of Minorities (the committee preparing the agenda for the Human Rights Commission) adopts a resolution on East Timor, calling for a negotiated settlement and requesting the Indonesian Government to grant improved access to East Timor.

Sep 4   In Lisbon, a spokesman for the newly-elected Social Democratic Government states that it has dropped the demand for East Timor's self-determination from its programme because it is seeking greater flexibility in negotiations with Indonesia and a rapid diplomatic solution to the problem.

Sep 8   The UN Secretary-General's report on East Timor is published. It concludes that limited progress has been made to diminish the differences in the positions held by both sides. The General Assembly decides to adjourn debate on East Timor for a further year.

Oct 5	20 prisoners are released from Dili prison. According to Amnesty International, 136 prisoners were held in Dili prior to the release of the 20: 63 in Becora prison, 73 in Comarca prison.
Nov 14	It is reported (in the *Jakarta Post*) that in the southern region of East Timor thousands of adults and children are short of food. Overall, 38,000 children in East Timor are in a state of malnutrition.
Dec 23	Accepting the credentials of the new Indonesian Ambassador to the Vatican, Pope John-Paul states: 'The church's universal mission of service leads her to hope that particular consideration will be given to the protection of the ethnic, religious and cultural character of East Timor' (*UCA News*, Hong Kong).
Dec 31	Governor Carrascalao concludes that 'although integration exists on paper . . . it still has to be given content' (*Kompas*, Jakarta).

1988

Jan 4	East Timorese refugees in Australia who are in contact with relatives in East Timor claim that Javanese are increasingly taking over the best housing and land in the centre of towns, and moving East Timorese out to suburban areas (*Diario de Noticias*, Lisbon).
Feb 18	Indonesian Government representatives invite members of the Portuguese parliament to send a delegation to East Timor on an 'observer' mission.
Mar 9	Reports from East Timor describe an upsurge of fighting, with increases in Fretilin ambushes, an infiltration of Fretilin troops into Baucau and Fretilin attacks in areas near the border with West (Indonesian) Timor.
Mar 9	The Plenary Session of the European Parliament approves a draft resolution condemning the Indonesian occupation of East Timor.
Mar 14	A former Portuguese civil servant, detained by the Indonesians after 1975 and then residing in the territory, manages to leave East Timor for Australia. Arriving in Lisbon, he claims that 200,000 East Timorese have been killed since the Indonesian invasion.
May 2–3	For the first time, the 12 EC governments adopt a common position on East Timor, agreeing to support the UN Secretary-General's efforts at achieving a fair and internationally acceptable settlement which 'will safeguard the rights of the people of East Timor and their cultural identity' (*O Seculo*, Lisbon, 4 May).
Jun 20	Governor Carrascalao asks President Suharto to declare East Timor an open province, in order to speed up the process of economic development.
Jul 29	It is reported that a new Indonesian military offensive has been underway in East Timor since May. It is entitled Operation Clean-Up (*Diario de Noticias*, Lisbon).
Sep 15	By 164 to 12 votes, with 15 abstentions, the European Parliament calls for the withdrawal of Indonesian troops from East Timor, and affirms that the people of the territory should exercise their right to self-determination.

Oct 30	182 members of the US House of Representatives and 47 members of the Senate send letters to Secretary of State George Schultz, stating their continuing concern over events in East Timor. They focus particularly on torture, imprisonment and denial of access to international human rights organizations.
Nov 5	President Suharto announces that from January 1989 eight of East Timor's 13 districts will be opened up to entry by Indonesians and foreigners.
Nov 16	The Council of Europe's Committee of Ministers, meeting in Strasbourg, refers to East Timor for the first time in its final communiqué, expressing its members' hope for a fair, global and internationally acceptable solution, respecting the interests of the East Timorese people.
Dec 12	It is reported that between 26 October and 21 November a total of 3000 people were arrested in connection with intelligence surveillance before, during and after a visit by President Suharto to the territory on 2–3 November.
Dec 29	The Indonesian Government grants East Timor 'equal status' with the provinces of the Indonesian Republic.
Dec 31	Fretilin units attack Dili's Lahane and Taibesse neighbourhoods. 84 Indonesian soldiers are killed and several East Timorese soldiers desert their Indonesian units.

1989

Feb 6	Mgr Belo writes to UN Secretary-General Perez de Cuellar, calling upon the UN to hold a referendum on the future of the territory.
Mar 16	The ICRC is allowed to visit one of Baucau's prisons for the first time in the town since the 1975 invasion.
Mar 17	A reporter travelling to Viqueque states that villagers have been ordered to build walls around their resettlement villages. He concludes that security is tight, with 40,000 troops stationed in the territory (*Daily Telegraph*, London).
Apr 26	In discussion with President Suharto, American Vice-President Dan Quayle raises the subject of East Timor, forcusing on the issues of political prisoners and 'repressive practices' in the territory (*Diario Popular*, Lisbon).
Jun 9	118 members of the US Congress write to President Bush requesting him to discuss East Timor with President Suharto during the latter's forthcoming visit to Washington.
Jul 15	Documents received by East Timorese refugees in Lisbon claim that 1500 people have been arrested in East Timor since the beginning of the year. Almost all of these have been interrogated and many of them have 'disappeared'.
Jul 15	A short Indonesian military offensive is carried out in advance of the Pope's visit to East Timor. Its primary aim is to capture Fretilin President Xanana.
Aug 5	In a speech to the Indonesian House of Representatives in Jakarta, Governor Carrascalao states that in East Timor malaria is endemic,

70 per cent of the population are infected with tuberculosis, of 61 districts only 40 have physicians and that the illiteracy rate is 92 per cent.

Aug 25   The UN Sub-Commission on Prevention of Discrimination and Protection of Minorities recommends to the UN Human Rights Commission that it continues to consider the human rights situation in East Timor.

Sep 5   Leaders of the East Timorese National Convergence are received officially by the Vatican State Office.

Sep 14   UN Secretary-General Perez de Cuellar releases a report on the current state of progress on the East Timor issue. It states that, despite difficulties, negotiations between the Portuguese and Indonesian governments are proceeding, concluding that a proposed visit by the Portuguese Parliamentary Mission to East Timor will help in creating an atmosphere conducive to the achievement of an internationally acceptable solution.

Oct 12   Pope John-Paul II visits Dili. He consecrates the cathedral and celebrates Mass in the open-air at Taci-Tolu, before a congregation of 100,000. At the end of the Mass, a demonstration takes place, supporting independence. The demonstrators are beaten by the police, and the scene is observed and photographed by foreign journalists.

Oct 13   40 young people are arrested after the Pope's visit, and interrogated. Some are tortured in order to extract confessions of involvement in the demonstration.

Nov 4   The Indonesian military organizes a demonstration outside Bishop Belo's residence, calling on him to release students who took refuge in his house after being chased by Indonesian troops following on from the demonstration during the Pope's visit. A counter-demonstration develops, and is suppressed by Indonesian troops.

Nov 5   Children and young people from St Joseph's primary and secondary schools are arrested by Indonesian troops after they forcibly enter the school.

Dec 11   The Australian and Indonesian governments sign a treaty to jointly explore the Timor Gap area.

Dec 17   100 members of the United States Congress call on the State Department to launch an official enquiry into claims of torture of East Timorese by the Indonesian military after the Pope's visit.

Dec 26   East Timorese students in Bali, Indonesia, stage a demonstration against suppression of students in Dili in November.

1990

Jan 17   During a visit to Dili, the US Ambassador to Indonesia meets with a group of demonstrators outside the Hotel Tourismo. They are dispersed violently after his departure. At least two are reported killed. The violence is witnessed by US diplomats and Australian tourists.

Feb 3   General Murdani visits East Timor and addresses a meeting of all
           the senior military and non-military personnel in the territory. He
           threatens brutal reprisals if there is any recurrence of the
           demonstrations held during the recent visits of the Pope and the US
           ambassador.

Feb   A joint statement on East Timor is made by 12 members of the EC
           to the UN Human Rights Commission. It notes the human rights
           violations in the territory and requests entry for human rights
           organizations.

Mar (mid-) A new offensive is launched by the Indonesian military, involving
           40,000 troops, 6000 East Timorese conscripts and two helicopter
           squadrons.

Apr 20   The ICRC reports that it was allowed to visit 82 prisoners in six
           detention centres in East Timor between January and March, and
           that all these prisoners were detained for security reasons.

Glossary

The following is a selected glossary of main abbreviations used in the text.

I = Indonesian word. T = Word in Tetum (the East Timorese *lingua franca*). P = Portuguese word. Remaining terms are Indonesian military acronyms.

ABRI	Indonesian armed forces
ACFOA	Australian Council for Overseas Aid
Apodeti	Associacao Popular Democratica (P) (Timorese Popular Democratic Association)
ASDT	Associacao Social Democratica Timor (P) (Timorese Social Democratic Association)
assimilados (P)	'assimilated' Timorese
ata (T)	Traditional Timorese term for slave
babinsa (I)	Village Guidance Officer
BAKIN	The Indonesian Military Intelligence Co-ordinating Agency
bapak (I)	Literally 'father', a term of respect
binpolda (I)	Local police officer
bupati (I)	Head of district
concelho (P)	Portuguese administrative division
Dato (T)	Traditional word for commoners, or 'the people'
Falantil	Forcas Armadas de Libertacao Nacional de Timor-Leste (P) (Fretilin's army)
Fretilin	Frente Revolucionara do Timor Leste Independente (P) (Revolutionary Front for an Independent East Timor)
Golkar	The Political Party of the Indonesian Military
GPK	Gerombolan Pengacau Keamanan (I) (literally, 'Security Disrupting Gangs' — the term used by the Indonesian military for Fretilin groups)
Hansip (I)	The civil guard in East Timor
ICRC	International Committee of the Red Cross
indigenes (P)	'unassimilated' Timorese
kabupaten (I)	A district in Indonesia's system of local administration
ketua (I)	Elder (in a village)
KODAM	Indonesian regional military command. East Timor is divided into seventeen Kodams
KODIM	District Military Command
KORAMIL	Sub-district Military Command

KOREM	Sub-regional Military Command
KOSTRAD	Strategic Reserve Command of the Indonesian army
liurai (T)	Ruler of a Timorese Kingdom
lulik (T)	Sacred object in Timorese animist religions
nao indigenes (P)	'assimilated' Timorese
NUREP	Indonesian term for a cell group within Fretilin
OPSUS	The Special Operations Unit of the Indonesian Government
postos (P)	Portuguese administrative posts
Ratih (I)	A people's unit, trained by the Indonesian military
suco (T)	A Timorese princedom
UDT	Uniao Democratica Timorense (P) (Timorese Democratic Union)
WANRA	Another term for *Hansip* (civil guard) in East Timor

Bibliography

General texts and articles on East Timor

This bibliography covers most but not all of the books and articles cited in the text, in addition to recommended further reading. The most complete bibliography available currently is provided by Sherlock (1980).

Alkatiri, Mari, 'East Timor: Survival and Resistance', *Kommentar*, Stockholm, February, 1982.

Amnesty International, *East Timor: Violations of Human Rights*, London, 1985.

Anderson, P., 'Portugal and the End of Ultra-Colonialism' (Part 2), *New Left Review*, No. 16, 1962.

Araujo, A. de, *Timorese Elites* (ed. J. Jolliffe and B. Reece), Canberra, 1975.

Arndt, H. W., 'Timor: Vendetta against Indonesia', *Quadrant*, Sydney, 23 December 1979.

Australian Council for Overseas Aid (ACFOA), *Report on Visit to East Timor for the ACFOA Timor Task Force*, ACFOA, Canberra, November 1975.

—— *Dossier on East Timor*, containing 26 documents, with eye-witness accounts from students in East Timor, Canberra, 1982.

Australian Parliament, Senate Standing Committee on Foreign Affairs and Defence, *Hearings on East Timor*, May–October, Canberra, 1982.

—— Senate Standing Committee on Foreign Affairs and Defence, *The Human Rights and Conditions of the People of East Timor*, Canberra, 1983.

Australian Government Publishing Service, *Official Report of the Australian Parliamentary Delegation to East Timor*, Canberra, 1983.

Barbedo de Magalhaes, A., *Timor Leste: Mensagem Aos Vivos*, Limiar, Portugal, 1983.

Barreto, J. L., *The Timor Drama*, published by *Timor Newsletter*, Lisbon 1982.

Boxer, C. R., 'Portuguese Timor: A Rough Island Story, 1515–1960', *History Today*, 10(5), May, 1960.

—— *Fidalgos in the Far East, 1550–1770*, Oxford University Press, London, 1968.

—— *The Portuguese Seaborne Empire*, Hutchinson, London, 1969.

Budiardjo, C. and Liong, Lim Soei, *The War Against East Timor*, Zed Press, London, 1984.

Callinan, B., *Independent Company: the 2/2 and 2/4 Australian Independent Companies in Portuguese Timor, 1941–3*, Heinemann, Melbourne, 1953.

Campagnolo, H., 'La langue des Fataluku de Lorehe (Timor Portugais)' Phd thesis, Rene Descartes Université, Paris, 1973.

Capell, A., 'Peoples and Languages of Timor', *Oceania* (Sydney), 14, 1943–4 and 15, 1944–5.

—— 'Portuguese Timor: Two More Non-Austronesian Languages', *Oceania* Linguistic Monographs No. 15, Sydney, 1972.

Capizzi, E., Hill, H. and Macey, D., 'Fretilin and the Struggle for Independence in East Timor,' *Race and Class*, XVII, 4, London, 1976.

Catholic Institute for International Relations, *I am Timorese/Je suis Timorais*, a set of six refugee interviews, London, 1990.

Chomsky, N., *East Timor and the Western Democracies*, Spokesman Pamphlet No. 67, Spokesman Books, Nottingham, 1979.

—— and Herman, E., *The Political Economy of Human Rights*, Vol. 1, containing a chapter on East Timor, Spokesman, Nottingham, 1979.

Clark, R. S., 'The "Decolonization" of East Timor and the United Nations Norms on Self-Determination and Aggression', *The Yale Journal of World Public Order*, Yale, 7/2, Fall 1980.

—— 'Does the Genocide Convention Go Far Enough? Some Thoughts on the Nature of Criminal Genocide in the Context of Indonesia's Invasion of East Timor', *Ohio Northern University Law Review*, 8, 1981.

Commissie Justitia et Pax Nederland, *East Timor, the Most Important Developments Since (Mid) 1983*, Justitia et Pax, Gravenhage, Netherlands, 1986.

Cowan, H. J. K., '"Le Buna" de Timor: une langue "Oueste-Papoue"', *Bijdragen tot de Taal, Land, en Volkenkunde*, 119, 1963.

Crawford, R. and Dyanidhi, P., 'East Timor: a Study in Decolonization', *India Quarterly*, New Delhi, 33/4, 1977.

Dunn, J. S., 'Portuguese Timor Before and After the Coup: Options for the Future', Legislative Research Service, Australian Parliament, Canberra, 1974.

—— *Portuguese Timor — the Independence Movement from Coalition to Conflict*, Dyason House Papers, Melbourne 2/1, 1975.

—— *The Timor Story*, Legislative Research Service, Australian Parliament, Canberra, 1976.

—— *East Timor — From Portuguese Colonialism to Indonesian Incorporation*, Legislative Research Service, Australian Parliament, Canberra, 1977a.

—— *The East Timor Situation. Report on Talks with Timorese Refugees in Portugal*, Legislative Research Service, Australian Parliament, Canberra, 1977b.

—— *Notes on the Current Situation in East Timor*, Legislative Research Service, Australian Parliament, Canberra 1979.

—— *East Timor: Reports on the Situation in 1980–1*, Legislative Research Service, Australian Parliament, Canberra, 1981.

—— *Timor, a People Betrayed*, Jacaranda Press, Milton, Queensland, 1983. (This book includes most of the material contained in Dunn's earlier monographs, above.)

Elliott, P. D., 'The East Timor Dispute', *The International and Comparative Law Quarterly*, London, 27/1, January 1978.

Evans, Grant, 'Eastern (Portuguese) Timor', Australian Union of Students, February 1975.

Feith, H., *The Decline of Constitutional Democracy in Indonesia*, Cornell University Press, Ithaca, 1962.

Forbes, H. O., 'On Some of the Tribes of the Island of Timor', *Journal of the Royal Anthropological Institute*, London, No. 13, 1883.

Forman, S., 'East Timor: Exchange and Political Hierarchy at the Time of the

European Discoveries', paper given to a conference on Trade in Ancient Southeast Asia, Ann Arbor, Michigan, March 1976 (later published in Hutterer (ed.), 1978).

Fox, J. J., *The Flow of Life: Essays on Eastern Indonesia*, Harvard University Press, Cambridge, Mass., 1980. (This text contains articles on Timor by anthropologists Brigitte Clamagirand, Shepard Forman, Gerard Francillon, Claudine Friedberg, H. G. Schulte-Nordholt and Elizabeth Traube.)

Francillon, G., 'Some Matriarchal Aspects of the Social System of the Southern Tetum', Phd thesis, Australian National University, Canberra, 1967.

Franck, T. and Hoffman, P., 'The Right of Self-Determination in Very Small Places', *International Law and Politics*, 8, 1976.

Franke, R. W., 'East Timor: the Responsibility of the United States', *Bulletin of Concerned Asian Scholars*, Charlemont, Mass., 11/2, 1983.

Freney, D., *Timor: Freedom Caught Between the Powers*, Spokesman Books, Nottingham, 1975.

Fretilin External Delegation, *Fretilin Conquers the Right to Dialogue*, Lisbon, 1983 (containing Fretilin's proposals for negotiations during the 1983 ceasefire, as outlined by Fretilin's internal leadership).

Fry, K. L. and Gietzelt, A., *Report on a Visit to Portuguese Timor*, mimeographed, November 1975, Canberra (nd).

George, A., *East Timor and the Shaming of the West*, Tapol Publications, London, 1985.

Glover, I. C., 'Prehistoric Research in Timor', in D. J. Mulvaney and J. Golson (eds) *Aboriginal Man and Environment in Australia*, Australian National University Press, Canberra, 1971.

Groeneveldt, W. P., *Historical Notes on Indonesia and Malaya Compiled from Chinese Sources*, Jakarta, Bhatara, 1960 (original published in Verhandelingen Van het Genootschap Van Kunsten en Wetenschappen, Batavia, 1839).

Hall, D. G. E., *A History of South-East Asia*, St Martin's Press, New York, 1968.

Hastings, P., 'The Timor Problem', *The Australian Outlook*, Canberra, Vol. 29 Nos. 1,2,3, 1975.

—— 'Timor and West Irian: the Reasons Why', in Mackie, J. (ed.), *Indonesia: the Making of a Nation*, 1980.

Hicks, D., *Tetum Ghosts and Kin*, Mayfield Publishing Company, Palo Alto, California, 1976.

Hill, H. M., 'Fretilin: the Origins, Ideologies and Strategies of a Nationalist Movement in East Timor', MA thesis, Monash University, Melbourne, 1978.

Hiorth, F., *Timor: Past and Present*, South-East Asian Monographs, No. 17, James Cook University, Northern Queensland, 1985.

Hoadley, J. S., *The Future of Portuguese Timor*, Occasional Paper No. 27, Institute of Southeast Asian Studies, University of Singapore, 1975.

—— 'Portuguese Timor and Regional Stability', *Southeast Asian Spectrum*, Bangkok, 3/4, 1975.

—— 'East Timor: Civil War — Causes and Consequences', *Southeast Asian Affairs*, Singapore, 1976.

—— 'Indonesia's Annexation of East Timor: Political, Administrative and Developmental Initiatives', *Southeast Asian Affairs*, Singapore, 1977.

Hutterer, K. (ed.), *Economic Exchange and Social Interaction in Southeast Asia*, Michigan, 1978.

IDOC (International Documentation Centre), *East Timor*, IDOC, Vol. XVIII, No. 1/87, Rome, 1987.

Indonesia, Republic of, *To Build a Better Tomorrow in East Timor*, Department of Information, Jakarta, 1979.

—— *The Province of East Timor: Development in Progress*, departments of Foreign Affairs and Information, Jakarta, 1981.

—— *East Timor Develops*, Regional Government of East Timor, Dili, 1984.

—— *Process of Decolonization in East Timor*, Department of Information, Jakarta, 1987.

Jolliffe, J., *Report from East Timor*, Australian National University Student Association, 1975.

—— *East Timor: Nationalism and Colonialism*, University of Queensland Press, 1978.

Kohen, A. and Taylor J., *An Act of Genocide: Indonesia's Invasion of East Timor*, Tapol Books, London, 1979.

—— and Quance, R., 'The Politics of Starvation', *Inquiry*, New York, February 1980.

Komite Indonesie, *East Timor: Holocaust on the Sly*, International Congress on East Timor, Amsterdam, September 1980.

Lawless, R., 'The Indonesian Takeover of East Timor', *Asian Survey*, University of California, Berkeley, 16/10, 1976.

Lawson, Y., *East Timor: Roots Continue to Grow*, unpublished manuscript, Amsterdam, 1990.

Lazarowitz, T., 'The Makassai: Complementary Dualism in Timor', Phd thesis, State University of New York, Stony Brook, 1980.

Lebar, F. M., *Ethnic Groups of Insular Southeast Asia*, Human Relations Area Files, New Haven, 1972–5 (section on Timor and its neighbouring island of Roti by David Hicks and James Fox).

Leifer, M., 'Indonesia and the Incorporation of East Timor', *The World Today*, London, 32/9.

Luwig, K and Horta, K., *Ost-Timor, Das vergessene Sterben*, Gesellschaft fur bedrohte Volker, Gottingen, Germany, 1985.

May, Brian, *The Indonesian Tragedy*, Routledge & Kegan Paul, London, 1978.

McDonald, H., *Suharto's Indonesia*, Fontana, Melbourne, 1980.

Metzner, J., *Man and Environment in Eastern Timor. A Geo-ecological Analysis of the Baucau–Viqueque Area as a Possible Basis for Regional Planning*, Development Studies Centre, Australian National University, Canberra, 1977.

Middelkoop, P., 'Trektochten Van Timorese Groepen', *Tijdschrift voor Indische Taat, hand-en Volkenkunde*, Batavia, 85 (2), pp. 173–272, 1952.

Montealegre, F., *Background Information on Indonesia, the Invasion of East Timor and US Military Assistance*, Institute for Policy Studies, Washington, 1982.

Morris, C., *Timor: Legends and Poems from the Land of the Sleeping Crocodile*, H. C. Morris, Victoria, Australia, 1984.

Munster, G. J., *Secrets of State*, Angus and Robertson, Sydney, 1982 (Chapter 6 on East Timor).

—— and Walsh, R. (eds), *Documents on Australian Defence and Foreign Policy, 1968–75*, Sydney, 1980 (pp. 165–223 on East Timor).

Nichterlein, S., 'Australia: Courtier or Courtesan? The Timor Issue Revisited', *Australian Outlook*, 36/1, Canberra, 1982.

—— 'The Struggle for East Timor — Prelude to Invasion, *Journal of Contemporary Asia*, Manila, Vol. 7, no. 4, 1977.

Nicol, B., *Timor: the Stillborn Nation*, Widescope International Publishers, Victoria, Australia, 1978.

Ormeling, F. J., *The Timor Problem*, Groningen, 1956.

Pardo J., *El Problema de Timor-Este*, Cuadernos de Debate Politico, No. 2, Iepala, Madrid, 1984.

Portuguese Parliament, *Report Presented by the Eventual Commission for the Following-Up of the Situation in East Timor*, Lisbon, 1986.

Pro-Mundi Vita, *East Timor*, Dossier No. 4, Belgium, 1984.

Ramos-Horta, J., 'East Timor: Decolonization Unfinished: a Case Study in International Law', MA thesis, Antioch University, New York, 1984.

——— *Funu: the Unfinished Saga of East Timor*, Red Sea Press, New Jersey, 1985.

Ranck, S., 'Timor — No Changes Overnight', *New Guinea*, Vol. 10, No. 1, Sydney, 1977.

Retboll, T., 'East Timor and Indonesia', *Bulletin of Concerned Asian Scholars*, US, 15/2, 1983.

——— (ed.), *East Timor, Indonesia and the Western Democracies*, International Working Group for Indigenous Affairs, Document No. 50, Copenhagen, 1980.

——— *East Timor: the Struggle Continues*, International Working Group for Indigenous Affairs, Copenhagen, 1984.

Roger, M., *Timor Oriental, hier la colonisation, aujourd'hui la resistance à l'agression Indonesienne*, Editions L'Harmattan, Paris, 1976.

Schulte-Nordholt, H. G., *The Political System of the Atoni of Timor*, Verhandelingen van het Koninlijk Instituut voor Taal- Land- en Volkenkunde, The Hague, 1971.

Sherlock, K., 'The Timor Collection', list of holdings on East Timor (unpublished typescript), Darwin, 1982.

Sidell, S., 'The United States and Genocide in East Timor', *Journal of Contemporary Asia*, Manila, 11/1, 1981.

Southeast Asia Chronicle, No. 74 (various authors), *East Timor: Beyond Hunger*, Berkeley, California, 1980.

Suter, K. D., *International Law and East Timor*, Dyason House Papers, 5/2, 1978.

——— *East Timor and West Irian*, Minority Rights Group, London, Report No. 42, 1979.

Taylor, J. G., *The Indonesian Occupation of East Timor: a Chronology, 1974–1989*, Catholic Institute for International Relations, London, and the Refugee Studies Programme, Oxford University, 1990.

Telkamp, G. J., 'The Economic Structure of an Outpost in the Outer Islands in the Indonesian Archipelago: Portuguese Timor 1850–1975', in *Between People and Statistics: Essays on Modern Indonesian History*, P. Creutzberg, Martinus Nijhoff, The Hague, 1979.

Thomaz, Luis Filipe F. R., 'The Formation of Tetun-Praca, Vehicular Language of East Timor', in N. Phillips and K. Anwar (eds), *Papers on Indonesian Language and Literature, Cahiers d'Archipel*, 13, Paris, 1981.

Traube, E., *Cultural Notes on Timor*, unpublished manuscript, New York, 1984.

United Nations, *East Timor*, Department of Political Affairs, Trusteeship and Decolonization, No. 7, New York, 1977.

Van Atta, D. and Toohey, B., 'The Timor Papers', *National Times*, Australia, 30 May and 6 June 1982.

Viviani, N., 'Australians and the Timor Issue', *Australian Outlook*, 30/2 1976.

Wallace, A. F., *The Malay Archipelago: the Land of the Orang-utan and the Bird of Paradise*, Dover, London, 1964.

Walsh, P., 'Indonesia in Timor', *Arena*, Victoria, Australia, 1981.

Weatherbee, D. E., 'Portuguese Timor: an Indonesian Dilemma', *Asian Survey*, 6/12, Berkeley, 1966.

—— *The Situation in East Timor*, Institute of International Studies, University of South Carolina, Occasional Paper No. 1, 1980.

—— 'The Indonesianization of East Timor', *Contemporary Southeast Asia*, Institute of Southeast Asian Studies, Singapore, 3/1, 1981.

Whitlam, E. G., 'Australia, Indonesia and Europe's Empires', *Australian Outlook*, Canberra, 34, 1980.

Periodicals

In addition to the newspaper articles, journals and texts cited in the book, reference is also made to specialist publications devoted to regular reporting and analysis of events in and about East Timor. For the reader's information, details of these publications are as follows:

East Timor Information Bulletin
Bi-monthly publication of the former British Campaign for an Independent East Timor. It contains detailed coverage of events and a useful chronology during the period of its publication, from 1975–9. Back copies are available from the author.

East Timor News
The bulletin of the East Timor News Agency in Sydney, Australia. Produced monthly, and then bi-monthly, from 1979 to 1985. It specialized in the publication of radio messages from Fretilin transmissions received in Northern Australia, but also collated press articles on East Timorese issues. Some back copies available from the author, or from PO Box A716, Sydney, Australia.

East Timor News
A monthly bulletin, also publishing memo sheets with reports from East Timor, analysing news coverage in the Portuguese press, and details of events concerned with East Timor in the international arena. The bulletin has been published since 1987. Available from Rua Pinheiro Chagas, 77–2 esq, 1000 Lisboa, Portugal.

East Timor Report
Published from 1982–5 under the auspices of the Australian Council for Overseas Aid (ACFOA). It contains valuable information from church sources in East Timor and Indonesia. Produced bi-monthly. Back copies available from ACFOA, 183 Gertrude Street, Fitzroy, Victoria 3065, Australia.

East Timor Update
The bulletin of the East Timor Human Rights Committee in Syracuse, USA. Produced irregularly from 1978–81, it contained coverage of events in and about East Timor, with particular reference to lobbying campaigns in the United States and the role of the American Government in the East Timor war. Some back copies available from the author.

Em Timor-Leste, a Paz e Possivel
Published bi-monthly in Portuguese and French, 1982 to present. Regular reporting of events in East Timor, with good access to East Timorese church sources. The

editors regularly produce issues on particular subjects, e.g. imprisonment and trials, human rights abuses. Copies available from Rua de Campolide, 215 4–DC, 1000 Lisboa, Portugal.

Tapol Bulletin
Bi-monthly bulletin of the Indonesian Human Rights Campaign, published regularly since 1972, with over 100 issues. *Tapol* carries articles providing rigorous and detailed coverage of events in East Timor, particularly as they relate to Indonesian politics. It contains feature articles on all aspects of the war in East Timor, from resettlement and transmigration to military organization and arms supplies, and has carried several detailed interviews with East Timorese refugees. Copies available from 111 Northwood Road, Thornton Heath, Croydon, Surrey, CR4 8HW, UK.

Timor Informations
The Bulletin of the French East Timor Committee and the longest-running regular bulletin on East Timor, from 1975 to the present. It produces updates on the conflict, and is particularly useful in the areas of national and international diplomacy. Copies available from Association de Solidarité avec Timor Orientale, BP 235, 07, 75327, Paris, Cedex 07.

Timor Information Service
Bi-monthly, from 1975–83, publishing letters and radio messages from East Timor, together with articles on all aspects of the war in East Timor. Back copies from PO Box 77, Clifton Hill, Victoria 3068, Australia.

Timor Link
Published by the Catholic Institute for International Relations, London. Produced quarterly, from 1985 to the present, and containing detailed, regular coverage of news from and about East Timor, utilizing church sources in East Timor and Indonesia. CIIR, 22 Coleman Fields, London N1 7AF, UK.

Timor Newsletter
Published monthly for two years, and then bi-monthly for the remaining two, from 1980–84, it contains news and reports from East Timor, with invaluable up-to-date information from East Timorese refugees in Lisbon, together with reports on the coverage of East Timorese issues in the Portuguese press. Back copies available from the author, or from Rua Damasceno Monteiro 14a – R/c, Lisboa, Portugal.

Index

Zed Books Ltd

is a publisher whose international and Third World lists span:

- **Women's Studies**
- **Development**
- **Environment**
- **Current Affairs**
- **International Relations**
- **Children's Studies**
- **Labour Studies**
- **Cultural Studies**
- **Human Rights**
- **Indigenous Peoples**
- **Health**

We also specialize in Area Studies where we have extensive lists in African Studies, Asian Studies, Caribbean and Latin American Studies, Middle East Studies, and Pacific Studies.

For further information about books available from Zed Books, please write to: Catalogue Enquiries, Zed Books Ltd, 57 Caledonian Road, London N1 9BU. Our books are available from distributors in many countries (for full details, see our catalogues), including:

In the USA
Humanities Press International, Inc., 165 First Avenue,
Atlantic Highlands, New Jersey 07716.
Tel: (201) 872 1441;
Fax: (201) 872 0717.

In Canada
DEC, 229 College Street, Toronto, Ontario M5T 1R4.
Tel: (416) 971 7051.

In Australia
Wild and Woolley Ltd, 16 Darghan Street, Glebe, NSW 2037.

In India
Bibliomania, C-236 Defence Colony, New Delhi 110 024.

In Southern Africa
David Philip Publisher (Pty) Ltd, PO Box 408, Claremont 7735,
South Africa.